Merry Christmas
Christopher

Love,

Uncle Bobby
&
Aunt Teri

MARIAN'S BIG

OF

WM. B. EERDMANS PUBLISHING CO.

BOOK
BIBLE
STORIES

by MARIAN M. SCHOOLLAND

Illustrated by Dirk Gringhuis

GRAND RAPIDS, MICHIGAN

Library of Congress
Catalog Card No. 47–28700
ISBN 0-8028-5003-0

SET UP AND PRINTED, MAY, 1947

Reprinted, July 1988

Manufactured in the United States of America

PREFACE

The stories told us in the Bible are some of the most beautiful and interesting of all stories. But they are much more than that. They are a revelation of God. They reveal His thoughts and plans; they reveal His manner of dealing with mankind; they reveal His very self — His love and anger, His mercy and care. In fact, the prime purpose of each Bible story is just that — to show us God.

In this book, Bible stories have been selected and simplified for the very young child. But in each story the author has earnestly sought to be true to the purpose of the Bible, to keep God at the center, to show Him to the child. The Old Testament stories tell how He guided and loved and tested and sometimes punished His people. The stories of Job and Esther have been included, for they, too, reveal things of God which little folk can understand. The New Testament is linked to the Old as a fulfillment of the promise made long years before, and further as a revelation of God in His Son, our Saviour — His mercy upon the sick and poor, His warning against sin, His power over all nature, and above all, the love which made Him our Redeemer.

If this book leads some little heart and mind to know and love God, it will not have been written in vain.

M. M. S.

CONTENTS

The Old Testament

The New Testament

Contents — Continued

LIST OF ILLUSTRATIONS

The Old Testament

In the beginning God created the heaven and the earth . . . . And God saw everything that He had made, and behold it was very good. —GEN. 1:1, 31.

Happy is that people whose God is the Lord. —Ps. 144:15.

1

FROM CREATION TO THE FLOOD

I

How the World Began

(Genesis 1)

Long, long ago, there were no people at all. There was not even a world. There was no sun in the sky; there was no moon; there were no stars. In all the wide, wide spaces there was nothing. There was only God. God was everywhere.

Then God made a plan. He said, "We shall make people. And We shall make a beautiful earth for them to live on. We shall make a sun and a moon and many stars to shine for them."

So God made a great big ball. We call that ball the earth or the world. We live on that big ball; we live on the earth.

At first the earth was all dark as darkest night. And it was covered with mist. But the Spirit of God was there. The Spirit of God moved in the darkness and the mist. Then God said, "Let there be light." And the light came. The light shone upon the earth. That was the first morning, the morning of the very first day.

The first day passed. The light slipped away. Night came, and the whole earth was dark again.

But morning came again — the second morning. The light shone again on the misty earth.

On that second morning, God spoke to the mist. When He spoke, some of it went up into the sky and became clouds. Some of it settled down on the earth and became water. So there was water up in the sky, in the clouds; and there was water everywhere on the earth.

Then the light slipped away again. It was dark night once more.

The third morning came. The earth was still covered with water. God spoke to the water. God told the water to come together in great deep places. When God spoke, the water ran together. It filled the deep places. The deep places became oceans and lakes and rivers. In between the oceans and lakes and rivers, there was dry land.

Then God spoke again, and plants came up out of the dry land. Trees and bushes and grass grew up. They covered the earth. The land was green between the blue oceans and rivers and lakes. Then night fell upon the beautiful earth.

Once again it was morning, the fourth day. On this day God set the great lights in the sky. He made the sun to shine by day. He made the moon and stars to shine at night, when the sun has gone down.

And so, on the fifth day, a bright sun arose to shine on the fresh green plants and on the flowers and on the blue waters. But there was not one bird to sing among the trees. And there was not one fish to play in the water.

Then God gave a command for fish to come, and for birds to come. And there they were! Fish were swimming in the water. Birds were flying in the air. When the sun went down that day, there were many fish. There were big fish and little fish. And there were many beautiful birds with bright colored feathers, red and blue and yellow. The birds sang praises to God.

On the sixth day, God made the animals. There were little furry ones, big long-legged ones, some with long necks and some with long tails. There were all kinds of animals. They played in the green grass. They climbed up into the trees. They ran all over in God's beautiful world.

That is how the world began. And when God looked at the earth and all the things He had made on it, He saw that it was all very beautiful and very good.

But His work was not yet finished.

II

How God Made People

(Genesis 2)

When God had finished making the animals, He said, "Now let Us make a man. He can take care of all these things that We have made on the earth."

This time God did not just speak, as He did when He made the fish and the birds and the furry animals. Instead, He took some of the ground. He shaped it into a man. He made a body; He made arms and legs and hands and feet on the body; He made a head with wonderful eyes and ears, a nose and a mouth. When He had shaped the man, God breathed His own breath into the man. And the man stood up before God. He was alive and big and strong. God called the man Adam.

Then God made a beautiful garden. It was called the Garden of Eden. There were all kinds of flowers in the garden, and there were very many beautiful trees with fruit. God brought Adam to this garden. He told Adam to take care of it. It was a place where Adam could surely be very happy.

Soon after that, God brought all the animals to Adam. The animals did not have names. God told Adam he could give them names. Adam saw the animals come. He saw how beautiful they were. The animals were not afraid of Adam, and Adam was not afraid of the animals. They came to Adam. They let him pet them.

Adam knew just the right name to give each animal as it came to him. Then they ran off to the trees and fields again with their

See accompanying illustration between pages 32 and 33

new names — the cunning little chipmunk, the rabbit with long ears, the sheep with curly wool, the big elephant, and the giraffe with his long neck.

But not one of the animals could talk to Adam. God knew that Adam would be lonesome without someone to talk with him. So God put Adam to sleep. While Adam was asleep, God took a rib from his side. He made a beautiful woman of the rib. After a while Adam awoke. Then God brought the beautiful woman to him, to be his wife and to live with him in the Garden of Eden. The woman's name was Eve.

Night came at the end of the sixth day. The moon and stars shone down upon Adam and Eve asleep in the beautiful garden.

Then morning came. The sun shone; the birds sang; Adam and Eve awoke. God looked down at His earth and all that was in it. He saw that it was all very beautiful and very good. And it was all finished.

God rested on that day. It was the seventh day.

III

An Ugly Creature Comes to the Garden

(Genesis 2, 3)

Adam and Eve were happy in the garden. There were beautiful flowers. There were all kinds of fruit, very good to eat.

"The fruit that grows in the garden is yours to eat," God told Adam. "But there is one tree of which you must not eat. That is the Tree of the Knowledge of Good and Evil. It grows in the middle of the garden. If you eat the fruit of that tree, you will surely die."

God often came to the garden. Sometimes He came in the evening. He would walk and talk with Adam and Eve, as we walk and talk with our friends.

But there was another person who came to the garden. That was Satan. Satan hated God. He hated God very much. Because he hated God so much, he wanted to spoil the beautiful earth that God had made.

One day Eve was walking alone in the garden. Satan came to her. He hid himself inside a serpent, and he talked to her from inside the serpent.

Satan said, "How lovely this garden is! How wonderful the fruit is! Did God tell you not to eat of the fruit of the garden?"

"Oh, no," said Eve. "He gave us all these beautiful fruits to eat. We may eat all we want. There is only one tree that we must not touch. That is the Tree of the Knowledge of Good and Evil. God says that if we eat of the tree, we will surely die."

"But that is not true," said Satan. "You will not die if you eat of that tree. You will become like God if you eat of that tree!"

Become like God? How wonderful that would be! Eve walked on and went to look at the Tree of the Knowledge of Good and Evil. The fruit was beautiful. Eve was sure that it would taste very good.

But God had said, "You must not eat of it."

Eve looked again. Then she put out her hand to touch one of the fruits. Then she picked it. It looked very good.

God had said, "You must not eat of it. You will surely die if you eat of it."

But the serpent had said, "No, you will not die."

Eve took a bite.

Then she called Adam. She gave him some. He ate of the fruit, too.

Then Satan was glad.

But Adam and Eve looked at each other, and they were ashamed. They were afraid, too. They had disobeyed God. What would happen to them now? God had said they would surely die!

Satan went away. He laughed.

IV

The Beautiful Earth Is Spoiled

(Genesis 3)

All that day Adam and Eve were not happy. Evening came, and they were afraid. They knew God would come to visit them. They ran to hide among the bushes. They did not want to see God.

But God called them. God called, "Where are you?"

They knew they could not hide from God. So they came out of their hiding place. They stood before God. They said, "We were afraid."

And they told God what they had done.

Adam did not say he was sorry. He said it was Eve's fault.

Eve did not say she was sorry. She told God it was the serpent's fault.

When they had told God all about it, God called the serpent.

God said to the serpent, "From this day on, you shall crawl upon your stomach. You, and all serpents to come, shall eat dust. The children of this woman shall be your enemies. And One of them will crush your head."

When God said that, He was thinking of the time when Jesus would come to be our Saviour and crush Satan's head.

God said to Eve, "Your happiness is spoiled. You shall have children. But you shall have much pain and sorrow."

Then He said to Adam, "Because you disobeyed me, thorns and weeds shall grow on earth. You shall have to work hard. And at last you shall die and become part of the earth again."

Then God sent them out of the garden. He put an angel at the garden gate. The angel had a flaming sword. No one could come into the garden.

God also had animals killed and made coats of their skins for Adam and Eve.

Adam and Eve were very sad. They went out of the garden with sad hearts.

Now they had to make their own garden. It was hard work. Weeds grew fast. Sharp thorns came on many plants. Adam had to work hard to get enough to eat.

The animals had been friends of Adam. But now they became wild. The lions and tigers growled at Adam and Eve. The little animals ran away from them.

So, by the sin of Adam and Eve, God's beautiful world was spoiled.

But, worst of all, God did not come to walk and talk with Adam and Eve as He used to do. Their sin had come between them and God. God had sent them away from Him. Their sin separated them from God. To be separated from God is death.

All death came into the world because of sin. But even then, so very long ago, God was planning to send His Son to be our Saviour, to save us from sin and to bring us back to God.

V

The Children of Adam and Eve

(Genesis 4)

God still loved Adam and Eve. He still watched over them. He let them pray to Him. He showed them how to make an altar of stones.

They were to burn their best animals on the altar, as an offering to God for sin. God heard their prayers, when they said they were sorry for their sins.

After a while God gave children to Adam and Eve. The first baby was a boy. Adam and Eve were very happy to have a baby. They called him Cain. The next baby was a boy, too. They called him Abel. Then there were many other children, both boys and girls.

When Cain grew up, he made a garden. He had fruits and vegetables. Abel became a shepherd. He had many sheep and lambs.

One day Cain and Abel were in the field together.

Cain said to himself, "Today I shall bring a gift to God on my altar."

So Cain took some of the grain and fruit of his garden. He laid them on the altar and burned them to God.

But Cain did not love God. As he watched the gift burn on the altar, Cain was not happy. He knew, deep down in his heart, that God did not want his gift. God wants us to love Him first. Then He will take our gifts.

Cain looked up. He saw Abel. Abel, too, was bringing a gift to God. Abel had taken a lamb from his flock. He was offering it on his altar to God. Cain watched him. He saw Abel lay the lamb on the altar and burn it. He saw that Abel's face was happy.

The lamb on the altar was a picture of Jesus dying for our sins.

But Cain said, "God takes Abel's gift. He does not want mine." And Cain was angry.

Then Cain heard a voice call to him. It was God's voice. God said, "Cain, why are you angry? If you do well, you will be accepted; if not, sin is at the door of your heart."

But Cain did not care. He was very angry. He doubled his fist and went to Abel. He talked to Abel. Anger filled his heart more and more. At last he hit Abel. Cain hit Abel so hard that Abel fell down dead.

Cain saw Abel fall. But he turned and went away.

Then God's voice called Cain again. God asked, "Cain, where is your brother Abel?"

Cain did not dare to say what he had done. He answered, "Must I take care of my brother?"

But God knew what Cain had done. God knows everything.

God said to Cain, "Because you have done this great sin, your garden will never grow for you again. You shall wander around, far from home. You must find your food here and there. You shall be a wanderer."

Then Cain was afraid.

Cain said, "What shall become of me? If I go and wander up and down, somebody will find me and kill me."

But God had mercy on Cain. God said, "I will not let anyone kill you." And He put a mark on Cain, so that no one would kill him.

So Cain left his home. He took his wife along. They wandered away to a far country.

Adam and Eve were very sorry to lose two of their boys. Now they knew that their sin had come upon their children.

VI

God Looks Down Upon the Earth

(Genesis 6)

Adam and Eve had many children. These children grew up and married and had children. Adam lived to be nine hundred and thirty years old. When Adam died, he had a great many children and grandchildren and great-grandchildren. There were very many people on the earth. They lived in cities and in towns and in the country.

In those days, when God looked down from heaven upon His earth, what did He see?

He saw that His beautiful earth was no longer the same as it was in the beginning.

There were many thorns and weeds where beautiful flowers used to be. Many of the animals were wild; they fought each other and even ate each other.

And what about the people? Some were very sinful, like Cain. Some were just having a good time, forgetting all about God. They did not pray. They did not bring gifts to God. They played and danced and did only what they wanted to do. They did not take care of God's plants and animals. They did not even think about God.

But there were still a few good people.

There was Enoch. Enoch lived close to God. He walked with God and talked with God every day, even if people laughed at him.

One day Enoch's children went to see their father. They could not find him. They hunted for him. He was not in his house. He was not in the field. He was gone. God had taken him up out of the world. God had taken him to heaven. So Enoch never died, because God took him.

Then there was Noah. Noah had an altar. He brought gifts to God upon the altar, and he prayed to God. God was pleased to see that Noah served Him.

God was very sorry to see all the other people living in sin. He loved the people and wanted them to love Him. But they would not.

Then God said, "I will send a great flood to wash all these wicked people from the earth. I will save only the good ones, only Noah and his family."

God made His plan. He told Noah about it. He told Noah to build a big, big boat — an ark.

God said, "Make a boat — a big boat. It must be three stories high. It must have a roof. It must have one window high up, and it must have one door. It must have little rooms. Put tar on it, all around, inside and out, so that no water can get into it. When the boat is ready, I shall send a very great rain. The rain will cover all the earth with a flood. You and your family will be safe inside the ark when I send the rain."

Noah listened to God. God told him just how to make the ark. Then Noah went to work.

Noah worked hard. He cut wood. He sawed, and he hammered. His three sons, Shem, Ham and Japheth, helped him.

Sometimes people came to see what Noah was doing. He told them about the flood that was coming. He told them to stop living in sin. He told them to live for God. They only laughed at him. They would not listen. They did not think the flood would ever come.

From heaven God watched. He gave the people a long, long time. He gave them one hundred and twenty years' time. He was kind to them. But they would not listen. They still lived in their sinful way. And Noah went on building the ark.

2

THE FLOOD TO ABRAHAM

1

The Flood

(Genesis 7)

Noah and his sons worked for a long, long time on the ark. The one hundred and twenty years went by. Then the ark was finished. It was a very big boat. It had a roof. There were rooms in it. There was a door and there was a window.

But the boat stood on dry land.

Then one day God came down and spoke to Noah again.

God said, "In seven days the rain will begin to fall. You must get everything ready now."

God wanted to let the animals live, too. He told Noah to take two of each kind that He had made, and bring them into the ark with Noah and his family.

Noah and his sons carried bushels and bushels of food into the ark. They needed food for themselves. They needed food for the animals. At last that was done.

Then the animals came. God sent them to Noah. They came two by two — a father and a mother rabbit, a father and a mother elephant, a father and a mother of each kind of animal that God had made. But God sent seven of some kinds. Noah took these into the ark, too.

When the animals were all in the ark, God told Noah to go in.

God said, "Take your wife, and your sons, and your sons' wives. You must all go into the ark. I will close the door. I will send the rain."

There was no sign of rain. But Noah went into the ark with his wife and his sons and sons' wives. Then God closed the door.

After a while the clouds came. Big dark clouds spread over the blue sky. They hid the sun. Then the rain began to fall. It came faster and faster. Soon it was pouring down.

All day long the rain fell. All night long the rain fell. All the next day the rain fell. And all the next day.

Water came up out of the ground, too. It came bubbling up.

Soon the water began to cover the earth. It ran over all the ground. It lifted the ark. The ark floated on the water. And still the rain poured down.

For forty days and forty nights the water came down from the sky and water came up from inside the earth. It lifted the ark higher and higher. It covered the housetops. It covered the tree-tops. The ark floated above the houses and the trees. All the people and all the animals that were left on the earth were drowned.

Then at last the rain stopped. Noah looked out of the window. He could see nothing but water. Water covered the whole earth. It covered even the highest hills. Everything was one great big sea. And the ark floated on the great big sea.

All the wicked people had drowned. Noah and his family and the animals inside the ark were safe.

II

God's Promise

(Genesis 8, 9)

The ark floated on the water for many, many days. Inside the ark, Noah and his sons took care of the animals every day.

But the water was like a great sea. When Noah and the other people looked out the window of the ark, they saw only water, water all around them.

Far to the left, and far to the right, as far away as they could see, there was only water. There was not one house, not one tree, not one green hill. There was just water, everywhere. And the ark was all alone on the water.

But above the water, and above the ark, there was the blue sky. At night the stars twinkled there, and the moon sailed slowly from east to west. And high above the stars, God watched over all.

God had not forgotten Noah. He saw the ark floating on the deep waters. And He sent a wind to dry up the waters.

The wind blew. The water began to dry up. The ark began to go down—down, down a little farther each day. One morning Noah looked out the window and called to his sons.

"Come and see! The water is going down! We can see the tops of the rocky hills!"

Noah was happy to see that the water was going down. Now he knew that God was not forgetting him.

After a while the ark came to rest on one of the hilltops.

Noah waited a little longer. Then one day he took a dove from the roomful of birds. He let the dove fly out of the window. He thought maybe the dove would find a tree to rest in, and would not come back.

But soon he saw the dove fluttering by the window. He opened the window and reached out his hand. The dove flew to Noah, and he took it in.

Now Noah knew that the trees were still covered with water.

Another week passed. Noah sent out the dove again. This time the dove stayed away until evening. Then it came back. Noah opened the window for it. The dove flew in. And Noah saw that the dove had an olive leaf in its bill.

Now Noah knew that the treetops were uncovered. The dove had found a leaf.

Another week passed. Again Noah sent the dove out. This time the dove did not come back at all. The water had dried up off the earth at last.

Then Noah opened the roof of the ark. He and his sons looked out upon the earth. It was clean and beautiful. Everywhere new plants were growing. How pleasant it all looked! They were all eager to get out of the ark. They had been in the ark for more than a year! But they did not go out. They waited. They waited for God to open the door.

At last God spoke to Noah. God told Noah to go out of the ark. What a happy day that was! Noah and his wife stepped out upon the clean new earth. Noah's sons and their wives stepped out. And then the animals! The great big ones, the little ones, and all the creeping things — they ran out to play on the green earth. The birds spread their wings and flew up into the blue sky and sang. What a day that was!

As soon as they were all out of the ark, Noah picked up stones and built an altar. On the altar he brought a thanksgiving gift to God. He took some of the animals that God had sent into the ark by sevens. He gave them as an offering to God on the altar.

God was pleased with Noah's gift. He came to talk with Noah again.

God said, "I promise you that I shall never again send such a flood to cover the whole earth. I will never again send a flood to kill all that lives upon the earth."

Then God pointed to the sky. Noah looked. He saw a beautiful big rainbow there. It was very beautiful. Its colors were very bright.

God said, "The rainbow is a sign of My promise. When I see the rainbow, I will remember My promise."

And never again has God sent such a terrible flood.

III

"We'll Build a Tower"

(Genesis 11)

Only eight people came out of the ark — Noah and his wife, Noah's three sons and their wives. Soon Noah's sons had children. These children grew up. They had children. And after a while there were many people on the earth again.

These people all lived close together, in one small part of the earth.

Adam knew just the right name
to give each animal.

*What a happy day that was when
they all came out of the ark!*

One day someone said, "Let's build us a big city and a big tower. Let's build a great big tower that will reach up to the sky, way up to heaven!"

"That will be fine," said another. "And we will all live around the tower. We will build a city around the tower."

So they began to build. They made bricks of clay. They baked the bricks in big hot ovens, till they were very hard. They laid the bricks in rows, one on top of the other. So the wall of the big tower was started.

God saw what they were doing.

God said, "We will not let them build a tower that reaches up to heaven. We will stop them. And We will scatter them all over, so that they will live all over the earth."

At that time all the people talked alike. No one talked German or French or English. They all talked the language of Adam.

But one night God touched their tongues. And in the morning they began to talk other languages. They did not all talk alike anymore.

They started to work in the morning, to build the tower. They talked to each other. And they could not understand each other! One man would ask for something, and they would not know what he wanted. One would say something, and others did not know what he said. They talked and talked, louder and louder. They became angry with each other. At last they shook their heads and gave up. They could not work that way. They had to stop building the tower because they did not talk alike.

Then they did not want to live together any longer. Some people moved north. Some moved south. Some moved west. Some moved east. They went to live in many places. God scattered them over His earth.

3

GOD AND ABRAHAM

I

A Friend of God

(Genesis 12-17)

The years went by. There were very many people upon the earth. They built houses and lived in big cities. Many had big farms. There were rich people and poor people.

But only a few people remembered God. Only a few people prayed to God.

There was a man named Abram. He lived in a country called Ur of the Chaldees. Abram prayed to God. Abram brought gifts to God upon his altar. And God called Abram His friend.

One day God said to Abram, "Abram, come out of the country where you live. Move to a country that I will show you. I will bless you. I will make a great nation of you. All the families of the earth shall be blessed in you."

What did God mean when He said, "All families of the earth shall be blessed in you?" He meant that He would give Abraham a child and grandchildren and great-grandchildren. These would have more children and great-grandchildren, till at last one of them would be Mary. And Mary's son was Jesus, who came to save us from sin.

Abram did not understand all about this. But he did love God. He did want God to bless him.

So Abram told his servants to get ready to move. He told his wife, Sarai, to get ready. He took all the gold and silver that he had. He took all his sheep and cows and camels. Abram was a rich man.

Abram told Lot, his nephew, that he was going to move. Lot said he wanted to go along. Lot took all his sheep and cows and camels.

They had to go slowly. The sheep could not go fast.

God led them to the land of Canaan.

In the land of Canaan Abram and Lot put up their tents. Abram made a new altar and brought his gifts to God on the altar. They lived in tents in the beautiful land of Canaan.

After a while Lot moved away from Abram. Lot went to live in the big city of Sodom.

One night Abram was sitting alone. He was thinking of God. He was thinking of God's promise. How could he ever have grandchildren? He did not have even one child.

Then God came to Abram. God said to Abram, "Come with me out under the sky."

Abram went with God into the dark night.

God said to him, "Now look up at the heavens. See if you can count the stars."

Abram looked up. The stars were shining bright. Some were very large and beautiful; some were smaller; some were so far away that Abram could hardly see them. There were very, very many.

"Can you count them?" God asked.

Abram shook his head. Count them? How could he count all those stars? There were so very, very many stars. Only God knew how many there were.

Then God said, "Your children's children shall be like that. There will be so many, that they cannot be counted."

Abram and Sarai had been married a long time. Yet they did not have even one child. But Abram believed God. He waited for God to keep His promise.

God talked to Abram again. He said, "After this your name shall be Abraham. That means 'Father of many.' And Sarai's name shall be Sarah. That means 'Princess.' And when your child comes, you must call him Isaac."

II

God Visits Abraham Again

(Genesis 18)

It was a very warm day. At noon, when the sun was high in the sky, Abraham sat in the doorway of his tent. He looked out over the green hills. The sheep and cows were resting there. Soon Abraham saw three men coming.

Abraham did not know the men. But he went to meet them.

Abraham said to the men, "Come and sit down. Sit in the shade under the trees. Rest a little while. I will get you something to eat and drink."

The three men sat down. Abraham went to tell Sarah to make dinner for them.

Sarah made dinner. Abraham brought it to the men under the trees. They ate the good dinner.

Then one of the men said to Abraham, "After a little while Sarah shall have a son."

Then Abraham knew that this man must be God Himself. Who else could give Sarah a baby? It was God. He had come down from heaven looking like a man. The other two were angels.

The men were ready to go away. Abraham walked slowly along with them.

God said, "Abraham is My friend. I shall tell him what We came to do."

And God said to Abraham, "There are two wicked cities down on the plain. We have come to destroy these wicked cities. We are going to destroy Sodom and Gomorrah."

Sodom! That was where Lot lived! Abraham thought of Lot. What would happen to Lot if God destroyed Sodom? Abraham was afraid Lot might be destroyed with the city.

The two angels walked on. Abraham stood still, talking with God.

Abraham said to God, "Maybe there are some good people in the city. Will You destroy the city if there are some good people there?"

God said to Abraham, "If I find ten good people in the city, I will not destroy the city."

Then Abraham went back home. And God went back to heaven.

III

Lot and the City of Sodom

(Genesis 19)

The two angels went to Sodom. Lot was sitting by the city gate. He saw two men come. He did not know they were angels.

Lot said to them, "Come to my house. Stay with me tonight. The day is almost gone. You cannot travel farther now."

So the two angels went with Lot. They stayed with Lot.

At night there was a noise by Lot's house. Lot heard someone knock on the door. Lot went to see who was there. It was a crowd of bad men.

The bad men said to Lot, "Bring those two men out to us — those two men who came to your house tonight." And they pounded on the door.

Lot opened the door. He told the bad men to go away.

But they would not go away. They tried to take hold of Lot. And Lot was afraid.

Then one of the angels pulled Lot inside the house. And he closed the door.

The angels made the bad men blind. They tried to get in, but they could not find the door. At last they went away.

The angels said to Lot, "Go to your married children. Tell them that they must get out of the city. God is going to destroy the city."

Lot went to tell them. But they laughed at him. They would not believe him. They would not believe what the angels said.

Early in the morning the angels called Lot. "Wake up!" they said. "You must hurry! Get out of the city as fast as you can!"

Lot did not like to leave his home. The angels had to take hold of his hand. They pulled him away. They took hold of his wife's hand, too. They told his two daughters to come along. They made Lot and his wife and his daughters hurry. They brought Lot and his wife and his daughters to the gate of the city.

"Now run!" they said. "Do not stop. Do not look around. Run to the mountains!"

How they ran! They could hear the roaring of fire behind them. They could smell the smoke. They knew God had sent fire from heaven. They knew the city was burning. Their house was burning.

Lot's wife stopped. She looked around. She wanted to see what was happening. And right there Lot's wife became a pillar of salt. She had disobeyed God.

But Lot and his two daughters did not look around. They ran till they came to the mountains. There they found a cave. They hid in the cave. But the wicked cities burned to ashes.

IV

Abraham Loves God Best

(Genesis 22)

Abraham and Sarah had a little baby at last — a little boy. They called him Isaac. That was the name God gave him.

Abraham and Sarah loved Isaac very much. He grew to be a very fine boy. He made them happy. They knew he was the beginning of the great nation that God had promised — a nation like the stars in number.

Many, many years later, Jesus, our Saviour, was born into this great nation which God had promised Abraham.

Then one day God called to Abraham.

Abraham answered, "Here I am."

God said to him, "Take your son, your son Isaac, whom you love so much. Go to a mountain. I will show you where to go. I want you to make an altar there. I want you to burn your son on the altar as an offering to Me."

Abraham had built many altars. He had killed many sheep to burn as offerings to God. But now God asked him to give his son. How could Abraham do that? He loved his son very, very much. But God had said it.

Abraham was up early the next morning. He cut some wood for a fire. He put some coals of fire in a jar. He took a big knife. All this he tied to a donkey. Then he called two of his servants. He called Isaac, too. He told them to get ready to go along.

They traveled all day. They slept under the stars at night. They traveled all the next day. On the third day God showed Abraham the mountain.

Then Abraham took the wood off the donkey. He gave it to Isaac, to carry on his back. He took the fire and the big knife in his own hands.

Abraham said to the servants, "You stay here with the donkey. My boy and I are going up there to worship God. We will come back."

Abraham and Isaac walked up the mountain together.

Isaac said, "Father, we have wood and fire. But where is the lamb that we are going to give to God?"

Abraham said, "God Himself will give us a lamb, my son."

On the mountain Abraham built an altar of stones. He laid the wood on the altar. Then he tied Isaac with ropes, as he always tied the sheep and lambs. He put Isaac on the altar. Everything was ready. Abraham took the big knife in his hand. He held it high over Isaac's head.

Then a voice called out of heaven, "Abraham, Abraham!"

It was God's voice.

Abraham said, "Here I am!"

God said, "Do not hurt the boy."

Abraham put the knife down.

God said, "Now I know that you love Me. I know that you love Me so much that you would give Me even your only son."

How happy Abraham was! He quickly cut the ropes. He took Isaac off the altar.

Then Abraham looked around for something to give to God on the altar. He saw a sheep in the bushes. He took the sheep and laid it on the altar. He burned the sheep as an offering to God.

Then Abraham and Isaac went down the mountain together.

So Abraham gave Isaac to God. And God gave Isaac back to Abraham. And Abraham loved God more than ever before.

V

An Old Man's Prayer

(Genesis 24:1-28)

Sarah lived to be a hundred and twenty-seven years old. When she died, Abraham and Isaac were lonely. Isaac had not married.

One day Abraham called his oldest servant. He talked to him about Isaac.

Abraham said, "Isaac should have a wife. But I do not want him to marry one of the girls of this country. These girls do not serve God. I want you to go to the country that I came from. Go to my people there. Find a girl there for Isaac."

The old servant said, "That country is far away. The girl may not want to come with me, so far from home."

Abraham said, "God will guide you. He will show you who is to be Isaac's wife. If the girl will not come, then you must come back alone."

So the old servant made ready to go. He took money. He took gifts for the people in that far-away country. He loaded everything on camels. With ten loaded camels he rode away.

It was a long, long journey. At last the old servant came to the country where Abraham used to live. He found a well in the field. He made his camels kneel down by the well. He sat down to wait. He knew that people would come to the well for water.

The old servant bowed his head to pray. He said, "O God, show me the girl who must be Isaac's wife. The girls will come for water. I will ask one of them for a drink. If she says, 'I will give your camels water, too,' let that be the right girl."

A girl was coming already. The old servant saw her. She was beautiful. She came with her pitcher on her shoulder. She went down the steps into the deep well. She came up with her pitcher full of water.

The old servant went to meet her.

He said to her, "Will you please give me a little drink from your pitcher?"

"Oh, yes," the girl said. She took the pitcher down from her shoulder and gave him a drink.

Then she said, "I'll give your camels water, too."

That was just what the old servant wanted her to say!

The girl went down into the well again. She brought water up and poured it into the trough for the camels. The old servant stood and watched her. He knew that she was the right one. He knew that God had heard his prayer.

At last the camels had enough. Then the old servant opened a bag that was on one of the camels. He took out a gold ring and two bracelets.

The girl was happy with the bracelets and the ring.

The old man said, "Now tell me who you are."

She said, "I am Rebekah. Nahor is my father."

The old servant was glad to hear that. He knew that Nahor was Abraham's brother.

He said to Rebekah, "I am Abraham's servant. Will there be room for me at your house?"

"Oh, yes," said Rebekah. "I'm sure there is room for you. There is room for all your camels, too. I'll run home. I'll tell them that you are here!"

She ran home. The old servant watched her. Then he bowed his head and thanked God for hearing his prayer.

4

ISAAC AND HIS FAMILY

I

Isaac Meets Rebekah

(Genesis 24:29-67)

Rebekah told her mother and her father and her brother about the old servant.

"There was an old man at the well," she said. "He asked me for a drink. I gave him a drink, and I gave his camels water, too. He came from our Uncle Abraham. And look, he gave me these!"

She showed the ring and the bracelets.

Her brother Laban listened. He liked the pretty presents. He said, "Why didn't you bring the man home?"

Then Laban ran to the well.

Laban said to the old servant, "Come home with me! Come to our house!" And he was very kind to the old servant.

Laban brought the old servant to the house. He gave him water to wash himself. He took care of the camels. And he told his servants to make a dinner ready for Abraham's servant.

But the good old servant would not eat. He said, "I must first tell you why I came here."

They all sat around to listen.

He told them about Abraham. He told how rich Abraham was. He told about Isaac, who was such a fine young man. He told how he had prayed to God by the well. And he told how Rebekah had said just the right words.

He said, "Now will you be kind to my master? Will you send Rebekah home with me to be Isaac's wife?"

Laban and his mother and his father looked at each other.

After a minute they said, "God has guided you. Now we cannot say no. You may take Rebekah to be Isaac's wife."

When the old servant heard this, he thanked God again. Then he was ready to eat his dinner.

The next morning, the old servant wanted to go back to Abraham right away.

But Rebekah's mother said, "Do not be in such a hurry. Let Rebekah stay with us a little while. Wait ten days for her."

The old servant shook his head. "Please do not stop me," he said. "My master is waiting. I want to go back right away. I want to bring Rebekah to Isaac."

"We will ask Rebekah," said Laban.

Rebekah said, "Yes, I will go right away."

Rebekah had to get ready quickly. Her maids helped her. She said good-bye to her mother and father and brother. She rode away on her camel with her maids. She followed the old servant to the far-away country where Abraham lived.

Isaac was waiting for the old servant to come back. He was walking in the field. And when he looked up, he saw camels coming.

Isaac went to meet the camels. Rebekah saw him coming. She put her veil over her face.

The old servant told Isaac how God had heard his prayer.

Isaac took Rebekah's hand. She got down off the camel. They walked away together to the tent. Then Rebekah lifted her veil. Isaac saw how beautiful she was. Isaac loved Rebekah, and she became his wife.

II

Twin Brothers

(Genesis 25)

God gave Isaac and Rebekah two children — twin boys.

When the babies came, Isaac and Rebekah were very happy. They called the twins Esau and Jacob. Esau was the first-born. He was just a little older than Jacob.

When the boys grew up, Jacob wished that he was the first-born. The first-born would get a special blessing. Jacob wanted that special blessing. But it was Esau's birth-right.

One day Esau went out hunting. Esau loved to go hunting with his bow and arrows. But this time Esau did not catch anything.

When Esau came home, he was very tired and hungry. Jacob was cooking some red soup. The soup looked very good to Esau.

Esau said, "Please give me some of that soup. I am very hungry."

Jacob thought of the special blessing. He thought maybe he could buy Esau's birth-right.

"I'll sell you some soup for your birth-right," he said.

Esau said, "You can have the birth-right. I'm too hungry to care."

Jacob said, "Are you sure?"

Esau said, "Yes, I mean it. Just give me some soup."

So Esau sold his birth-right and the special blessings. Jacob gave Esau all the soup he wanted. Esau did not care about the blessing then.

III

The Special Blessing

(Genesis 27)

Isaac became blind. He was a very old man. He knew that soon he would die. He thought of the birth-right blessing. So he called Esau.

Esau came to him.

Isaac said, "I am old, my son. I want to give you my blessing before I die. Take your bow and arrows. Hunt a deer. Then cook me some good meat. I will eat it, and then I will bless you."

Esau hurried away with his bow and arrows.

But Rebekah had heard what Isaac said. Rebekah wanted Jacob to have the blessing. She called Jacob.

Rebekah said to Jacob, "Listen, Jacob. Your father is going to give Esau the blessing. Esau is gone hunting. He will bring meat for your father. Then your father will bless him."

Then she told Jacob what to do. She said, "Go get two little goats. Bring them to me. I will make meat ready for your father. You can bring it to him before Esau gets back. Then he will give you the blessing."

"But, Mother," said Jacob, "my father might touch me. Then he will know that I am Jacob. I am smooth, and Esau is hairy."

"Don't be afraid," said Rebekah. "I will take care of that."

So Jacob went to get two little goats from the flock. He brought them to his mother. She cooked the meat. She cooked it the way Isaac liked it.

Rebekah took the skin of the little goats. She put the hairy goat skin around Jacob's neck and on his hands. She told Jacob to put on Esau's clothes. Then she gave Jacob a platter with meat.

Jacob went to his father's tent.

"Father!" he called at the door.

"Who are you, my son?" Isaac asked.

Jacob said, "I am Esau, your first-born son. I have brought you meat, as you told me to do."

Isaac said, "How quickly you are back! How did you get back so soon?"

Jacob said, "God helped me in the hunt."

Then Isaac said, "Come near me, my son, so that I can feel you."

Jacob was afraid. But he went to his father's bed.

Isaac tried to see if this was really Esau. But he could not see. So he reached out his hand and touched Jacob's hand. He felt the goat's hair on Jacob's hand.

Then Isaac said, "The voice is like Jacob's voice. But the skin is hairy like Esau's."

Isaac took the platter of meat and he ate. Jacob stood by him.

When Isaac finished eating he said, "Come near me now and kiss me, my son."

Jacob bent over his old father and kissed him. Isaac smelled the woodsy smell of Esau's clothes. He thought it must really be Esau.

Isaac said, "Your clothes smell like the field, and God will bless the field for you." And he went on to give Jacob the special blessing. He promised that God would give Jacob all good things.

So Jacob really had the blessing. But then he hurried away. He was afraid Esau would come.

Jacob had just left when Esau came. Esau had a platter of meat. He brought it to Isaac's tent.

At the tent door Esau called, "My father! Here is the meat that you told me to get. It is ready for you to eat, so that you can bless me."

Isaac opened his blind eyes wide. "But who are you, my son?" he asked.

Esau said, "I am Esau, your first-born son."

Isaac knew that was Esau's voice. Isaac's old hands began to shake. He said, "Then who was it that was just here? Someone came. He brought me meat. I ate it, and blessed him."

Esau thought, "That was Jacob!" And he knew that Jacob had stolen the blessing.

Then Esau said, "Oh, Father, give me a blessing, too."

Isaac shook his white head. He said, "I have given Jacob the great special blessing. I cannot give it to you." And he had only a little blessing for Esau.

Esau was very angry. He said, "My father is old. Soon he will die. Then I will kill Jacob."

Someone heard what Esau said, and told it to Rebekah.

Rebekah said to Jacob, "Esau is angry because you stole the blessing. You must go away. Go to the far country, where your Uncle Laban lives. Stay there as long as Esau is angry."

Jacob was afraid of Esau. He went to say goodbye to his father Isaac. He said good-bye to his mother Rebekah. And he went away.

IV

Jacob's Dream

(Genesis 28)

Jacob walked and walked. He went farther and farther away from home. When night came, he was in a strange country. He was tired. He was all alone. He had no place to go.

It grew dark. Jacob had no place to sleep. At last he took a stone for a pillow. He lay down under the stars. He was very lonesome. But after a while he fell asleep.

Jacob began to dream. In his dream he saw a ladder. It was a big, wonderful ladder. It stood on the earth, and the top of it reached way up to heaven.

On the ladder Jacob saw bright shining angels. The angels were walking up and down the ladder. The bright light from heaven shone on them.

But who was at the top of the wonderful ladder? It was Someone even brighter than the angels. It was the Lord God Himself.

God spoke to Jacob from the top of the ladder. God said to Jacob, "I am the God of your grandfather Abraham; I am the God of your father Isaac; I will be your God, too. Some day I will give you this country — this country where you are sleeping now. It will be yours. You and your children will live here."

And God said, "I will go with you wherever you go."

Then Jacob awoke. He rubbed his eyes. He looked around. There was no ladder. There were no angels. It had been only a dream.

But Jacob knew that God had really come to him in the dream. He knew that God had really talked to him.

Then Jacob was afraid. But he was happy, too.

Jacob said, "God is here. I thought I was all alone, but God was with me all the time. He sees me. He will go with me."

Jacob took the stone he had used for a pillow. He set it up on end. The stone was his altar. He poured oil on the stone. The oil was his gift to God.

And Jacob said, "If God goes with me and takes care of me, then I will serve Him. I will give Him a tenth part of all that He gives to me."

V

Jacob Finds a New Home

(Genesis 29)

Jacob went on his way again. After a while he came to the far country where Rebekah used to live.

Jacob saw flocks of sheep lying on the grass. They were near a well. Shepherds were sitting by the sheep.

Jacob went to the shepherds. He sat down with them and began to talk.

Jacob asked, "Do you know a man called Laban?"

The shepherds answered, "Yes, we know Laban. He lives near here. Look, here comes his daughter, Rachel. She is bringing the sheep to the well."

They pointed, and Jacob looked. He saw a young woman coming toward the well. She was leading a flock of sheep. She was a pretty young woman.

Jacob said to the shepherds, "Why don't you give your sheep water, and take them back to the pasture?"

The shepherds said, "There is a big stone on the well. We wait until all the sheep are here. Then we take the stone off the well."

But when Rachel came, Jacob took the big stone off the well. Then he gave her sheep water. Rachel watched him. She wondered who he was.

When all the sheep had finished drinking, Jacob talked to Rachel.

Jacob said, "Do you know who I am? I am your cousin, Jacob. I am a son of Rebekah, your aunt."

Rachel had often heard her father talk about Rebekah, her beautiful aunt.

"Oh!" she said. "I must run home and tell my father that you are here!" And away she ran.

Jacob watched her go running across the fields. After a while he saw a man come running back. That was Laban, his uncle.

Laban was very glad to see Jacob. He threw his arms around Jacob and kissed him.

"You must come with me," he said. "You may stay at my house. My house will be your home."

So Jacob went with his Uncle Laban. God had brought him to a new home.

Jacob worked for Laban, and lived with him for many years.

See accompanying illustration
between pages 64 and 65

VI

Jacob Meets Esau

(Genesis 30-33)

Jacob worked hard for Laban. He took care of Laban's sheep. He found green pastures for them. He gave them water from the well. He watched over the little lambs.

Laban had two daughters, Leah and Rachel. Laban gave both his daughters to Jacob, to be Jacob's wives. (God had not yet told men to take only one wife.) Laban also paid Jacob with sheep and goats.

Jacob lived with Laban for many years. God gave Jacob twelve children and He made Jacob a very rich man. God was with Jacob, as He had promised.

Then one day God spoke to Jacob. God told Jacob that it was time for him to go back to his own country to his father Isaac. Jacob told Leah and Rachel.

It was not easy to move. There was much to get ready — the sheep and goats, the little children, all the household goods. It was a long, long way to Canaan where Isaac lived.

But at last they were ready to go. The servants drove the sheep and goats. Leah and Rachel and the children rode on camels.

The ride was fun for the children. But Jacob thought of Esau. When he thought of Esau, he was afraid. Would Esau still be angry?

Jacob thought and thought about it. At last he called some of his servants. He said to them, "You go ahead and see if Esau is there. Tell him that I am coming."

Jacob hoped that Esau would not be angry.

The servants rode away. After a while they came back. They said, "Esau is coming to meet us. He has four hundred men with him!"

Then Jacob shook with fear. Four hundred men! That was almost an army!

Jacob went to God in prayer. Jacob said, "O God, I am afraid. Esau is coming to meet us with four hundred men. Maybe he will kill me, and Leah, and Rachel, and the children. Thou hast been very good to me. Thou hast given me all that I have. Thou hast promised to go with me. Now I pray Thee to take care of us all."

Then Jacob told his servants to take some of the best sheep and goats and camels — a big flock. Jacob said, "Go to meet Esau. Tell him that these sheep and goats and camels are a present for him. Then maybe he will not be angry."

The servants went away with the sheep and goats and camels.

That night Jacob went out alone under the stars to pray. And an Angel of God came to him there.

All night long Jacob and the Angel of God wrestled together. When morning light came up in the eastern sky, the Angel blessed Jacob. Then He went away.

Jacob looked across the fields that morning. Far away he saw a cloud of dust. Esau was coming.

Jacob went to meet Esau. He bowed down to the ground before Esau.

Esau jumped off his camel. He ran to Jacob. He threw his arms around Jacob and kissed him. He was not angry any longer.

So God took care of Jacob again.

Jacob and Esau talked for a long time. Then Esau went back home. Jacob followed slowly, because his sheep and lambs could not go fast.

VII

Joseph, the Dreamer

(Genesis 37:1-11)

Jacob put up his tents in the land of Canaan. He lived there with his big family. Jacob's twelve sons grew up. They helped him take care of the sheep.

Jacob loved Joseph best of all his sons. He loved Benjamin very much, too. Benjamin was the youngest. But he loved Joseph best of all.

One day Jacob gave Joseph a beautiful coat. It was a coat of many bright colors. Joseph was happy with the coat. He liked to wear it.

But Joseph's brothers were angry. They said, "Our father does not give us such pretty things." And they began to hate Joseph.

One night Joseph had a dream. In his dream he was out in the field. His brothers were there, too. They were all cutting the ripe grain. They tied the grain into golden sheaves. Each one had a sheaf of grain. When they had tied their sheaves, the other sheaves bowed before Joseph's sheaf.

Joseph told his brothers about his dream. That made them still more angry with him. They said, "What do you think your dream means? Do you think we will all bow down to you?"

After a while Joseph had another dream. He saw the sun, moon and eleven stars bow down to him.

Joseph told his brothers about that dream, too. Then they were more angry than ever. They said, "Do you think your father and mother and eleven brothers will bow down before you?"

And Joseph's brothers hated him more and more.

Joseph told his father Jacob the dreams. Jacob scolded Joseph. Jacob said to Joseph, "You must not think that your mother and I and your brothers will ever bow down to you."

But Jacob remembered the dreams that Joseph dreamed. Sometimes he wondered what those dreams could mean.

VIII

Joseph's Brothers Sell Him

(Genesis 37:12-35; 42:21, 22)

Sometimes Joseph's brothers went far away from home to find grass for the sheep. One day they went to Shechem. They did not come back at night. They stayed away for a few days.

Then Jacob called Joseph.

Jacob said to Joseph, "Your brothers went to Shechem. Now I will send you to Shechem to see if they are well."

Shechem was a long way off. Joseph put on his beautiful coat of many colors. Away he went, down the lonely road.

Joseph came to Shechem at last. But his brothers were not there. He looked for them in the fields and on the hills. He could not find them.

Joseph did not know what to do. He did not want to go back home. He must see if all was well with his brothers.

A man came walking along the road. He saw Joseph. He said to Joseph, "What are you looking for?"

Joseph said, "I am looking for my brothers. My father said they were in Shechem. He sent me to see if they are well."

"Oh," said the man, "I know them. They were here, but they went away. I heard them say that they were going to Dothan."

The man showed Joseph the way, and Joseph went to Dothan.

There Joseph saw the sheep grazing in the green grass. And he saw his brothers sitting near the sheep.

Joseph's brothers saw Joseph coming.

"Look," they said, "here comes the dreamer." They still hated Joseph.

When Joseph came near, they saw that he wore his coat of many colors. That made them angry.

One of the brothers said, "Let's kill him. Let's kill him and tell our father that a wild animal killed him."

And another said, "Yes, let's kill him. And then we'll see if his dreams come true!"

But Reuben, the oldest, did not want them to harm Joseph.

Reuben said, "We must not kill our brother. Let us put him into the empty well instead."

Reuben said to himself, "When no one is looking, I will take him out of the well and send him home to our father."

Joseph came running. He began to tell his brothers how he had hunted and hunted for them.

But before he could tell it all, his brothers grabbed hold of him. They tore his beautiful coat off him. They threw him into the well.

There was no water in the well, but it was deep and dark.

Joseph was afraid down in the deep dark well. He called to his brothers. He begged them to take him out.

But Joseph's brothers would not listen. They sat eating, up in the sunshine. Down in the dark well, Joseph cried and begged.

After lunch Reuben went away for a little while.

While he was away, some strange men came riding along. Joseph's brothers saw them coming. The strange men came nearer and nearer, riding on their camels.

Suddenly Judah said, "I know what to do with Joseph. We must not kill him. Let's sell him to these men."

The others said, "Yes, yes. Let's sell him."

Reuben was not there.

When the men on camels came near, Joseph's brothers pulled Joseph out of the well. They dragged him to the road. They stopped the men on the camels.

"Look," they said. "We want to sell this boy. Will you buy him?"

The men looked at Joseph. Joseph begged his brothers not to sell him.

The men said, "Yes, we will buy him."

The men counted out some money. They gave the money to Joseph's brothers. Then they took Joseph and rode away.

After a while Reuben came back. He went straight to the well and called Joseph. But Joseph did not answer. Joseph was not in the well.

Reuben hurried to his brothers. "What did you do with Joseph?" he asked.

They told him what they had done.

Then Reuben was sad. He said, "How can we go home and tell our father?"

But his brothers said, "We know what to do."

They caught a little goat and killed it. They took Joseph's coat and put goat blood on the coat.

They said, "We will send this to our father. He will know it is Joseph's coat. He will think that a wild animal killed Joseph."

So they sent the coat to Jacob.

Jacob looked at the coat, and he was sure that it was Joseph's coat.

Jacob said, "Surely a wild animal has killed Joseph."

Then Jacob was sad for many, many days. He thought that Joseph was dead.

5

JOSEPH IN EGYPT

I

Joseph Is a Slave

(Genesis 39, 40)

The strange men took Joseph far away from home. They took him to the land of Egypt. There they sold him. A man named Potiphar bought Joseph. Joseph became Potiphar's slave.

Joseph was sad because he was far away from home. But he trusted God. He was a good slave. God blessed Joseph. And Potiphar was kind to Joseph. God blessed Potiphar, too, because he was kind to Joseph.

But one day Potiphar's wife became angry with Joseph. She lied about him to Potiphar. Potiphar believed her lie. He became angry with Joseph, too. And he put Joseph in prison.

Joseph still trusted God, even in prison. And God blessed Joseph in prison. The keeper of the prison was kind to Joseph. He let Joseph walk around inside the prison. He let him help with the work.

One day King Pharaoh sent two men to prison. He was angry with these two men. They were his butler and his baker.

Joseph saw the butler and the baker in prison. Sometimes he talked with them.

One morning Joseph came to the room of the butler and baker. He found them looking very sad.

Joseph asked them, "What makes you look so sad this morning?"

"Oh," said the butler, "we had such strange dreams last night. We are afraid the dreams mean something bad."

Then Joseph said, "Only God knows what your dreams mean. Tell me your dreams."

Joseph knew that God would show him the meaning of the dreams.

The butler said, "In my dream there was a grape-vine. The grape-vine had three branches. Leaves and little flowers grew on the branches. The little flowers grew into grapes. When the grapes were ripe, I picked them. I squeezed the juice of the grapes into Pharaoh's cup. And I gave the cup to Pharaoh."

Joseph said, "You saw three branches in your dream. The three branches mean three days. After three days, Pharaoh will take you out of prison. He will make you his butler again. You will give him his cup of wine again."

How happy the butler was to hear that! He would soon be out of prison!

Joseph said to him, "When you are out of prison, think of me. Tell Pharaoh about me. Maybe Pharaoh will take me out of prison, too."

Then the baker told his dream. He said, "In my dream I had three baskets on my head, one on top of the other. In the baskets there was bread and cake for Pharaoh. But the birds came and pecked at the bread and cake. Then I awoke."

Joseph looked sad when he heard the baker's dream. He said, "The three baskets mean three days. After three days Pharaoh will take you out of prison. But he will not make you his baker again. He will hang you. And the birds will peck at you."

Then the baker was very sad.

The three days went by. Pharaoh sent for the butler and the baker. He took them both out of prison. He hanged the baker. He took the butler back to the palace to work for him again.

The butler was happy to be out of prison. But he forgot all about Joseph.

II

Joseph in Pharaoh's Palace

(Genesis 41)

Every day the butler brought Pharaoh his wine. But the butler never thought to tell Pharaoh about Joseph. So two long years went by, and Joseph was still in prison.

Then, one night, Pharaoh dreamed a strange dream. In his dream Pharaoh was standing by the river. He saw seven fat cows come walking out of the water. Then he saw seven thin cows come out. The seven thin cows ate up the seven fat cows. And the seven thin cows were still thin.

Pharaoh awoke. He thought, "What a strange dream!"

Then Pharaoh fell asleep again, and began to dream again. This time he saw a tall corn plant with seven big fat ears of corn on it. Then seven thin ears grew beside the seven fat ears. And the seven thin ears swallowed up the seven fat ears.

Pharaoh awoke again. "Surely," he thought, "such strange dreams must have a special meaning."

God often spoke to people in dreams in those days.

So Pharaoh called his wise men. He told them the dreams. "Now," he said, "tell me what the dreams mean."

But the wise men shook their heads. They could not tell the meaning of the dreams.

Just then the butler came to bring Pharaoh his wine. He heard about the dreams. And then he thought of Joseph.

Quickly the butler went to Pharaoh.

The butler said, "O Pharaoh, I am ashamed. There is something I should have told you long ago. Once upon a time you were angry with me and with the baker. You put us both into prison. There was a man in prison whose name was Joseph. One night the baker and I each had a dream. Our dreams were very strange. But Joseph told us the meaning of the dreams. And, O Pharaoh, everything happened just as Joseph said it would."

Then Pharaoh said, "Send for this Joseph."

They sent to get Joseph out of prison. Joseph washed himself and put on clean clothes. When he was ready, he followed Pharaoh's servant. They went to the palace. They went into the room where the great Pharaoh was.

Joseph bowed before Pharaoh.

Pharaoh said to Joseph, "I have heard that you can tell the meaning of dreams."

But Joseph said, "I cannot tell the meaning of dreams. Only God can do that."

So Pharaoh told Joseph the dreams. He told about the seven thin cows that ate up the seven fat cows. He told about the seven thin ears of corn that swallowed up the seven fat ears.

Then Joseph said, "God has sent Pharaoh the dreams. The dreams tell what is going to happen. The two dreams mean the same thing. There will be seven fat years. The rain will fall; the grain and fruit will grow; there will be plenty of food. Then there will be seven thin years. The rain will not fall; the grain and fruit will not grow; there will not be enough food."

Pharaoh listened carefully.

Then Joseph said, "This is what Pharaoh should do: he should choose a wise man to save food in the fat years. He should build big barns, and fill them with food. Then, when the seven thin years come, and nothing grows, there will be food in the barns."

Pharaoh thought that was a good plan.

Pharaoh said, "Joseph is the wisest man in all Egypt. Let Joseph take care of the food and build the barns."

So Pharaoh made Joseph governor of Egypt.

Pharaoh took a ring off his own finger and put it on Joseph's finger. He put a chain of gold around Joseph's neck. He gave Joseph beautiful clothes to wear. And he let Joseph ride in Pharaoh's chariot.

Pharaoh told all the people of Egypt to do just as Joseph said.

So Joseph, the slave, became governor of Egypt.

The seven fat years came. Joseph built big barns and filled them with food.

Then the seven thin years came. Nothing grew in the fields and gardens. But Joseph opened the barns. There was food enough for everybody.

III

Joseph's Dreams Come True

(Genesis 42)

Far away, in the land of Canaan, Joseph's father and his brothers needed food. Nothing grew in their fields and gardens. The little children were hungry.

One day Jacob heard that there was food in Egypt. Jacob said to his sons, "We do not need to go hungry. There is corn in Egypt. Go to Egypt and buy some corn."

Ten of Joseph's brothers said they would go. They took empty sacks for the corn, and rode away on their donkeys. They left Benjamin at home. Jacob did not want Benjamin to go so far away.

After a long, long ride, the ten brothers came to Egypt. There they heard about the great governor of Egypt. They heard that he was almost like a king.

They had to go ask the governor to let them buy corn. So Joseph's brothers went to see Joseph. But they did not know that he was Joseph. They bowed low before the great governor.

Joseph looked at those ten men. And he knew who they were. He knew that they were his own brothers.

But Joseph made believe that he did not know them. In a rough voice he said, "Where did you come from? Who are you?"

They said, "We came from Canaan to buy food. We are all brothers."

Then Joseph looked angry and said, "You are spies. You have come to spy the land."

The brothers said, "Oh, no! We are not spies. We are honest men. We have an old father at home, and one more brother. We had another brother, too, but he's gone."

Joseph acted as if he did not believe them. He said, "You are spies." And he put them all in prison.

There they sat in prison. They thought about their poor old father. They thought of Joseph, too. They wondered if he was a slave somewhere in this strange land.

Joseph left them in prison for three days. Then he said, "You may go home now — all but one. I will keep one in prison. If you come back for more corn, you must bring your youngest brother with you. Then I will know that you are honest men. Do not dare to come back without your youngest brother!"

Joseph told his servants to fill the sacks with corn. He told them to put the money back in the sacks. Then he sent nine brothers home. He kept Simeon in prison.

The nine brothers put the sacks of corn on their donkeys. They rode away home. But they were sad. They said to each other, "This has happened to us because we sold Joseph."

At night they stopped to sleep at an inn. They had to feed their donkeys. One of the men opened his sack of corn. And there, on top of the corn, he saw his money.

He called to his brothers, "Look what is in my sack!"

They looked, and when they saw the money they were afraid. That rough governor would surely say that they had stolen the money!

They went on home. They told their father Jacob all about the governor of Egypt. They said, "He is a hard man. He said we may not come back unless we take Benjamin with us."

Jacob shook his head. He said, "Joseph is gone. Simeon is gone. Now you talk about taking Benjamin. If anything happens to Benjamin, I shall die of sorrow."

They opened their sacks for food. And they found more money. Each man had money in his sack. Then they were more afraid than ever to go back.

IV

Joseph's Brothers Come Again

(Genesis 43, 44:1-3)

Every day they ate of the corn of Egypt. There were many families and many children. Soon all the corn was gone.

Then Jacob said to his sons, "You must go to Egypt for more corn."

Judah said, "We have to take Benjamin along. The governor is a hard man. He will not let us buy corn unless we take Benjamin along."

Jacob did not want to let Benjamin go. But there was no more food. The brothers promised to take care of Benjamin.

At last Jacob said, "Go then. Take a present along for the governor. I pray that God will take care of you. Perhaps the governor will let Simeon and Benjamin come back."

So Joseph's brothers went to Joseph again. They bowed down before him once more. Benjamin bowed, too.

Joseph was glad to see Benjamin. He wanted to put his arms around him and kiss him. But Joseph did not. He kept his secret. He did not tell them that he was Joseph.

Joseph said to his servant, "Take these men to my house. Make a big dinner for them."

All the brothers went to Joseph's house. Simeon came, too, out of prison. Joseph's servants made a big dinner.

Joseph put all his brothers in a row at the table, with the oldest first and the youngest last. The brothers were surprised. How could this governor know how old each one was? But they sat down to eat.

Joseph was kind to them. He asked them about their father. He told them that he, too, worshipped God. He gave them plenty to eat and drink. They were all happy.

Then Joseph talked to his servant in secret. He said to the servant, "Fill the sacks with corn, and put the money back in again. And put my cup, my silver cup, in the sack of the youngest man."

The servant did just as Joseph said. He put the money in the sacks. He put Joseph's silver cup in Benjamin's sack.

In the morning the brothers put the sacks on their donkeys. They rode away. They were happy. They were glad that Simeon and Benjamin were both safe. They hurried to get home to their father Jacob.

They did not know that the silver cup was in Benjamin's sack.

V

The Silver Cup

(Genesis 44:3-34; 45, 46)

Joseph's brothers went as fast as they could. They had good news for their father Jacob. Simeon was with them, and Benjamin was safe, and their sacks were full of corn.

But they had gone only a little way, when they heard someone coming behind them. They looked, and they saw the governor's servant, on horseback, coming after them.

He caught up with them, and he looked very angry.

When the sheep had finished
drinking, Jacob talked to Rachel.

*How happy Jacob was to see his
son Joseph again!*

In a loud voice the servant said, "Why did you steal my master's cup? His silver cup?"

Joseph's brothers stared at the man! "Oh, no, sir," they said. "We would not do such a thing. We would not steal anything from your master."

They said, "You may look in all our sacks. If you find it, you may kill the one who has it in his sack. And the rest of us will be your slaves."

The servant of the governor shook his head. "If I find it," he said, "the man who has it in his sack will be my master's slave. The rest of you may go home."

Then he began to hunt. He opened Reuben's sack first. Reuben was the oldest. The silver cup was not in Reuben's sack. Then he opened the sack of the next-to-the-oldest. The silver cup was not in his sack. He opened the next and the next and the next. He did not find the silver cup. Now there was only Benjamin's sack left.

All the brothers stood around. They were sure the cup was not in Benjamin's sack. But the man opened the sack — and there was the cup! It was in Benjamin's sack!

Joseph's servant said, "I'll take Benjamin back with me."

Then Joseph's brother said, "We'll all go back. We can't let Benjamin go back alone."

So they all turned around and rode back to Egypt, back to the hard governor.

When they came to the governor, they fell down on their faces.

Joseph talked to them in an angry voice. He said, "How did you dare to steal my cup?"

Then Judah said, "We do not know what to say. The Lord is punishing us for our sins. We will all be your slaves."

Joseph said, "No. I do not want you all to be my slaves. I want only the one who had my cup in his sack. He will be my slave."

Then Judah said, "Please listen to me. Our father is an old man. Benjamin is his youngest son. He will surely die if we do not take Benjamin home with us. He loves Benjamin very, very much."

Then Judah told about Joseph. He said, "There was another son once. My father loved him most of all. But he is gone. Now if Benjamin does not come back, my father will die of sorrow. Let me stay and be your slave. But send Benjamin home."

Then Joseph's eyes filled with tears. He sent the Egyptian servants out of the room. When he was alone with his brothers, he began to cry.

"I am Joseph!" he said. "I am your brother, Joseph!"

Joseph's brothers stared at him. Could this be their brother? This great governor? Could this be the Joseph they sold to Egypt?

And they were afraid. What would Joseph do to them? They did not know what to say.

But Joseph said, "Do not be afraid. You meant to do harm to me. But God turned everything for good. Now you can go get my father. You can all come to Egypt. There is food enough here for you all."

They talked a long time. There was so much to tell.

At last Joseph's brothers hurried home. They could hardly go fast enough. They were so eager to tell Jacob about Joseph.

Jacob saw them coming, and he walked to meet them. Jacob was an old man.

Jacob's sons called out to him, "Joseph is alive! Joseph is alive, and he is the governor of Egypt!"

Jacob could hardly believe that!

His sons said, "Joseph is sending a chariot. He wants you to come to Egypt. He wants all of us to come to Egypt. He is sending his chariot for you to ride in."

And after a little while the chariot came. Then Jacob believed that Joseph was alive.

Jacob was very happy. He said, "I will go to see Joseph. He is really alive."

And in the night God spoke to Jacob. God said to him, "Go down to Egypt. I will bless you there."

So Jacob and his sons and all their children went to Egypt. When Joseph heard they were coming, he took his chariot and rode to meet them. The horses ran down the road swiftly, pulling the chariot. And there, at last, Joseph saw them coming.

Then Joseph jumped down and ran to his old father. How happy Jacob was to see his son Joseph again! Jacob and Joseph threw their arms around each other. They kissed each other, and they wept for joy.

*See accompanying illustration
between pages 64 and 65*

6

THE CHILDREN OF ISRAEL LEAVE EGPYT

I

A Baby in a Basket

(Genesis 49, 50; Exodus 1, 2)

Jacob and his sons, and all their children, lived in Egypt for many years. Jacob became very old. Then he called all his sons to his bedside. He told them that God would some day bring them back to Canaan. And he told them that some day God would send a Saviour.

Then Jacob blessed his sons. And he died.

After a while Joseph and his brothers died, too. God took them away, one by one.

The children of Joseph and of his brothers lived in Egypt. There were very many children. God blessed them. They became a great nation. They were called the children of Israel.

Then there was another Pharaoh. The new Pharaoh did not like the children of Israel. He said, "There are too many of them."

This Pharaoh made the children of Israel his slaves. He made them work very hard. They had to make bricks. They had to build cities with the bricks. They worked very, very hard.

Pharaoh also made a cruel law. The law said that every baby boy must be thrown into the river to drown.

One day a very dear baby boy was born. His mother and father loved the baby. They would not throw him into the river.

The mother hid the baby. She kept him a long time.

But after a while the mother did not dare keep the baby any longer. He was three months old. Sometimes he cried very loud. Pharaoh's soldiers would surely hear him.

The mother thought and thought about it. One morning she went to the river and picked some reeds. She took the reeds home. She wove the reeds into a basket.

She made the basket very strong. When it was finished, she filled all the cracks with pitch. Then it was like a little boat.

The mother made a bed in the little basket. She put the baby in it, and covered him carefully. Then she took the basket to the river.

The baby's sister, Miriam, went along.

At the edge of the river they put the basket down. It rocked on the little waves among the reeds. The mother did not want it to float away. So Miriam stayed to watch. And the mother went home.

Miriam hid in the bushes. After a while she heard voices. She saw ladies come to the river. It was the princess, Pharaoh's daughter. She and her maids were coming to bathe in the river.

Would they see the basket? Miriam watched. One of the maids walked near the basket. Then she ran back to the princess, to tell her something. And Miriam heard the princess say, "Go and get it."

The maid got the basket, and Miriam watched her bring it to the princess. She saw the princess lift the cover. And she heard the baby cry.

Then the princess said, "It is one of the babies of the children of Israel." And Miriam knew that she felt sorry for the baby.

So Miriam came out of her hiding place and went to the princess. She said, "Shall I go find a nurse to take care of the baby?"

The princess said, "Yes, go find a nurse."

Miriam ran home. "Oh, Mother!" she said, "the princess found the basket! And she wants a nurse!"

Miriam's mother hurried back with Miriam.

The princess said, "Take this baby home with you. Take care of him for me. I will pay you. When he is old enough, bring him to me."

How happy the mother was! She bowed to the princess, and hurried home with her baby.

She loved her baby. She took good care of him. She taught him about God.

But when he was old enough, she had to give him to the princess. She brought him to the palace. The princess called him Moses, and said that he was her boy.

II

The Burning Bush

(Exodus 2, 3, 4)

Moses lived with the princess until he was a man. He went to school in the palace. He learned all the wisdom of Egypt. But he did not forget God.

All this time Pharaoh was cruel. He made the children of Israel work very hard. They were his slaves.

Moses wanted to help the children of Israel. He did not want to live in the palace while they worked so hard. But he did not know how to help them. So he ran away to the country. He became a shepherd.

One day, when Moses was with the sheep, he saw a burning bush. The bush burned and burned, but it did not burn up. That seemed very strange. Moses went near the bush to see it better.

Then suddenly Moses heard a voice call, "Moses! Moses!"

Moses looked around. He did not see anyone. But he said, "Here I am!"

Then the voice said, "Do not come near the bush. Take your shoes off your feet, for you are standing on holy ground."

Moses took off his shoes. He knew it must be God who spoke to him. He knew it must be God who made the bush burn so strangely. He put his hands over his face.

God said to him, "I am the God of Abraham, Isaac and Jacob. The children of Israel are My people. They cry to Me because Pharaoh makes them work very hard. Now I have come to help them."

Moses listened. He was glad that God had come to help His people.

God said, "I shall bring them to the land of Canaan. And I have chosen you, Moses, to take them out of Egypt."

Then Moses said, "Oh, no! Do not ask me to do that! How can I do that? They will not follow me. And Pharaoh will not listen to me."

God said to him, "I will go with you. I will bring them to a beautiful land."

But Moses was afraid. He said, "The people will not believe me. They will not believe that God talked with me."

Then God gave Moses two signs to show the people.

God said, "Throw your rod on the ground."

Moses had the rod in his hand. It was a dry stick that he used for the sheep. Moses threw it on the ground.

Then the rod turned into a snake. The snake crawled on the ground. Moses began to run away from it.

But God said, "Take hold of the snake by its tail."

So Moses caught hold of it. And the snake became a rod again.

That was one sign he could do for the children of Israel.

Then God said, "Put your hand inside your coat."

Moses put his hand inside his coat. He took it out. He

looked at it and saw that it was white as snow. An awful disease, leprosy, had come on his hand.

God said to Moses, "Put your hand inside your coat again."

Moses put his hand inside his coat again. When he took it out, it was all better. The disease was gone.

That was another sign he could do for the children of Israel.

Then God said, "When you talk to the children of Israel, you can do those two signs. Then they will believe that I sent you."

And God promised to send Moses' brother, Aaron, to help him.

So Moses brought his sheep home, and he went to Egypt.

III

Pharaoh Says "No" to God

(Exodus 5, 6)

Moses went to Egypt. On the way he met Aaron. God had sent Aaron to meet Moses. Then Moses and Aaron went on to Egypt together.

Moses and Aaron went to the children of Israel first.

The children of Israel had not heard about God for a long, long time. They did not have a Bible. They thought God had forgotten them.

Moses told them that God was going to help them, that God was going to take them out of Egypt, that God would give them a beautiful land to live in.

Then Moses showed them the two signs.

He threw his rod on the ground. It became a snake. He picked it up, and it became a rod again.

After that, he put his hand inside his coat. When he took it out, all the children of Israel saw that it was white like snow. Then he put his hand inside his coat again, and it became well.

So the children of Israel knew that God had sent Moses. And

they were very happy. They wanted to get away from cruel Pharaoh.

Then Moses and Aaron went to Pharaoh. They told Pharaoh what God had said.

Pharaoh said, "Who is God? I do not know Him. I will not let the children of Israel go!"

Pharaoh sent Moses and Aaron away. He was angry. He made the children of Israel work harder than ever.

Moses felt sorry for the people. They worked so very, very hard. Moses prayed to God. He said, "O God, Pharaoh will not let the people go. He makes them work harder than ever."

But God said, "I am God Almighty. I will bring My people to Canaan. But first I will show Pharaoh great wonders."

IV

God's Wonders in Egypt

(Exodus 7-10)

God said to Moses, "Tomorrow, early in the morning, you must go to the river. Pharaoh will come there to wash himself."

And God told Moses just what to say and do.

Early in the morning Moses and Aaron went to the river. Pharaoh came to wash himself. Moses and Aaron went to meet Pharaoh.

Moses said to Pharaoh, "The Lord God says, 'Let my people go.' But you will not listen to Him. Now He will show you that He is truly the Lord."

Then Aaron hit the water of the river with his rod.

And the water became red. It turned to blood. Everywhere in Egypt the water turned to blood, even all the little puddles and ponds.

The people could not drink the water. The fish in the river died. The water smelled bad.

But Pharaoh would not let the people go.

Moses went to Pharaoh again. He said to Pharaoh, "Thus saith the Lord, 'Let My people go, or I will send frogs.'"

Pharaoh would not listen.

So Aaron held his rod out over the river. And frogs came hopping out of the water. More and more frogs came. Hundreds and hundreds of frogs came. They hopped everywhere—into the houses, into the bedrooms, even into the beds. There were frogs everywhere.

Then Pharaoh said to Moses, "Pray to your God. Ask Him to take these frogs away."

Moses did pray to God. And all the frogs died.

But when the frogs were dead, Pharaoh hardened his heart. He would not let the people go.

Pharaoh did not want to obey God.

*   *   *

God sent other awful wonders upon Egypt.

He sent lice. Aaron hit the ground with the rod, and the dust became lice. The lice crawled all over. There were lice on the men, women and children, and on the animals, too.

After the lice died, God sent flies. Great clouds of flies came buzzing into the houses of the Egyptians, and into the palace of Pharaoh. They buzzed around Pharaoh's head. They flew into his food.

But the flies did not go to the homes of the people of Israel.

Then Pharaoh again called for Moses and Aaron. He begged them to take the flies away.

Pharaoh said, "I will let the children of Israel go. Only ask your God to take these flies away."

And Moses said, "I will ask God, and He will take the flies away tomorrow."

The next day Moses prayed, and God took away the flies. But Pharaoh hardened his heart again. He would not let the people go.

Then God sent sickness upon the animals of Egypt. Many of Pharaoh's sheep and cows and goats and camels died. All over Egypt, animals became sick and died.

The animals of the people of Israel did not die.

But Pharaoh still hardened his heart. He would not let the people go.

After that, God said to Moses and Aaron, "Take handfuls of ashes from the furnace. Throw the ashes up high into the air."

Moses and Aaron took ashes. They went to Pharaoh. They threw the ashes up high into the air before Pharaoh. The ashes blew away. And where the ashes fell, it made boils on men and animals.

But still Pharaoh would not let the people go.

Once more Moses went to see Pharaoh.

Moses said to Pharaoh, "You must let God's people go. If you do not let them go, God will send more wonders. He will send a great storm."

But Pharaoh would not listen.

The next morning Moses went out-of-doors. He held his rod up high toward heaven. Then big dark clouds came. The clouds spread all over the sky. They hid the sun. The thunder began to rumble. Lightning shot from the clouds. Balls of lightning rolled along the ground.

Then rain came pouring down. Big hailstones began to fall. The hailstones broke trees and knocked down the grain in the fields.

Pharaoh was afraid. The awful thunder shook his palace. The lightning was like fire from heaven. Pharaoh trembled.

"Go call Moses!" Pharaoh said to his servants.

Moses came. And Pharaoh said to him, "I am a wicked man. Pray to your God that this awful thunder and lightning and hail may stop. Then I will let the children of Israel go."

Moses said, "As soon as I am outside the city, I will pray. Then the storm will stop."

Moses did pray to God. Then the thunder and lightning and hail stopped. The dark clouds rolled away. The sun shone again.

But when Pharaoh saw the sunshine, he hardened his heart again. He would not let the people go.

Then God sent grasshoppers into the land of Egypt — great big grasshoppers. They ate all the grain and the grass that was left after the storm. They came into the houses of the Egyptians. They were everywhere. People could not walk without stepping on grasshoppers.

But Pharaoh would not let the people go.

After the grasshoppers, God sent a great darkness. The darkness came down like a big thick blanket and covered Egypt. Egypt was darker than darkest midnight. People could not see each other. They could not make a light. They could not get up to work or eat. For three days the terrible darkness covered Egypt.

Pharaoh decided to let the people go for sure this time. But when the darkness left he again hardened his heart. He would not let the people go.

V

The Angel of Death

(Exodus 11, 12)

God had sent nine wonders upon Egypt. He would send one more. He told Moses about it, and He sent Moses to tell Pharaoh. This one would be the worst of all.

Moses went to Pharaoh and said, "The Lord God says, 'About midnight I will go through the land of Egypt, and all the first-born shall die. In every house the first-born, the oldest child, shall die.'"

Then Pharaoh was very angry. He said to Moses, "Go away! Don't you dare come to see me again!"

And Moses said, "I shall never see you again." Moses knew that this time Pharaoh would let them go.

So Moses told the children of Israel to get ready. He told them just what they should do.

Each family must kill a little lamb. They must take some of the blood and put it around the outside of the doorway, some on each side of the door and some above the door. Then they must go inside, and lock the door.

Moses said, "God will come to Egypt in the night. In every house of Egypt the first-born shall die. But God will pass over every house that has blood around its doorway."

Moses told the people to roast the lamb for supper. He told them to put their coats on and be ready to go. He told them to eat supper standing up, and to pack all their goods.

The people of Israel did just as Moses said. Each family killed a lamb. They put blood on the doorway — above the door and on each side. They roasted the lamb. They packed all their goods. They put on their coats. They were ready to go. And then they ate their supper.

That night God's Angel of Death came to Egypt. The Angel of Death went to every house. If there was no blood on the door, the Angel of Death went in — and the oldest child of the family died. If the Angel of Death saw blood on the door, he passed over that house.

In the middle of the night the Egyptians awoke. Each family found its oldest child dead. Then they moaned and cried.

Pharaoh awoke, too. He found his son, the prince, dead.

Then Pharaoh sent for Moses in the night. He told him to take all the people of Israel, and go. He told them to hurry. He was afraid of God now.

The people of Egypt were afraid of God, too. They helped the people of Israel hurry away. They gave them presents of gold and silver and clothes.

Everybody had to carry something. Then away they went — mothers and fathers, boys and girls, little babies on their mothers' arms. They marched away in a long, long row. All their sheep and cows and goats marched along, too. They all went out of Egypt. At last they were free.

That was a wonderful night. The children of Israel never forgot that night. Each year they have a feast — the Passover Feast. At the Passover Feast they remember that the Angel of Death passed over their houses when He saw the blood. They were saved by the blood of the lamb.

And we, too, are saved by the blood of the Lamb — God's Lamb, our Saviour Jesus Christ.

VI

A Cloud Leads the Way

(Exodus 13, 14:1-14, 19, 20)

All the next day the children of Israel marched along the road, farther and farther away from Pharaoh. They were very happy. They were free at last!

Sometimes they stopped to eat along the way. At night they stopped to rest. Then they went on again.

Just ahead of the people there was a Cloud. The Cloud looked like a pillar. And it moved on ahead of the people. Each day the Cloud moved on farther, and the people followed it. The Lord led His people by that Cloud. At night the Cloud was like a glowing fire. Then it gave light for the people.

At last the Cloud stopped by the Red Sea. There the people put up their tents. They could rest now. They were far away from Pharaoh.

But away back in Egypt, Pharaoh thought about the people of Israel. He wished he had not let them go. He thought and thought about it.

"Why did we let them go?" he said. "We will go catch them, and bring them back."

So Pharaoh called his servants and his soldiers. He told them to get ready quickly. And with all his chariots and his soldiers, Pharaoh went after the children of Israel.

Soon the children of Israel, resting in their tents, heard a noise. It was a noise like rolling thunder. It was the noise of many feet, of men and horses marching. And it came nearer and nearer!

The people ran to Moses. They cried, "Pharaoh is coming! He is coming with all his chariots and his soldiers!"

The people did not know what to do. The Red Sea was in front of them. Pharaoh was behind them. Where could they go? They were terribly afraid.

Moses said to them, "Just be quiet. Wait and see what God will do for you."

Then Moses prayed to God.

The Egyptians came nearer and nearer. The children of Israel shivered with fear.

And then the Cloud moved. At first it was in front of the children of Israel. It moved till it was behind them. There it stopped, right between the children of Israel and the Egyptians. For God would not let Pharaoh harm His people.

Night came. The Cloud began to glow like a fire. It gave light to the children of Israel. But it was dark on the side toward the Egyptians.

So the children of Israel were safe.

VII

A Path Through the Sea

(Exodus 14:15-31; 15:1-21)

The Egyptians were angry. They wanted to catch the children of Israel. But they could not, because the Cloud was in the way.

In the night, God spoke to Moses. He told Moses to hold out his rod over the water of the Red Sea. God said He would make a path through the Red Sea.

Moses did as God said. He went to the edge of the Red Sea and he held out his rod over the water. Then an east wind began to blow. It blew very hard. It blew all night long. God used the wind to blow a path in the Red Sea. It piled the water into two high walls. And it made a dry path between the two high walls of water.

The children of Israel stood on the shore, watching. They saw how the wind made a path between the two high walls of water.

At last Moses told them to go ahead, to walk on the path between the two high walls of water.

The people obeyed Moses. They walked down the path on the bottom of the Red Sea between the two high walls of water. The Cloud gave them light. All through the long night the people marched along the path. By morning the long, long row of people had crossed the Red Sea. They were safe on the other side.

Pharaoh saw that path between the two high walls of water. Pharaoh saw the people walk on the path. He said, "We can walk there, too!"

So Pharaoh and his men drove the chariots into the path between the two high walls of water. Pharaoh and all his men followed the children of Israel. The children of Israel, standing on the other side, saw Pharaoh and all his men come.

Then God said to Moses, "Hold out your rod over the Red Sea again."

Moses held his rod over the Red Sea again, and the two high walls of water broke. They fell together with a great splash and the water covered the path. The water covered Pharaoh and all his men. They drowned in the Red Sea.

Then the children of Israel knew that Pharaoh could never harm them again. They all thanked God. Miriam, Moses' sister, played her timbrel while they all sang praises to God.

7

ON THE WAY TO THE PROMISED LAND

I

Bread from Heaven

(Exodus 16:1-15)

The children of Israel went on and on towards the land of Canaan, the land which God had promised them. Sometimes they put up their tents to rest. But when the Cloud moved, they followed the Cloud.

After a while they came to a wilderness. A wilderness is a very dry country. In this wilderness there were no trees, there was no corn or wheat. The children of Israel were afraid they would not find enough food.

So they grumbled. They said to Moses, "Why did you bring us to this wilderness? We had enough to eat in Egypt. Why did you take us out of Egypt?"

Moses said to them, "When you grumble, you grumble against God. It is God who brought you out of Egypt. Let us all come before God, to find out what He will say."

The people looked at the Cloud. They saw that it was glowing bright. The glory of God shone in the Cloud.

God spoke to Moses. He said, "Tell the people that I shall send them bread tomorrow. Tomorrow they will know that I am truly God."

*See accompanying illustration
between pages 96 and 97*

Then the people went back to their tents to wait until the next day.

The people said to each other, "How can God give us bread here in this wilderness? Where will He get enough bread for so many people?"

In the morning, when the people came out of their tents, they saw little white things lying on the ground.

They called to each other, "Look! What are those little white things on the ground?"

They picked up some of the little white things. But no one knew what they were.

Then Moses said, "This is the bread that God said He would send you."

It was bread from heaven!

The people tasted it. They said, "It tastes like bread and honey. It is very good." They called it manna.

II

Trust and Obey
(Exodus 16:16-36)

All the people went out to pick up manna and eat it.

Moses said to them, "You must take enough for breakfast, dinner, and supper. After a while it will be gone. But do not take any for tomorrow. Take just enough for one day."

Some of the people said to each other, "There is so much manna. Let's pick up some for tomorrow." And they took enough manna for two days.

But others said, "We must obey and trust God." They took just enough for one day.

After a while the sun came and melted the manna away.

The people ate manna for breakfast, dinner, and supper.

Those who took just enough for one day had none left.

Those who took enough for two days had some left. They put it into jars, to save it.

In the morning the people woke up and looked out of their tent doors. Yes, there it was, plenty of manna on the ground again!

The people who had none left ran out to pick some up.

The people who had some left went to their jars. But they found the manna in their jars sour and full of worms. They had to throw it away. Then they were ashamed.

So there was fresh manna every morning, all week long.

But on the sixth day Moses said to the people, "Today you must pick up enough manna for two days. Tomorrow is the Sabbath day. God will not send manna tomorrow, because He does not want you to work on the Sabbath day. So this morning you must pick up enough for two days."

Some of the people trusted God again. They obeyed Moses. They picked up enough manna for two days.

Others said, "The manna spoils. Why should we pick up some for tomorrow? We know it spoils." And they picked up just enough for one day.

The Sabbath morning came. The people opened their tent doors and looked out. And there was no manna on the ground. Some of the people went to hunt for manna, but they could not find any. Then they were ashamed. And they had nothing to eat.

The people who had saved manna went to their jars. They found the manna good to eat. It was not spoiled at all.

So God taught His people that they must obey Him and trust Him.

III

God Talks to His People

(Exodus 19, 20, 24)

The people of Israel traveled on and on. They followed the Cloud.

After a while they came to a high hill. That was Mount Sinai. The Cloud stopped by Mount Sinai. There the people put up their tents.

Then Moses said to the people, "In three days God Himself will come down to Mount Sinai. He will talk to you from the top of the Mount. You must wash yourselves and put on clean clothes. Be ready when He comes."

The people obeyed Moses. On the third day they were ready. They went out and stood by Mount Sinai.

On top of the Mount they saw a big dark cloud that was like smoke. It covered the top of the Mount. They saw lightning flash in the cloud. They heard the thunder roll. The whole Mount seemed to be on fire with the glory of God.

The people were afraid. But they waited to hear God speak.

Moses said to them, "Do not try to climb the Mount. Do not even go close to it. The Mount is holy because God is there."

So the people stood still. They saw the Lord come down upon the mountain in fire. They saw great clouds of smoke roll up.

After a while someone blew a trumpet. The trumpet blew loud and long. And then God spoke.

God's voice was loud, like thunder. He said, "I am the Lord, thy God. You shall not worship any other gods . . ."

The people stood very still. They trembled at the voice of God. They listened, and God gave the Ten Commandments.

But they said to Moses, "We are afraid. Let God talk to you. Then you can tell us what He says. We are afraid when He talks to us."

So the people stood farther away from the Mount. And God talked to Moses. He told Moses just how His people must serve Him and worship Him. He promised to bless His people.

Then God said to Moses, "Come up to Me in the Mount. I will give you My law on tablets of stone."

Moses told Aaron to take care of the people and to wait for him. Then he climbed up the Mount.

The people watched Moses go. They looked at the dark cloud on the top of the Mount. They saw the glory of God shining in the dark cloud. And they saw Moses climb up and up.

At last Moses went into the dark cloud. Then the people could no longer see him. They went quietly back to their tents.

Up on the Mount, God wrote the Ten Commandments on tablets of stone. And God talked with Moses.

IV

The Golden Calf

(Exodus 32, 33, 34; Deuteronomy 9)

The people could hardly wait for Moses to come down from the Mount. They said, "When he comes, he will tell us all that God commands us."

But Moses did not come down that day. And he did not come down the next day. A week passed, and still he did not come down. A whole month passed, and still he did not come down.

Then the people said to Aaron, "We do not know what has become of Moses. We are tired of waiting. Perhaps he will never come back."

And they said, "We want you to make us a god to lead us."

Aaron said, "Do you want me to make a god for you? All right. Bring me gold, and I will make you a god. Bring me your golden earrings. Bring me your bracelets and your golden chains."

The people took the earrings out of their ears. They gave them to Aaron. They gave Aaron their golden bracelets and other jewelry.

Aaron took all the earrings and other jewelry. He melted the gold and made a golden calf. It was a calf like the calves that the Egyptians worshipped as gods.

When the people saw the golden calf, they were happy. They said, "Look! This is the god that brought us out of Egypt!"

And Aaron said to them, "Tomorrow we shall have a big feast."

The next morning all the people came to the feast. Aaron made an altar. The people brought gifts to burn on the altar — gifts for the golden calf. They ate and drank. Then they held hands and danced around the golden calf. They sang songs. They said, "This is our god! This is the god that brought us out of Egypt!"

Moses, up on the Mount, could not see what the people were doing.

But God saw.

God said to Moses, "Go down to your people. They have forgotten Me already. They have made a golden calf, and are worshipping it."

Then Moses went down. In his hands he carried two stone tablets. On these tablets God Himself had written His law.

Moses came out of the cloud. He heard the people sing. He went on down, and soon he could see the golden calf, shining in the sun. And he saw the people dancing around the golden calf.

Then Moses was very angry. He threw down the stone tablets so that they broke in many pieces. He hurried down the Mount. He went right to that golden calf. He threw it down. Then he ground it to powder. And he put the gold powder in the water that the people had to drink.

Moses said to Aaron, "Why did you do this? Why did you lead the people to sin?"

And he said to the people, "You have sinned a very great sin. I will go and pray to God. Perhaps He will forgive you."

Moses went to pray. The people stood and watched him. They were sorry for their sin.

Moses prayed for a long time. He asked God to forgive Aaron and to forgive the people. God was very angry because of their sin.

But because Moses prayed so earnestly, the Lord said to Moses, "I will forgive them. I will go with them to Canaan."

After that God called Moses up to the Mount again. Moses made two new tablets of stone for the law. Moses was with God on Mount Sinai for forty days. The people waited for him.

When he came down, his face shone like the sun. The people knew that he had been with God.

V

Making a Tent for God

(Exodus 35-40; Leviticus 8)

One day Moses called all the people of Israel together. He said to them, "The Lord wants us to build a big tent for Him. We shall call this tent the Tabernacle. In this Tabernacle we shall meet God, pray to Him, and bring our gifts to Him."

God had told Moses just how to make the Tabernacle.

Moses said to the people, "Would you like to bring gifts to God? Then you may bring things for the making of the Tabernacle. You may bring things that we can use."

The people were glad that they could bring something to God. They had many beautiful things. The people of Egypt had given them silver and gold and many other beautiful things. They brought these to God.

Some brought silver and gold. Some brought beautiful wood. Some brought the soft fur of animals. Some brought their jewels.

The people brought so much that Moses had to tell them not to bring any more. There was enough for the making of the Tabernacle.

Then the people worked. Some of the women made cloth for curtains — blue and purple and red cloth. Some of the men carved wood.

God chose wise men to make the Tabernacle. These men worked for many, many days. They made two beautiful altars — a small one and a large one. They made a golden lamp that had seven lights. They made a box called an Ark. They covered the Ark with gold. They made two angels of gold bending over the Ark. They made a table of gold. And they made beautiful robes for the priest who would serve in the Tabernacle.

All the people were happy to work for God. They remembered how much God had done for them.

The people did everything that Moses told them to do. At last everything was made. Moses looked at everything, and he said it was just as God wanted it.

They set up the tent. It was very big. They hung beautiful curtains to make two rooms. All the way around these rooms there was a space called "the court." Moses and his helpers put all the furniture in place — the altars, the golden table, the lamp, and the Ark. Then the Tabernacle was ready.

Aaron was the High Priest or minister. Moses put the High Priest's robe on Aaron. It was a beautiful robe — blue and purple, embroidered with gold. There were little bells sewed on the bottom edge of the robe. The little bells tinkled when Aaron walked. Moses put a golden crown on Aaron's head. And he hung a breastplate of shining jewels around his neck.

Then Moses lit the seven lamps. And he burned sweet spices on the little golden altar.

The people brought animals to offer to God on the large altar. Aaron made the offerings ready. All the people stood outside, watching.

When the offerings were on the altar, Moses and Aaron lifted up their hands over the people to bless them.

And then God Himself sent fire from heaven to burn the offerings. The people saw the fire come down from God. And when they saw the fire come down from God, they fell on their faces to worship God.

The people were happy with the beautiful Tabernacle. It was their church.

VI

Afraid of Giants

(Numbers 13)

After a while the people of Israel came near to the land of Canaan. They had traveled for many, many days. But now they would soon be in the new land. How happy they were!

God said to Moses, "Choose twelve men, one from each of the twelve tribes of Israel. Send these twelve men ahead to Canaan. They will see what the land is like, and tell you about it."

Moses chose twelve men. He sent them to see the land of Canaan. These men were spies.

The twelve spies went away to see the land of Canaan.

The people could hardly wait for the twelve spies to come back. A week went by. Two weeks went by. A whole month went by. Every day the people looked for the spies.

At last, there they came! Men and women and children ran to meet them.

What were the spies carrying? Oh, a great big bunch of grapes. Two men carried the bunch of grapes, so that they would not crush them. They carried it on a stick between them. The spies had other fruit, too. They had big golden-brown figs, and rosy pomegranates. These wonderful fruits grew in Canaan, in their new country!

The spies went to Moses and Aaron. The people all followed them. They wanted to hear what the spies would say.

Moses and Aaron were glad to see the spies. Moses and Aaron looked at the wonderful fruit. What a wonderful country this must be — this country that God was going to give to His people!

Then the spies told their story. They said, "We went all through the land. We went to the cities and we went to the farms. Canaan is truly a rich country. It has wonderful fruit trees and wonderful gardens."

The people thought, "And that will be our country! We are almost there!"

But the spies shook their heads. They said, "It is a wonderful country. But the people who live there are strong people. They have big cities. They have walls around their cities — big, strong walls. And some of the people are giants."

Giants! When the people of Israel heard about the giants, they were afraid. Big cities with walls! And giants! How could they ever chase the giants out? How could they ever go into that country? All the people began to talk at once.

But one of the spies lifted up his hand and told them to be quiet. That was Caleb.

Caleb said, "Listen to me! We can take that land. It is true that the people are strong. But we can take the land. Let us go right away!"

Ten of the spies said, "No! We cannot take the land. The people are much stronger than we are. Some of them are very big giants. They are so big that we felt like little grasshoppers!"

Then all the people began to cry and wail. How could they fight against giants? What could they do? Where should they go? Should they go back to Egypt?

All night long the people cried and wailed.

Some said, "We wish we had stayed in Egypt."

Some said, "If we try to go to Canaan, we will all be killed."

Some said, "Let's go back to Egypt!"

The people could not sleep that night. They were afraid of the giants. They forgot that God is greater than any giant.

VII

"Because They Did Not Believe"
(Numbers 14:1-39)

The people were afraid to go to Canaan. They were afraid of the giants. All night long they cried and wailed.

In the morning the people went to Moses and Aaron. The people were angry. They said to Moses and Aaron, "Why did you bring us out of Egypt? Does God want us all to die here in the wilderness?"

That made Moses and Aaron very sad.

But Caleb, the good spy, was there. Joshua, another good spy, was there too. These two good spies told the people not to be afraid.

Caleb said, "The land of Canaan is a wonderful land. There are fine fruits in Canaan. We can be very happy there. If God loves us, He will give that land to us. We can go take it."

And Joshua said, "We do not need to be afraid. The Lord is with us. Why should we be afraid if the Lord is with us?"

But the people would not listen. They began to throw stones at Caleb and Joshua. They cried, "We will not go. We do not want our children killed. We will not listen!" They shouted at Moses and Aaron.

Then, suddenly, a bright light shone all around the Tabernacle. It was the glory of God shining there. The people stopped shouting. They did not even talk. They stood very still. They were afraid of God.

Out of the bright light God spoke. God said to Moses, "Will these people never trust Me? I have done great wonders for them. Why will they not believe Me and trust Me?"

And God said, "I will punish them. They shall no longer be My people."

Then Moses prayed for the people. Moses begged God to have mercy on the people and to forgive them.

And God said, "I will forgive them. But they shall never see the beautiful land of Canaan. All of them, except those that are under twenty years old, must die in the wilderness. Caleb and Joshua shall see Canaan, too, because they have trusted Me."

And God said that the people of Israel should go back to the wilderness.

Moses told the people what God said. Then they were very, very sorry. Slowly they went to their tents. Their heads were bowed. Their hearts were sad.

VIII

Too Late

(Numbers 14:40-45)

The men of Israel were up early the next morning.

They went to Moses and said, "We are ready to go to Canaan now. Yesterday we would not go. We sinned then. Now we are ready."

But Moses shook his head. Moses said, "No, you cannot go now. God has told you to go back to the wilderness. You must obey Him."

The men wanted to go just the same.

Moses said, "God will not go with you. It is too late now."

Then the men said, "We will go anyway!"

So they went. They marched toward the land of Canaan.

The people that lived in the hills saw the men of Israel come. These hill people came running down the hills, ready to fight. When the men of Israel saw them, they were afraid. They turned around and ran back.

The men of Israel could not fight against the hill people because God was not with them.

The men of Israel were ashamed. They went to their tents. They were sorry they had not trusted God yesterday.

Then all the children of Israel took up their tents, and they went back into the wilderness.

8

IN THE DESERT

I

The Wonder of Aaron's Rod
(Numbers 17)

Day after day Aaron was busy in the beautiful Tabernacle. The people brought animals as gifts to God. Aaron took the animals. He burned them to God on the big altar, for the sins of the people. Every morning and every evening Aaron burned sweet incense to God on the little altar. Aaron was the High Priest.

But after a while some other men thought they should have a turn to be High Priest. They said, "Why do Moses and Aaron do all the work in the Tabernacle? We are just as good and just as holy as Moses and Aaron."

Moses and Aaron heard it. And it made them sad. For God had made Aaron High Priest.

But the Lord said to Moses, "Tell the head men of Israel to bring rods to you — one rod for each tribe of Israel."

That would be twelve rods.

Moses told the men to bring the rods. The rods were dead sticks. Each man put his name on his rod. One of the rods was Aaron's. Aaron's name was on it.

Moses took the twelve rods and put them in the Tabernacle. Then he told the people to come back in the morning to see the rods.

In the morning the people came to the Tabernacle. They wondered what had happened to the rods.

Moses went into the Tabernacle. He came out with the twelve rods in his hand. One of the rods had green leaves. The other eleven rods were still dead sticks.

94

Moses gave each man his own rod, the rod with his name on it.

Last of all was the rod with green leaves. That rod was Aaron's. Moses gave it to Aaron, and all the people saw the green leaves. They came closer and saw that the rod had blossoms, too, and little brown almond nuts. God had made Aaron's rod grow.

The people knew that God had made Aaron's rod grow. Now they knew that Aaron was truly the High Priest. He was the one God Himself had chosen.

The people went back to their tents. And Moses put Aaron's rod back in the Tabernacle.

II

Moses and Aaron Sin

(Numbers 20:1-13)

Years went by. The children of Israel were still living in the wilderness. They were still living in tents. The older people died. The children grew up.

Then God led them to the edge of Canaan again. They put up their tents near Canaan. Now they had only to cross through the land of Edom. Then they would be in the Promised Land.

But the wilderness was very dry. The people could find no water.

Then the people went to Moses and Aaron.

Did they ask Moses and Aaron to pray for water? No. Instead, they grumbled and they scolded.

The people said to Moses and Aaron, "Why did you bring us here? There are no trees. There is no grass for our animals. We can't find water to drink."

Moses and Aaron were sorry to hear the people grumble and scold. They went to the Tabernacle. There they fell on their faces before God to pray.

Then God said to Moses, "Call all the people together. Tell them to come to the big rock that is in the wilderness. You must talk to the rock. Then the rock will give water."

Moses called the people to come to the rock. Moses had Aaron's rod in his hand — the rod that had the leaves and blossoms and almond nuts on it.

The people were still grumbling and scolding. Moses heard them, and he was angry.

Moses lifted Aaron's rod up high. He said to the people, "Must we get water out of this rock for you?"

And then he hit the rock. He hit it twice.

A spring of water came pouring out of the rock. It was clean, cold water. The people ran to get a drink. How good it was! So fresh and cool!

There was plenty of it — enough for all the people. Enough for all the animals, too.

But Moses had hit the rock. And God had told him to speak to the rock.

So God said to Moses and Aaron, "You did not do what I told you to do. I told you to talk to the rock. But you hit it with the rod, twice."

Then Moses and Aaron were ashamed. They did not know what to say.

God said to them, "Because you did not obey Me, you shall not go into the land of Canaan."

That made Moses and Aaron sad. But they knew that God does what is right. They knew they had not obeyed God. They deserved His punishment.

When God told them it was time to move on, they took the Tabernacle down again. The priests blew the trumpets to call the people to break camp. They folded their tents. They formed a long line and they marched on. God led them on with the Pillar of Cloud.

At night the Cloud glowed
brightly as a Pillar of Fire.

When God told them to move on,
the Cloud moved on before them.

III

A Long Way Around

(Numbers 20:14-29)

The children of Israel were by the land of Edom. Canaan was on the other side of Edom.

Moses sent a messenger to the king of Edom. He said to the king. "We are on our way to another land. May we go through your country?"

The king of Edom said, "No!"

Moses said to the king, "We will be very careful. We will not eat any fruit off your trees. We will not harm anything. The Lord led us out of Egypt. Please let us go through your land."

The king of Edom said, "You may not go through my land. If you do, my men will fight you."

So the children of Israel had to go around Edom. They had to go many, many miles farther to get to Canaan.

After a few days, the children of Israel stopped by a mountain. They put up their tents by this mountain. It was Mount Hor.

There God said to Moses and Aaron, "It is time for Aaron to die. Go up to the top of Mount Hor. Take Eleazar, Aaron's son, with you. Eleazar shall be High Priest after Aaron is gone."

Up the mountain they went: Moses, Aaron, and Eleazar. All the people stood below, watching. Aaron wore the High Priest's robe. It was a beautiful robe, you remember. It was made of fine blue cloth. It was embroidered with purple and scarlet thread. Little golden bells hung down from the hem. The little bells tinkled when Aaron walked. This was the robe he wore when he brought gifts to God in the Tabernacle.

When they were up on the mountain, Moses took the beautiful robe off Aaron. He put it on Eleazar. Now Eleazar would be High Priest.

After that, Aaron died. God took Aaron's soul to heaven. And Aaron was buried there, up on the mountain.

Moses and Eleazar went down the mountain together. The people saw them come — just Moses and Eleazar. Then they knew that Aaron had died. They went quietly to their tents. The people were sad. They loved Aaron.

IV

A Shining Snake

(Numbers 21:1-9)

The children of Israel still had a long way to go. They were getting very tired.

One day they said to Moses, "Why did you bring us out of Egypt? We had good things to eat in Egypt. Now we have only this manna. We are tired of this manna."

Manna was the bread that God sent from Heaven. It was wonderful bread. God sent it each morning, except on the Sabbath day.

But the children of Israel wanted melons and vegetables and garlic. So they grumbled and complained.

God heard them grumble and complain. He saw how cross and angry they were. We may not grumble and complain.

The people grumbled and complained every day. Then one day, when they were cross and angry again, God sent snakes into the camp.

The snakes crawled all around between the tents. They bit many people. The snake bites were poison. Some people died. Some were very sick.

Then the people cried to Moses. They said, "We have sinned! It was sinful of us to grumble and complain. Pray to God for us. Ask Him to take the snakes away."

Moses did pray.

And God said to Moses, "Make a snake of shining brass. Put it on a high pole. Tell the people to look at it when a snake bites them."

Moses quickly made a snake of shining brass. He put it on a pole. The pole was high, so that the people could see the shining snake from afar.

Then Moses sent word around, "If a snake bites you, look at the brass snake on the pole. Look at the shining brass snake. Then you will not die."

The snakes had bitten many people — mothers and fathers, and even little children. When they heard about the shining snake on the pole, they looked at it. Then the snake bites healed. The pain stopped. The people did not die.

Many, many years later Jesus said, "Just as Moses put the brass snake up on a pole in the wilderness, so Jesus, the Son of man must be lifted up, so that whosoever believeth on Him may have everlasting life" (John 3:14).

V

Two Armies Fight Israel

(Numbers 21:10-35)

The people of Israel went on farther and farther toward the land of Canaan. At last they came to the land of King Sihon.

Moses sent a messenger to King Sihon. The messenger asked King Sihon, "May we go through your country?"

King Sihon was a wicked man. He did not care about God. He said to the messenger, "No, you may not go through my land."

The messenger said, "We will be careful. We will not touch anything that is yours. We will just walk along the road."

But King Sihon called his soldiers and began to fight Israel.

The men of Israel fought hard. God was with them. They chased King Sihon and his soldiers. They took the cities of King Sihon and all his land.

Then another king, King Og, began to fight Israel, too.

The Lord said to Moses, "Do not be afraid."

So the men of Israel fought against the two kings. They took the cities and the land of King Og, too.

God gave the land of King Sihon and the land of King Og to the children of Israel because Sihon and Og were wicked kings who did not serve God.

Then the children of Israel moved their tents. They made their camp by the river Jordan. Right across the river was the land of Canaan.

All the people who lived in Canaan were afraid of the children of Israel. They had heard about the wonderful God of Israel.

VI

A Strange Prophet

(Numbers 22)

Balak was king of Moab. The people of Israel were near Moab. And Balak was afraid. He had heard about Sihon and Og. He had heard about the great God of Israel. No wonder he was afraid.

Balak said, "We must do something to stop these Israelites. They will take Moab, too, if we do not stop them."

Balak said he would send for a prophet. He would tell the prophet to curse Israel. He thought that the prophet could make bad things happen to the children of Israel by cursing them.

There was a prophet named Balaam. Balaam was not a true prophet of God. Sometimes he spoke truth. Sometimes he spoke lies.

Balak sent messengers to Balaam. Balak said, "A big army of people has come near my country. They have come from Egypt. I want you to come and curse them."

Balaam said to the messengers, "Wait until morning. Then I will tell you if God will let me go."

That night God spoke to Balaam. God said to Balaam, "You must not go with the messengers. You may not curse Israel."

So Balaam sent the messengers away in the morning.

But Balak sent other messengers. They said, "Balak will give you much gold. He can make you a great man. Come and curse Israel."

Balaam said again, "Wait until morning. Then I will tell you if God will let me go."

Balaam wanted the gold very badly.

That night God spoke to Balaam. God said to Balaam, "You may go with the messengers. But you may say only what I tell you to say."

In the morning Balaam went along with the messengers. He rode his donkey.

While Balaam was riding along, suddenly there was an Angel of God in the middle of the road. The Angel of God had a sword in his hand.

Balaam did not see the angel. But the donkey did see the angel. The donkey was afraid. He went off the road, and ran into the field.

Balaam hit his donkey with his whip. He made the donkey go back to the road.

But the Angel of God stood in the road again. He stood where the road was narrow. There was a grapevine on one side, and there was a wall on the other side.

The donkey saw the angel again. The donkey could not run into the field. So he squeezed up against the wall. That hurt Balaam's foot. Balaam hit the donkey again.

Then the angel went on and stood in a very narrow place. The donkey could not get out of the way at all. So the donkey fell down, with Balaam on his back.

Then Balaam was angry. He hit the donkey hard.

The donkey turned his head to look at Balaam. And God made the donkey talk. God put words into the donkey's mouth.

The donkey said, "Why did you hit me three times?"

Balaam said, "Because you do not obey me. If I had a sword, I would kill you."

The donkey said, "Did I ever act like this before?"

Balaam said, "No."

And then God opened Balaam's eyes, so that Balaam saw the Angel of God in the road. And he saw the sword in the angel's hand.

The Angel of God said to Balaam, "The donkey saved your life, three times."

Balaam said, "I did not see you. If you want me to, I'll go back."

But the Angel of God said, "You may go to Balak. But remember, you may say only what God tells you."

So Balaam went on. He came to Balak. Balak was very glad to see Balaam. He made a big dinner for him.

Balak said, "Tomorrow I will show you the people of Israel. Then you must curse them for me."

VII

What the Strange Prophet Said

(Numbers 23, 24)

Early in the morning, Balak took Balaam up on a high hill. From the top of the hill, they could see the tents of the Israelites. The valley was full of tents, rows and rows and rows of tents, shining in the sun.

Balak said, "See what a great people they are. Now curse them for me. Then I will make you a rich man."

Balaam said, "You must build seven altars. We will burn gifts to God on the altars. But I can only say what God tells me to say."

Balak told his servants to build seven altars. Then they burned their gifts to God.

But Balak and Balaam were not good men. They did not serve God truly. So God did not want their gifts.

But God did speak to Balaam. He put words in Balaam's mouth, just as He had put words into the donkey's mouth.

Balaam stood still and listened to God's voice.

Balak and all his princes stood around the altars. They waited to hear what Balaam would say.

Then Balaam began to speak. He said, "How can I curse this people? God has blessed them. I cannot curse them."

And Balaam spoke wonderful things in a poem about God's people.

Balak did not like that. He said to Balaam, "I told you to curse them. You are not cursing them at all!"

Balaam said, "I told you that I can only say what God tells me to say."

Balak said, "We will try again."

Balak took Balaam to another high hill. He made seven new altars. They brought gifts to God on these seven new altars.

Again Balaam listened for God's voice. Balak and his princes waited to hear what Balaam would say. God put words into Balaam's mouth.

Balaam said, "God does not tell lies. He does not change His mind. God has blessed these people. God will do wonders for them."

And Balaam spoke another poem about the wonderful things God would do for the children of Israel.

Balak said, "Stop! You are not cursing the people at all! You are blessing them!"

Balaam said, "I told you that I can only say what God tells me to say."

Balak said, "We will try again."

Balak took Balaam to another high hill. He made seven new altars. They brought gifts to God on the seven new altars.

Again Balaam listened for God's voice. Balak and his princes waited to hear what Balaam would say. God put words into Balaam's mouth.

Balaam said, "God brought these people out of Egypt. He will bless them and make a great nation . . ."

That made Balak angry. Three times Balaam had blessed the people. Balak shouted, "Stop! Stop!"

But Balaam could not stop. God had put more words into his mouth. He said, "There shall come a Star out of Jacob. He shall rule over all nations. . . ."

Long, long afterwards that Star came. That Star was Jesus, our Saviour. He shall rule over all nations.

When Balaam had said all the words that God put into his mouth, he went home. Balak was angry. Balak did not make Balaam a rich man.

VIII

God Takes Moses Away

(Numbers 27:12-14; Deuteronomy 31-34)

Moses knew that it was time for him to die. He knew that God was not going to let him enter Canaan.

One day he called all the people together. He wanted to say goodbye to them.

All the people came to hear Moses. Fathers and mothers and boys and girls all came to listen to Moses.

Moses was a wonderful old man. His hair and beard were white. But he stood very straight. His eyes were bright. He was still strong.

Moses talked to the people. He told them all about the wonders God had done in Egypt and in the desert. He told them that God would bring them to Canaan very soon. He told them that they should love God very much. He told them that they must never, never forget God, and they must never, never serve idols.

Moses said, "If you love God and serve Him, He will bless you very much in the new land."

Then Moses called Joshua. Joshua, you remember, was one of the two good spies. Joshua came and stood by Moses.

Moses said to all the people, "When I am gone, Joshua will be your leader. The Lord has chosen him. Joshua will lead you into Canaan."

Moses laid his hand on Joshua's head. He blessed Joshua. And all the people said that they would obey Joshua.

After that, the Lord said to Moses, "Come up on top of Mount Nebo. From the top of Mount Nebo, I will show you the land of Canaan."

Moses went up the mountain. He went alone. All the people saw him go.

From the top of Mount Nebo, Moses looked across the river Jordan. He could see the land of Canaan. He could see the green hills, the big cities, the beautiful farms with trees and grain. It was a wonderful country.

And there, on top of Mount Nebo, Moses died. God took his soul to heaven. And God buried Moses up there on the mount.

The children of Israel were sad when they knew Moses was dead.

But Joshua was their leader now. And they obeyed Joshua.

See accompanying illustration between pages 128 and 12⁹

9

INTO CANAAN

I

Two Spies Visit a Big City

(Joshua 2)

Joshua was the new leader of the children of Israel.

One day the Lord said to Joshua, "Tell the people to get ready. In three days you will cross the river Jordan."

How happy the people were! They were almost in the land of Canaan at last!

But first Joshua sent two spies to Canaan. He sent them to Jericho, the city that was just across the river. He wanted to know all about this city.

The two spies went to Jericho. They found that it was a very big city, with very high walls all around it. There were houses built right on top of the walls.

The two spies went through the big gate of the city. They walked on the city streets. At night they went to a house that stood on the wall. A woman named Rahab lived there.

Rahab let the men come in, to sleep in her house.

But someone told the king of Jericho about the spies. The king tried to find them. He closed the big gate of the city. He sent soldiers to find the spies. They went to Rahab's house.

Rahab saw the king's soldiers coming. Quickly she sent the two spies up to the roof of her house. The roof of Rahab's house was flat. Rahab often sat on the roof, as we sit on our porches.

Rahab told the spies to lie down on the roof. Then she covered them with stalks of flax.

When the king's soldiers came to Rahab's house, they did not find the spies. Rahab said that they were gone. Then the king's soldiers went away.

Rahab said to the spies, "The king of Jericho and all the people are afraid. They have heard about the children of Israel. They have heard about the wonderful things God does for you. They have heard about Sihon and Og. We know that God will give you the city of Jericho."

Then Rahab said to the spies, "I have been good to you. Will you be good to me? When you take Jericho, will you save me, and my father and my mother, and my brothers and sisters?"

The two spies said, "When the Lord gives us the city, we will be good to you. We will save you, and we will save everybody that is in your house."

Then the two spies wanted to go away. The king might send his soldiers to look for them again. Rahab took a long red rope. She let the rope down out of her window, outside of the city wall. The spies climbed down the rope, and they were out of the city.

Rahab let the rope hang out of the window. She said, "They will come back and see the red rope. Then they will know which is my house."

The two spies went to the mountains. They hid away for three days. Then they went back to Joshua.

They told Joshua all about Jericho. They said, "The Lord will surely give us Jericho. The people are afraid of us already."

II

The River Stops Running

(Joshua 3, 4)

It was time to go across the river. The people of Israel took down their tents. They packed all their things. They stood by the river — a long, long row of people, and a long, long row of sheep, goats and cows.

But the water of the river Jordan was deep, and it flowed swiftly. The people stood waiting.

The priests had taken the Tabernacle down. They had folded the curtains. They had covered all the furniture with beautiful blue cloths. Then everybody was ready.

Four priests came marching to the edge of the river. They carried the golden Ark between them. No one could see the Ark. It was covered with a blue cloth.

Slowly the priests walked to the river. They walked down the bank and into the water. There they stopped. They stood still with their feet in the water.

Then a strange thing happened. The water that came flowing down stopped. It did not flow past the feet of the priests. It began to pile up, like a wall of water, far away to the right. God made the water stay up there, and soon the priests were standing on dry ground.

Then the priests walked on. They carried the Ark to the middle of the river bed. The ground was dry all the way. In the middle of the river bed the priests stopped again.

The wall of water grew higher and higher. God did not let the water flow down.

Now it was time for the people to cross the river. They marched into the dry river bed — the long, long row of people, and the long, long row of sheep and goats and cows. They marched past the priests. They marched on to the other side of the river. And the water did not come down.

Joshua chose twelve men to pick up stones. He told each to bring a big stone out of the middle of the river bed. Each man carried one big stone on his shoulder. They piled the big stones up on the river bank.

Then, last of all, the priests came out of the river bed with the Ark.

And when everybody was safely on the other shore, the wall of water broke. The river flowed again, deep and fast. How happy the people were! God had brought them into Canaan at last! He had brought them over the river in a wonderful way.

Then Joshua said to the people, "When your little children grow up, they will see this pile of stones. They will ask you where these stones came from. You must tell them that the stones came from the middle of the river when God made the river stop running for you."

The people put up their tents by the river that night. They looked around at this new country — their own country. They found good things to eat — corn and fruit and other good things.

The next morning there was no manna on the ground. They did not need manna now. God never sent manna again.

III

The Walls of Jericho Fall

(Joshua 6)

The people of Jericho saw the tents along the river bank. They were afraid. The people of Jericho were wicked people. They had been wicked for many, many years. They served idols. They did not love God at all. Now, at last, God was going to punish them.

The king of Jericho closed the gates of the city. No one could come in. No one dared to go out.

Then God told Joshua what to do. Joshua called the priests and all the soldiers. He told them to get in line. They would march around the city.

First came hundreds of soldiers. Then came seven priests, each with a horn to blow. Then came four priests carrying the Ark. And then came more soldiers, thousands of them.

When they were in line, the seven priests blew their horns. The whole army began to march. The men did not talk. They only marched — tramp, tramp, tramp. All the way around Jericho they marched. Then they went back to their tents.

The next day they formed in line again. The priests blew their horns. And away they went, tramp, tramp, tramp. They marched all the way around the city again.

The next day they did the same. And the next day, and the next. For six days they marched around the city, one time each day.

Then Joshua said to the men, "Tomorrow you must get up early in the morning. We are going to march around the city seven times tomorrow. Then we will all shout. And God will make the walls of Jericho fall."

Joshua remembered Rahab. He said to the two spies, "You must go to Rahab's house, and take care of her."

And he said to the soldiers, "There will be many beautiful things in the city. But you may not take anything for yourself. The gold and silver and brass and iron belongs to God. All the rest must be burned, because the city is wicked."

Very early on the next day the soldiers were ready. Away they went again, tramp, tramp, tramp. The priests blew the horns as they went. No one talked. They marched around the city seven times — around and around and around.

Then Joshua gave the signal. And all the men shouted. They shouted as loud as they could. And the walls of Jericho fell with a great crash.

The two spies hurried to Rahab's house. They took care of her and her family.

The men of Israel ran into the city. They killed the wicked people. They set fire to the city. They burned everything, for God had commanded them not to take anything.

Aachan was one of the men who set fire to Jericho. Aachan did not like to burn everything. He went into a rich man's house and saw a beautiful robe. He took the robe and kept it. Then he found some silver money. He kept that, too. Then he found a big piece of gold, worth much money. He kept that, too.

When Jericho was all burned, the men went back to their tents.

Aachan did not show anyone what he had. He took the robe and the silver money and the gold to his tent. He dug a hole in the ground under his tent, and hid the things in the hole.

IV

The Soldiers of Israel Run Away

(Joshua 7, 8)

Ai was a little city near Jericho. Joshua sent spies to see it. The spies said, "Ai is such a little city that we can take it easily."

So Joshua sent a small army to take Ai.

But the men of Ai came out to fight against the soldiers of Israel. And the soldiers ran away! Some were killed. The others ran back to camp to Joshua. They could not take Ai.

Joshua could not understand that. Surely, God was not with them. God's people do not run away when God is with them. So Joshua went to the Tabernacle to ask God about it.

God said to Joshua, "Someone has sinned. I told them not to take anything out of the city of Jericho. But someone disobeyed Me. I cannot go with you until you take the sin out of the camp."

In the morning Joshua called all the people together. He told them what God had said. He told them that someone had sinned.

Joshua said, "That is why God did not go with our soldiers to Ai."

Then the people all stood waiting. And God pointed out the man who had sinned. It was Aachan.

Joshua said to Aachan, "Tell me, what did you do?"

Aachan said, "I have sinned against the Lord. When I was in Jericho, I saw a beautiful robe and some silver money and some gold. I took them. They are in my tent."

Joshua sent a man to Aachan's tent. He found the robe and the silver money, and the gold.

Joshua took Aachan outside the camp. Aachan had to be punished. All the people went along. There they stoned Aachan until he died.

After that, God was with the children of Israel again. He gave them the little city of Ai.

V

A Foolish Promise

(Joshua 9)

The people of Gibeon heard about Joshua and the Israelites. They heard about Jericho — how the walls had fallen down. They heard about Ai — how Joshua had taken it. They said, "Joshua will come and take our cities next." And they were afraid.

The people of Gibeon said to each other, "Perhaps we can fool Joshua."

So they decided to send messengers to Joshua. They dressed the messengers in very old clothes — the oldest clothes they could find. They gave the messengers old shoes to wear — the very oldest shoes they could find. They gave them dry, moldy bread to take along. And they tied old wine bags to their donkeys. Then the messengers rode away to Joshua.

The messengers from Gibeon came to the camp of Israel. They went to Joshua. They said to Joshua, "We have come from a far, far country. We have heard about the Lord, your God. We have heard what He did to the Egyptians and to Jericho and to Ai. We want to be your friends."

Joshua said to them, "Did you really come from a far country?"

Then they showed Joshua their dry, moldy bread and their old wine bottles, and their old shoes and their old clothes.

They said to Joshua, "Our bread was fresh, just out of the oven, when we left our country. Our wine bottles were new. And just see how our clothes are worn out by the long journey! And look at our shoes!"

Joshua looked at the old bread and the other old things. He thought that these men had really come from a far country. Joshua did not ask God what to do. But he promised these men that he would not take the cities of Gibeon.

The messengers went back home. They had fooled Joshua.

Three days later, Joshua found out. He found out that Gibeon was near-by. The messengers had not come from a far country at all.

Joshua was sorry he had made them a foolish promise.

Some of the people of Israel wanted to take the cities of Gibeon. But Joshua said to them, "No. We promised that we would not harm them. Now we may not take their cities. We cannot break our promise."

Joshua said to the people of Gibeon, "Why did you lie to us? We will keep our promise. We will not take your cities. But because you lied to us, you shall be our servants. You shall cut wood for us and carry water for us."

So Joshua kept his promise. But it was a foolish promise because Joshua forgot to ask God before he made the promise.

VI

In the New Country

(Joshua 18:1; 21:43-45; 23, 24)
(Psalm 105)

The children of Israel fought many more battles. Joshua led them, and God was with them. God took the land of Canaan away from the heathen nations. They did not worship Him. He gave it to His own people, the children of Israel.

Joshua divided the land among the people so that each had a share. Then they built their own homes. They made their own gardens. They were happy in their new country.

The children of Israel put up the Tabernacle, too. They all came together at Shiloh, and put up the Tabernacle there. They worshipped God in the Tabernacle at Shiloh.

Years went by. Joshua became an old man. He knew that he would soon die. So one day he called all the people of Israel together.

The people came to Joshua. They stood out-of-doors — a great big crowd. Joshua was a wonderful old man. The people were glad to listen to him.

Joshua made a speech. He said, "Long, long ago, the Lord promised Abraham that He would give this land of Canaan to you. He has kept His promise. He brought you out of Egypt. He made a path for you through the Red Sea. He chased the heathen people out of the land. He gave the land to you. Now you must choose whom you will serve. Will you serve the idols of the people that used to live here?"

And Joshua added, "As for me and my house, we will serve the Lord."

The people answered, "We will not serve the idols. The Lord God brought us out of Egypt. We will serve Him."

Joshua said to them, "If you forsake the Lord and serve idols, then He will punish you."

But the people said, "We will serve the Lord our God. We will obey His voice."

Then Joshua took a big stone. He set it up under an oak tree.

He said, "This stone is a sign that you have promised. I will set it here to remind you of your promise."

After that the people went home.

But the stone stood there to remind the people that they had made a promise to serve God and to obey Him.

When Joshua was one hundred and ten years old, he died.

And the children of Israel served the Lord. They were very happy in their new country.

10

TROUBLE IN THE NEW LAND

I

The Israelites Forget Their Promise

(Judges 6)

For many years the children of Israel served God and were happy. But after a while they forgot God. They made friends with the heathen people. They began to serve the idols of the heathen people.

Then God sent other heathen people to punish the children of Israel.

One time, when the children of Israel forgot God and served idols, the Midianites came. The Midianites put up their tents in the land of Canaan. There was a big army of Midianites. The children of Israel were afraid of them. The children of Israel ran to the mountains to hide. Some even lived in caves.

The Midianites took everything that the children of Israel had. They took all the wheat and corn. They did not leave enough for the children of Israel to eat.

Then the children of Israel cried to God. They asked God to help them. And God heard them. He sent them help. He sent an angel.

There was a young man, Gideon, who had a little bit of wheat. He hid it from the Midianites and threshed it.

While Gideon was threshing the wheat, the angel came to him. The angel looked like a man. He carried a staff in his hand. Gideon did not know that it was an angel.

The man said to Gideon, "The Lord is with thee."

Gideon said, "How can that be true? If the Lord is with us, why does all this trouble come? The Lord lets the Midianites steal all that we have."

The man looked at Gideon and said, "You shall save the children of Israel from the Midianites."

Gideon was surprised. He said, "How can I do that?"

The man said, "Surely, I will be with you."

Gideon began to think that this man must be an angel. He said, "Please show me a sign. But wait until I get you a present."

The man said, "I will wait."

Gideon hurried to his home and made lunch for the man. He brought meat and bread and broth.

The man said, "Put the meat and the bread on that rock, and pour the broth over it."

Gideon put the meat and bread on the rock. He poured the broth over it.

Then the man touched the food with the end of his staff. And fire came up out of the rock and burned the food.

Then Gideon knew that it was an angel. But then the angel was gone.

Gideon was afraid when he thought about the angel talking to him.

That night God spoke to Gideon. And Gideon arose in the night. He broke down the altar that his father had made for an idol. Gideon built an altar to God, and worshipped God.

II

Gideon Gets Ready for Battle

(Judges 6, 7)

Gideon sent messengers through the country. He asked all the men to come and help him fight the Midianites. Many men came.

Gideon wanted to be sure that God was sending him to fight the Midianites. So Gideon prayed to God and said, "Tonight I will lay a piece of sheep wool on the ground. If the wool is all wet with dew in the morning, and the ground is dry, then I will know that God has truly sent me."

Before he went to sleep, Gideon laid the piece of wool on the ground. In the morning he was up early. He hurried out to look at the wool. He found it all wet, and the ground around it was dry.

But Gideon wanted to be still more sure. He prayed again and said, "Please do not be angry with me, O God. Let me try once more. This time let the wool be dry, and the ground be wet."

Before Gideon went to sleep, he laid the wool on the ground. He was up early in the morning. He hurried out to look at the wool. This time he found the wool dry, and the ground was wet.

Then Gideon and his big army went to fight the Midianites.

But God said to Gideon, "Your army is too big. I do not need such a big army. Tell them that anyone who is afraid may go home."

Gideon told his men that those who were afraid could go home. More than half of the men went home.

God said to Gideon. "There are still too many. Take them to the spring to drink. And watch how they drink."

Gideon took all the men to the spring. Some of them knelt down on their hands and knees to drink. Some just picked up water in their hands. Gideon put all those who knelt down in one group. All those who took water in their hands he put in another group.

When they were all through drinking, there was a big group of those who knelt down. The other group was much smaller.

God said to Gideon. "Send home the big group. The little group is all I need."

So Gideon sent the big group home. Then he had only a very small army left — only three hundred men. The Midianite army was very, very big.

Gideon was up on a hill with his little army. The Midianites were down in the valley with their very, very big army.

How could such a little army fight such a big army?

III

God Gives the Victory to Gideon

(Judges 7)

Gideon could not sleep that night. He thought of his little army, and of the big army of the Midianites.

God said to Gideon, "If you are afraid, go down and listen to what the Midianites are saying. Take your servant with you."

Gideon called his servant. Together they crept quietly down the hill in the dark. They could see the Midianites lying asleep in the valley, a great big army. They crept closer and closer. After a while they heard two men talk.

One man said, "I had a strange dream. I dreamed that a little loaf of barley bread came rolling down the hill. It hit a tent, and knocked it over."

The other man said, "That little barley bread must be Gideon. God is going to give the whole army of the Midianites to Gideon."

When Gideon heard that, his heart was happy. He and his servant hurried back up the hill. They were no longer afraid.

Gideon called his little army of men. "Get up!" he said. "The Lord has given the Midianites to us!"

Gideon gave each man a trumpet. He told each one to take an empty water jar and a torch. They put the torches inside the jars to hide the light. Then Gideon sent some of the men to the other side of the valley. The little army made a circle around the camp of the Midianites.

In the middle of the night, when they were all ready, Gideon gave the signal. Then the men took their torches out of the water jars and held the lights high. They threw down the jars, breaking them on the rocks with a loud noise. They blew their trumpets as hard as they could. And they all cried out, as loud as they could, "The sword of the Lord and of Gideon!"

The awful noise scared the Midianites. They all woke up. They saw the bright lights and they heard the noise all around them. They were very much afraid. They did not know what was happening. They began to fight each other. And they all ran away as fast as they could go.

So the Lord saved the children of Israel from the Midianites, when they prayed to Him.

IV

Baby Samson

(Judges 13)

After the Midianites were gone, the children of Israel served God for many years. But after a while they forgot again. They began to sin against God. Then God sent the Philistines to bother them.

But some of the children of Israel still served God.

One day God sent an angel to visit an Israelite woman. He talked to her and said, "You shall have a baby. When that baby grows up, he will fight against the Philistines. But you must not let him drink wine, and he must never have his hair cut."

The woman hurried home to tell her husband, Manoah. She said to Manoah, "A man came to me. His face was like the face of an angel. He told me that I shall have a baby. The baby will fight against the Philistines when he grows up. But he must never drink wine, and he must never have his hair cut."

Manoah could hardly believe the story his wife told him. So he prayed to God. He asked God to send the man again.

Soon after that, the woman was out in the field one day. The angel came again. The woman ran home to get her husband. Together they ran back to the angel.

Manoah said to the angel, "Are you the man who said that we are to have a baby? Then please tell us what we must do to the baby. How must we take care of him?"

The angel said, "Your wife must not drink any wine. You must not let the boy drink any wine. And you must never cut his hair."

Manoah did not know that it was an angel talking to him. So he said, "Let me get you something to eat."

The angel answered, "I will not eat of your food. But you may give a gift to the Lord."

Manoah went to get a little goat. He prepared it as an offering and laid it on a rock by the angel. Manoah burned it as an offering to God.

Then, while Manoah and his wife watched, the angel went up to heaven with the smoke of the fire.

Then they knew it was an angel.

After a while the baby came. Manoah and his wife called him Samson. God blessed the baby. He grew up to be a strong man. He did not drink wine. And they did not cut his hair.

V

Samson the Strong Man

(Judges 14-16:3)

Samson's hair grew long. And God made Samson very strong.

One day Samson was walking in the country. A young lion roared at him. Samson was not afraid. He caught hold of the lion by its mouth, and killed it.

The Philistines often came to steal things from the people of Israel. Samson chased them away. Sometimes Samson would fight alone against many Philistines.

One day the Philistines caught Samson. They tied him with new ropes. But Samson laughed. He broke the ropes and walked away!

Another time, Samson went to a city of the Philistines. They closed the gate while he was in the city. They thought, "Now we have caught him!" But Samson went to the gate at night. He picked up the gate and walked away with it! He carried it to the top of a big hill!

People said, "What makes Samson so strong?"

Samson did not tell them. He obeyed God. He did not drink wine. He never had his hair cut. And as long as he obeyed God, the Spirit of God made him strong.

VI

Samson the Weak Man

(Judges 16:4-21)

After a while Samson loved a woman named Delilah. The Philistines went to Delilah. They said to her, "You must find out what makes Samson so strong. If you help us catch him, we will pay you much money."

See accompanying illustration
between pages 128 and 129

So Delilah asked Samson what it was that made him so strong.

Samson said to her, "If they will tie me with seven green twigs, then I will be weak like other men."

When the Philistines came again, Delilah hid them in her house. After a while Samson came. Delilah tied Samson with seven green twigs.

When Delilah had tied Samson, she called to him, "Samson, the Philistines are coming!"

The Philistines came running out of their hiding place.

But Samson broke the green twigs, and the Philistines could not take him.

Then Delilah said to Samson, "You lied to me. Now tell me what makes you so strong. What can I tie you with?"

Samson said, "If they tie me tight with new ropes, then I will be weak like other men."

Delilah hid the Philistines in her house again. She took new ropes and tied Samson tight. Then she called, "Samson, the Philistines are coming!"

The Philistines came running out of their hiding place.

But Samson broke the ropes as if they were threads. And the Philistines could not take him.

Delilah tried again. She said to Samson, "You are just making fun of me. Tell me, what can I tie you with?"

Then Samson said, "If you weave my hair on a loom, as you weave cloth, then I will be weak."

Samson had very long hair. When he was asleep, Delilah took the heavy loom and wove Samson's hair on it. Then she called him. "Samson, the Philistines are coming!"

The Philistines came running out of their hiding place.

Samson awoke. He stood up, and he walked away with the big loom hanging in his hair. The Philistines could not take him.

Delilah said to him, "How can you say you love me? You make fun of me. You do not tell me the truth."

Samson did not want to tell her his secret. He did not want to tell her that he never drank wine and that his hair had never been cut. But every day she teased him to tell.

Then, one day, Samson told this wicked woman all about it. He told her how God had talked to his mother. He told her that God made him strong. He told her that if he cut his hair, God would take his strength away.

Delilah was sure that he had told the truth this time. She sent for the Philistines again. She hid the Philistines in her house.

When Samson was asleep, Delilah called a man to come and cut his hair. He cut it all off.

Then Delilah woke Samson up. She called him, "Samson, the Philistines are coming!"

Samson awoke. He stood up. He was going to chase the Philistines away again. But his strength was all gone. The Spirit of God was gone.

The Philistines took Samson. They brought him to prison. They put his eyes out and bound him with brass bands. They made him work in the prison.

VII

Samson's Last Deed

(Judges 16:22-31)

The Philistines were very happy when Samson was in prison. They said, "Our god gave Samson to us. We must make a great feast and bring gifts to our god, Dagon."

Dagon was an idol. But the Philistines thought that Dagon was greater than the Lord.

So they made ready for a great feast. Very many people came. They gathered in a very big house for the feast. They praised their god, Dagon. They offered sacrifices to him.

Then they said, "Bring Samson here. Let's have fun with him."

They sent someone to prison to get Samson. He came out of the prison with a little boy. The little boy held Samson's hand to lead him because Samson was blind. The boy took him to the house and let him lean against the pillars of the house.

When the Philistines saw Samson, they laughed at him. He had been so strong. Now he was weak and blind. His hair was growing again, but his eyes were gone. The Philistines were glad. They made fun of him.

Then Samson said to the little boy, "Let me feel the two pillars that the house stands on."

The little boy helped Samson put his arms around the two pillars.

Samson bowed his head and prayed. He said, "O God, let me be strong once more — just once more."

Then he bent his body low and he pulled on the two pillars as hard as he could. The pillars cracked; they broke. The house came tumbling down with a crash. It fell on the Philistines and killed them. It killed Samson, too.

But Samson had done one last work for God. He showed the Philistines that God was stronger than Dagon.

11

JOB, A MAN WHO SERVED GOD

I

Job's Troubles

(Job 1)

Once upon a time there was a man named Job. He was a rich man. He had very many sheep and camels and oxen and servants. He had seven sons and three daughters. And, best of all, Job was a good man. He loved God and served God. He tried every day to do just what God would want him to do.

One day Satan talked with God in heaven. Satan said to God, "Job is a good man because he is rich. If You made him poor, then he would be angry; then he would not love You anymore."

God said to Satan, "You may go and make Job poor. But you may not hurt him."

Then Satan went down to earth. And in one day he sent all kinds of trouble upon Job.

Job was home. His sons and daughters were gone to a party together. And a man came running to Job with the first bad news.

The man said, "We were in the field, plowing. And some bad men came out of the hills. They stole all the oxen. They killed all the servants. I am the only one left!"

Just then another man came running. He said, "A fire came from heaven and burned up all the sheep and the servants that were with the sheep. I am the only one left!"

126

Then another man came running. He said, "Some strong men came and stole all the camels, and killed the servants. I am the only one left!"

Another came running and said, "Your sons and daughters were all in the house of the oldest son, and a wind came and blew the house down. They are all dead. I am the only one left!"

Then Job fell upon the ground.

But Job was not angry. He prayed. He said, "God gave me all my riches. Now He has taken it all away. I will praise His name." Job still loved God.

II

Job Is Sick
(Job 2-37)

Satan went to talk with God again.

God said to Satan, "Did you see Job? He is a good man. He still serves Me, even though you made him poor."

Satan said, "But if You make him sick, then he will turn against You."

And God said to Satan, "You may make him sick. But you must not let him die."

Then Satan went down to earth. And he made Job sick. There were big sores all over Job's body, so that Job did not know what to do. He felt very bad.

Then Job's wife said to him, "Do you still believe in God?"

Job said to her, "God sends us the good things. He sends us the bad, too. We must take the bad that He sends, as well as the good."

And Job did not sin against God. But he could not understand why God let so much trouble come upon him.

After a while Job's friends came to see him. They were sorry for him. But they did not understand Job's trouble at all.

Job's friends said, "You have surely done some very wicked thing. God has sent this trouble to punish you for some sin."

Job shook his head. He knew that his trouble was not because of his sin.

Job said, "God is very great. He holds the earth in His hand. He made all the stars. He is much greater than man. We cannot understand Him. He knows how I serve Him every day."

Job's friends said, "The sinful man has trouble. God makes all his days dark and unhappy, because he is wicked."

But Job knew God was good to him. Job trusted God.

Job said, "God is good. He does what is right. I know that some day I shall see God."

III

God Speaks to Job

(Job 38-42)

While Job and his friends were talking, there came a big whirlwind. And out of the whirlwind God spoke.

God said, "I will ask you some questions. Let us see if you can answer them.

"Do you know where light comes from? Do you know what makes the wind blow? Can you lead the stars through the sky? Can you make the rain and the thunder?"

God asked many more questions. But Job could not answer them. His friends could not answer, either.

At last Job said, "I am very, very small. I cannot answer God. God is very great. He can do all things. He is very wonderful, and I cannot understand Him."

And Job bowed his head before God.

After that, God made Job a rich man again. He made Job richer than he had been before. He gave him seven sons and three daughters, and very many sheep and camels and oxen.

God blessed Job because Job trusted Him even when troubles came.

From the top of Mount Nebo, Moses
could see the Promised Land.

Samson grew up to be very strong.
One day he killed a lion.

12

RUTH, GRANDMOTHER OF DAVID

I

Ruth and Naomi

(Ruth 1)

There was a famine in the land of Israel. The rain did not fall, the grain did not grow, and the fruit did not ripen. There was not enough for the people to eat. Some of the people moved away to other countries.

The family of Elimelech moved to Moab. Elimelech took his wife, Naomi, and their two boys. They lived in Moab for a long time.

After a while Elimelech died. The two boys grew up. They married girls of Moab, Ruth and Orpah.

Soon both boys died, too. Then Naomi was left alone with Ruth and Orpah.

Naomi was very sad. The people of Moab did not serve God. They had idols. So Naomi wanted to go back home to Canaan, to her own people.

Ruth and Orpah said they would walk along with their mother-in-law.

After they had walked a while, Naomi said to the girls. "Now you must go back to your homes, back to your mothers."

The girls loved Naomi. They did not want to go back. But Naomi told them they would be happier in their own land. So at last Orpah kissed Naomi and went back.

But Ruth would not go. She said to Naomi, "Where you go, I will go. Where you live, I will live. Your people shall be my people. Your God shall be my God."

So Ruth went on with Naomi. They went together to the city of Bethlehem, where Naomi used to live.

The people of Bethlehem hardly knew Naomi. She looked so sad. She had lost her husband and her two sons. They felt sorry for her.

But Naomi had Ruth. Ruth loved Naomi and tried to make her happy.

II

God Blesses Ruth
(Ruth 2-4)

It was harvest time. The grain in the fields was ripe. The reapers went out to cut it and tie it into bundles.

When the reapers tied the grain into bundles, they dropped some of it. Poor people came to pick up the grain that the men dropped. They could have that grain to take home.

Ruth said to Naomi, "Let me go out to some field and pick up grain after the reapers."

Naomi said she should go. Ruth went to the field of a man named Boaz. He was a rich man. Ruth followed the reapers in the field and picked up the grain that they dropped.

After a while Boaz came out to his field. He saw Ruth. And he asked his men, "Who is this young woman?"

The men said, "That is Ruth. She came from Moab with Naomi."

Then Boaz went to talk with Ruth. He was kind to her. He said to her, "I have heard about you. I know that you have been very good to your mother-in-law. The Lord will bless you because you have been good to her." And Boaz told Ruth to come again tomorrow, to pick up the grain that the men would drop.

Boaz went back to the reapers. He said to them, "Do not bother the young woman. Let her pick up grain tomorrow again. And drop an extra handful for her now and then."

So Ruth was busy all day. When she went home in the evening, she had almost a bushel of grain.

Ruth went to the fields of Boaz again the next day, and every day until the harvesting was done.

And after that, Boaz married Ruth. So God blessed Ruth because she was kind to Naomi, and because she had chosen God as her God.

After a while, Ruth and Boaz had a baby boy. This boy grew up and became the grandfather of a great king — King David.

13

SAMUEL, GOD'S PROPHET

I

God Answers Hannah's Prayer

(I Samuel 1)

Elkanah was a man who served God. Each year he went up to Shiloh to bring God an offering in the Tabernacle. Hannah, his wife, went with him.

But Hannah was not happy. Hannah had no children. She wanted very much to have a baby.

So Hannah prayed in the Tabernacle. She said, "O Lord, if Thou wilt give me a child, then I will give him back to Thee, to serve Thee all his life."

She prayed for a long time. She prayed in her heart, without talking aloud. She just moved her lips.

Near her, on a seat, sat the old priest Eli. Eli saw Hannah. He watched her lips move. He wondered what she was doing.

After a while, Eli said to Hannah, "Did you drink too much wine?"

But Hannah said, "Oh no. I did not drink any wine. I was praying."

Then Eli said, "May God give you what you asked for."

When Hannah heard the old priest say that, she felt better. She went home with a happy heart. And before another year was gone, Hannah had a baby boy. She called him Samuel.

Elkanah went to Shiloh again. Hannah did not go along this time. The baby was too small to go so far.

But when the baby was a little bigger, Hannah took him along to Shiloh to the Tabernacle. He was still a very little boy.

Hannah and Elkanah brought an offering to God in the Tabernacle. And they brought Samuel to the old priest Eli.

Hannah said to Eli, "Do you remember me? Do you remember how I stood in the Tabernacle, praying? I prayed for a baby. And the Lord sent me this little boy."

Hannah gave Samuel to Eli. She said, "Now I want to give my little boy to the Lord, to serve the Lord in His Tabernacle as long as he lives."

When Hannah and Elkanah went home, little Samuel stayed with Eli in the Tabernacle.

II

A Voice in the Night

(I Samuel 3)

Eli was a good priest. But his two sons were bad men. They were priests, but they sinned against God. And Eli did not punish them.

Samuel was Eli's little helper. He did many things for Eli in the Tabernacle. Once a year his father and mother came to see him. Each year his mother brought Samuel a little coat that she made for him. Samuel was happy in the Tabernacle with Eli.

One night, when Samuel had just gone to bed, he heard a voice calling him: "Samuel!"

Samuel jumped up and ran to Eli. "Here I am," he said.

But Eli said, "I did not call you. Go back to bed."

Samuel went back to bed. He closed his eyes to go to sleep. Then he heard the voice again: "Samuel!"

Samuel went to Eli again. "Here I am," he said. "You called me."

Eli said, "No, I did not call you. Go lie down again."

Samuel went back to bed. He closed his eyes. But the voice called him again: "Samuel!"

Again Samuel went to Eli.

"Here I am," he said. "You surely must have called me."

Then Eli knew that it was the Lord calling Samuel. Eli said to Samuel, "Go lie down. If you hear the voice again, you must say, 'Speak, Lord. Thy servant is listening.'"

Once again Samuel went back to bed. He lay very still. Then the voice came again, "Samuel! Samuel!"

This time Samuel did not get up. He said, "Speak, Lord. Thy servant is listening."

Samuel had never heard the voice of the Lord before. He lay still to listen.

The Lord said, "The sons of Eli are very sinful. Eli does not punish them. Now I will punish Eli's sons."

Then the Lord went away. Samuel lay very still in his bed. He could not sleep. In the morning he got up to do his work. He opened the doors of the Tabernacle.

Eli called to Samuel "Tell me," he said, "what did the Lord say to you? Tell me all about it."

Then Samuel had to tell Eli that God would punish his two sons.

That made Eli feel sad. But he knew that God does right. He knew that his sons were wicked. So he said, "It is well. Let the Lord do what He thinks is good."

Samuel grew up. And the Lord often came to Samuel. All the people heard that the Lord came to Samuel. They knew that Samuel was a prophet.

III

The Philistines Take the Ark

(I Samuel 4)

After a while the Philistines came to fight again. They were strong. They made the men of Israel run.

Then the men of Israel said, "Let us get the Ark out of the Tabernacle. The Ark will save us!"

So they went to get the Ark. Eli's two wicked sons carried it to the army camp.

When the men of Israel saw the Ark, they were happy. They clapped their hands and cheered. They were sure they would win the battle now.

The Philistines heard the noise. They said, "The men of Israel have the Ark of their God. Now we must fight very, very hard."

The Philistines knew that God could do wonderful things for Israel.

But God had not told the sons of Eli to take the Ark to the camp. And God did not go with the Ark. The Ark could not help the children of Israel. The Philistines chased the children of Israel again.

Some of the men of Israel were killed. The two sons of Eli were killed. And the Philistines took the Ark.

Then one man ran to Shiloh as fast as he could. He told the people about the battle. He told them that the men of Israel had run away. He told them that the sons of Eli were dead. He told them that the Ark was gone.

The people wept aloud.

Eli heard the people weep. He was waiting for someone to tell him about the battle. He was afraid something might happen to the Ark.

Eli was blind. But he heard someone come. He called, "What is the matter? Why do the people weep?"

The man from the army came to Eli. He told Eli about the battle, about his two sons, and about the Ark.

When Eli heard that the Philistines had the ark, Eli fell over backwards, and died.

That was a very sad day for Israel.

IV

What Happened to the Ark

(I Samuel 5, 6, 7:1)

The Philistines were glad that they had the Ark. They took it to one of their cities.

The god of the Philistines was an idol called Dagon. They had built a house for Dagon. They put the Ark of God in the house with Dagon.

In the morning the Philistines went to the house of Dagon to see the Ark. They opened the door — and there was Dagon, the idol, lying on the floor. It had fallen down before the Ark of God.

The Philistines set Dagon up again.

The next morning the Philistines went to the house of Dagon again to see the Ark. They opened the door — and there was Dagon, lying on the floor again. It had fallen down before the Ark of God again. This time Dagon's head and hands were broken off.

Then the Philistines were afraid of the Ark.

After that, many of the Philistines became sick. That made them still more afraid of the Ark. They knew that God did not want them to have the Ark.

So the Philistines sent the Ark to another city. But the people of that city became sick, too. They did not want the Ark. They sent it to another city.

When the people of the other city saw the Ark, they said, "We do not want it! It will make us sick, too!"

Then the leaders of the Philistines had a meeting. They said they would send the Ark back to the land of Israel.

The Philistines made a new cart for the Ark. They put some gold in the Ark. They said, "Maybe the God of Israel will make us well if we give Him some gold." And they brought two cows to pull the cart.

Each of the two cows had a calf. A cow does not like to leave its calf. The Philistines said, "If the cows go away, then we know that the God of Israel did make us sick."

Nobody got in the cart to drive the cows. They just let the cows go all by themselves. They watched to see if the cows would go away from their calves.

The cows mooed. They started away, walking straight down the road. They left their calves behind. They pulled the new cart with the Ark straight to the land of Israel. Then the Philistines knew that God was taking the Ark home.

The people of Israel saw the cart coming. They saw the Ark on the cart. And they were happy.

V

A Day of Prayer

(I Samuel 7)

Twenty years went by. The Philistines still came to steal and to fight. The people of Israel prayed to God for help.

One day Samuel sent a messenger all through the land of Israel. He said to the people of Israel, "If you will throw all your idols away, and if you will serve God with your hearts, then God will help you. Come to me in Mizpeh, and I will pray for you."

The people put away their idols. They went to Mizpeh. Many, many people came on that day.

The people said to Samuel, "We have sinned against the Lord."

Then they bowed their heads and prayed to God. All day long they prayed. They did not eat. They fasted.

The Philistines heard about the people of Israel. They knew that the people of Israel were praying and fasting. The Philistines said, "Now is a good time to fight the people of Israel. They are not ready to fight."

So the Philistines came with a big army.

The people of Israel heard the Philistines come. And they were afraid.

They called to Samuel, "Pray for us! Pray for us! Do not stop praying! Maybe God will save us."

Samuel made an altar. He burned a little lamb on the altar, and he prayed to God.

The Philistines came near. Then suddenly there was a big crash of thunder. There was more thunder, louder and louder. It was right over the heads of the Philistines. It seemed to chase the Philistines. Then they were afraid. They turned and ran away. And the thunder followed them until they were far away.

When the Philistines were gone, Samuel took a big stone and set it up.

Samuel said, "This is where the Lord helped us."

Then the people went back to their homes.

And the Philistines did not come back for a long, long time.

14

SAUL, THE FIRST KING

I

Hunting for the Donkeys
(I Samuel 9)

Saul was a young man, big and tall and strong.

Saul's father had many animals. One day two of his donkeys ran away.

Saul's father said to Saul, "I want you to go hunt for those donkeys."

Saul went to hunt for them. He took a servant with him. They hunted and hunted. They were a long way from home, and they did not find the donkeys.

At last Saul said to the servant, "I think we should go home. My father will begin to hunt for us."

The servant said, "There is a man who is a prophet. We could ask him about the donkeys. Maybe he can tell us where they are. He is a man of God."

They went to the city where the man of God was.

By the city gate, they met some girls. They said to the girls, "Is the prophet here?"

The girls said, "Yes, he is here." And they told Saul where to find the prophet.

Inside the city they met an old man. It was Samuel, the prophet. But Saul did not know who the old man was.

Saul said to the old man, "Can you tell us where the prophet is?"

Samuel said, "I am the prophet. Come with me and eat with me. Do not worry about the donkeys. They are found already."

Saul was surprised. How did Samuel know that the donkeys were lost?

Samuel said to Saul, "You are the man that all Israel is wishing for."

Saul was still more surprised.

Saul said, "I do not know what you mean. Is all Israel wishing for me? They do not even know me."

Samuel did not answer. He took Saul and the servant along into his house. There were other people there. But Samuel gave Saul the best place at the table.

Then Samuel said to the cook, "Bring the meat on the table now. This is the man I was waiting for."

Saul was more and more surprised. How could Samuel know about the donkeys? How could Samuel know that Saul was coming? Surely this Samuel was a great man of God. He knew things that only God could tell him.

That night Saul and his servant stayed with Samuel.

II

Saul Made King

(I Samuel 10)

Early in the morning Samuel called Saul. Saul could go back home now.

Samuel walked along with Saul and his servant a little way.

Outside the city, Samuel stopped. He said to Saul, "Tell your servant to go on ahead a little. Then I will tell you what God has said."

The servant went on ahead. Saul and Samuel stood still.

Samuel had a jar of oil hidden in his robe. He took it out and poured the oil on Saul's head.

Samuel said, "The Lord has anointed you to be king of His people. The Spirit of the Lord will come upon you. God will be with you."

Then Samuel went back. Saul went on home. And the Spirit of the Lord came upon Saul. But Saul did not tell anyone what Samuel had done.

After a while, Samuel sent a messenger to all the people of Israel. He told them to come to him at Mizpeh.

A great crowd of people came. They piled their baggage all together in the field. Then they all went to listen to Samuel. They had asked Samuel for a king. Perhaps he had found a king.

Samuel said to them, "You asked for a king. God will give you a king. He has chosen a man named Saul."

The people were glad of that. But where was Saul? They looked for him, and they could not find him.

Then they asked God where Saul was. God told Samuel that Saul was hiding behind the baggage.

Someone ran to the baggage and found Saul. Saul came and stood by the people. He was taller than anyone else. The people all looked at him — he was so big and tall and fine-looking. They thought he would be a very good king.

Then the people all began to shout, "God save the king! God save the king!"

When the people were quiet again, Samuel talked to them. He told them that they must obey the new king. Then he sent them all home.

Saul went back home, too. But he was ready to be king when the people needed him.

III

Saul Disobeys God

(I Samuel 15)

Saul was a brave man. The people of Israel were happy with their new king.

One day Samuel said to Saul, "The people of Amalek are wicked. They must be punished. God sends you to punish them. You must destroy them and everything that they have."

Saul had a very large army. He called all his soldiers, and they marched to Amalek. They destroyed the city of Amalek.

But they did not destroy everything. They took the best sheep, and the best lambs, and other things that they liked. They wanted to keep the good things.

That night, when the soldiers were in their tents again, God spoke to Samuel.

God said to Samuel, "Saul has disobeyed me. I told him to destroy everything in Amalek. But he has kept many things."

Samuel was very sorry to hear that. He was so sorry that he could not sleep. All night long Samuel prayed to God.

In the morning, Samuel went to Saul.

Saul came to meet Samuel. Saul said to Samuel, "God bless you, Samuel, I am glad you have come. I have done all that God told me to do."

Samuel looked at Saul. He said, "What do I hear? I hear the bleating of sheep and lambs. Where did these sheep and lambs come from?"

Saul said, "Oh, my men wanted to save some of the best sheep and lambs. They want to offer them to God upon the altar. But we did destroy everything else. We did just as God said."

Samuel shook his head. He said, "God told you not to take anything. He told you to destroy everything. Why did you not obey Him?"

Saul said, "But I did obey God. I went to Amalek. I destroyed it, as God told me to do. But the people wanted some of the sheep. They wished to sacrifice them to God."

Samuel shook his head again. "You did not obey God," he said. "You did not destroy everything. God does not want your sacrifices. He wants you to obey Him. Obedience is better than sacrifice."

Then Saul said, "Yes, I have sinned. Please forgive me. And please go with me to the camp, and we will pray to God."

Samuel said, "No, I do not want to go with you. God will make another man king instead of you."

But Saul begged Samuel to go to camp with him. So Samuel went. And they worshipped God together.

After that Samuel went back home. He was sad. He was sorry that Saul had not turned out to be a good king — a king that obeys God.

15

STORIES ABOUT DAVID

I

A Shepherd Boy

(I Samuel 16:10, 11; 17:34, 35)

In the little town of Bethlehem, there lived a boy named David. David had seven brothers. David was the youngest. David's father, Jesse, had many sheep. David often helped his brothers take care of the sheep.

David liked to be out in the fields and in the hills with the sheep. He loved to watch the clouds and the birds and the trees. He loved the little lambs, too. Sometimes, when the sheep were lying down in the grass, David would play his harp and sing. He sang praises to God.

But it was not always easy to take care of the sheep. Sometimes David had to lead them a long, long way to find water. Sometimes a little lamb would get lost, and David would have to hunt and hunt for it. Sometimes, at night, a lion would roar.

Once a bear came to the sheep fold. It caught a little lamb. David heard the little lamb cry. He ran after the bear. God made David strong. He took the little lamb out of the bear's mouth, and he killed the bear.

Once a lion came to the sheep fold. The lion caught a little lamb. David heard the little lamb cry. He ran after the lion. God made David strong again. He took the little lamb out of the lion's mouth, and he killed the lion.

David was a very good shepherd boy.

II

Samuel Anoints David to Be the New King
(I Samuel 16:1-13)

One day a white-haired old man came to Bethlehem. The people of Bethlehem saw him coming. They ran to meet him.

Soon everybody heard that the white-haired old man had come. The people told each other, "Samuel has come! Samuel, the great prophet, has come to Bethlehem!"

Samuel said to them, "We will have a feast together and worship God. Tell all the people to get ready."

The people were very glad to have a feast and to worship God with Samuel. They hurried to get ready.

Jesse got ready, too. And his sons got ready.

But somebody had to take care of the sheep. David was the youngest. His father told him to stay with the sheep.

So Jesse and his seven sons went to the feast. David went to the field to watch the sheep.

There were many people at the feast. Samuel said to them, "God sent me to anoint one of the sons of Jesse. I have a jar of oil. I will pour it on the head of the one God chooses. He will be king of Israel some day."

Jesse told his boys to walk past Samuel.

The oldest came first. He was a fine-looking young man. Samuel thought, "This must be the one."

But God said to Samuel, "This is not the one."

Then the next one came. But God said, "That is not the one."

All seven sons of Jesse walked past Samuel, one by one. And God did not choose any of them.

Then Samuel said to Jesse, "Are these all the sons you have?"

Jesse said, "No; I have one more. But he is just a boy. He is in the field, taking care of the sheep."

See accompanying illustration
between pages 160 and 161

Samuel said, "Send for him."

Someone ran to the field to find David. David hurried home to wash and dress himself. Then he went to the feast.

Samuel saw David coming, and he heard God say, "This is the one. Anoint him."

When David came near, Samuel poured the oil on his head.

Then the Spirit of God came upon David. And the Spirit of God lived in David's heart ever after that.

But when the feast was over, David went back home. He took care of his father's sheep again.

III

David and the Giant

(I Samuel 17)

Years went by. David was still a shepherd. And Saul was still king.

But there was war again. The Philistines came to fight against Israel.

Saul called out his army. Three of David's brothers were soldiers. There was a very big army to fight against the Philistines.

David stayed at home. He was not a soldier. But sometimes his father sent him to the camp to bring food to his brothers. David liked to go and see the army.

One morning Jesse said to David, "Get ready and go to the camp. Bring this food to your brothers, and see if they are all well."

David hurried to get ready. Then he took the food and went to camp.

What a busy place the camp was! There were so many tents and so many soldiers. David put his packages down by all the baggage. Then he went to find his brothers.

While David was talking with his brothers, he heard a loud voice. He looked around to see who was talking so loud. And he saw a big man standing in the valley. He was a very, very big man — bigger than any man David had ever seen. He was a giant. And behind the giant, on the hill, was the whole army of the Philistines.

The big giant was talking. David listened.

The giant said, "Send someone to fight me! If one of your men can fight me, and can kill me, we will all be your servants."

Then he laughed and said, "You don't dare! Not one of you dares to fight me! You say you have a wonderful God, but you dare not come and fight me!"

The soldiers all shivered when they heard the giant talk. They shook their heads.

They said, "Listen to him! That is Goliath. Every morning he comes out and says the same thing. Nobody dares to fight him."

David said, "Why doesn't somebody fight him?"

The soldiers laughed at David. They said, "What? Don't you see his big spear and his big sword? Why, he is a big giant. He would kill any one of us right away."

But David said, "We are God's people. Doesn't somebody dare to fight this giant who makes fun of God?"

Then they brought David to King Saul.

David said to King Saul, "I will go fight with this giant."

Saul said, "How can you? You are not big enough."

David answered, "Once a bear stole a lamb, and I killed the bear. Once a lion stole a lamb, and I killed the lion. God helped me then. He will help me kill this giant."

Then Saul told David he could go.

David went to the creek first. He picked up five smooth stones. He had his sling-shot in his hand. And he went to meet the giant.

The giant saw David coming, and he laughed. How could such a young boy fight such a big man?

Goliath, the giant, said to David, "Do you think I am a dog?"

David said, "I am coming in the Name of God."

Then David put a stone in his sling-shot. He ran, and he threw the stone. It hit the giant in the forehead. And the giant fell dead.

Then the men of Israel all shouted for joy.

But the Philistines began to run away. The soldiers of Israel chased the Philistines until not one was left.

That night the people of Israel sang songs about David. And Saul took David to live in the king's house.

IV

David Runs Away

(I Samuel 18-20)

Saul had a son named Jonathan. When David lived in the house of King Saul, David and Jonathan became friends.

But after a while Saul began to hate David. He hated David because he knew that some day David would be king.

Then it happened that Saul became very sick. An evil spirit came to bother him.

Saul's servants said, "Music will chase the evil spirit away. We must find someone who can play sweet music."

They knew David could play. So they called David to play his harp for Saul.

When David played his harp, the evil spirit went away.

After a while the evil spirit came to bother Saul again. The servants called David again, to play his beautiful music for Saul.

But this time the evil spirit did not go away. Saul looked at David and hated him more than ever. Suddenly Saul took his spear and threw it at David.

David saw the spear come. He stepped aside. And the spear went into the wall. But after that David could not play for Saul again. He was afraid Saul would kill him.

Jonathan said to David, "I do not think that my father really wants to harm you. I will ask him. If he does, I will help you run away."

So they made a plan. Jonathan said he would go talk to King Saul.

Jonathan said, "When I come back, I will bring my bow and arrows, and I will bring my little boy. I will shoot an arrow, and tell my little boy to get it. If I shoot it just a little way, that means you can stay here. If I shoot it far, that means you must go away."

Jonathan went to talk to Saul. David hid in the bushes and waited.

Soon Jonathan came back. He had his bow and arrows. And the little boy was with him.

David watched Jonathan. He saw Jonathan take an arrow and shoot it. The arrow flew far away, out into the field.

Jonathan called to the little boy, "The arrow is far away! Run and get it!"

The little boy ran to get the arrow. Then Jonathan gave him the bow and arrows and sent him home.

When the little boy was gone, David came out of his hiding place. He knew he would have to go away. The arrow told him that.

Jonathan came to meet David. They kissed each other and said goodbye. They were sad. Then David went away.

V

Saul Hunts for David
(I Samuel 22, 23)

David went away into the wild country. He found a cave in the hills, and he lived in the cave. After a while other men came to live with David. They made David their leader.

When Saul heard that David was gone, Saul was angry. He called his soldiers and went to hunt for him. He hunted and hunted.

Jonathan knew where David was. One day Jonathan went to visit David. But he did not tell Saul where David was hiding.

Somebody else did tell Saul.

Then Saul went to the hills. He made a ring of soldiers all around the hill where David's cave was.

Saul said, "Now I shall surely get him. We will make the ring smaller and smaller until we find him."

But a man came running to Saul. It was a messenger from home.

The messenger said, "You must hurry back home! The Philistines are coming! They are going to fight against us!"

So Saul had to take his soldiers and hurry back home. He did not get David. God would not let him catch David.

Afterwards, Saul went hunting for David again. He hunted all through the rocks and hills. David and his men were hiding in a big cave. Saul hunted day after day, and could not find him.

VI

David Spares Saul's Life
(I Samuel 24)

One day, when David was deep in the dark cave, he heard someone come in. David crept forward to see who was there. There was light by the mouth of the cave. David saw a man. It was Saul! Saul had come into the cave to rest. Saul did not know that David was there.

David went back to his men and said, "Saul is in the cave!"

The men said to David, "Now you can kill Saul. God sent him to you."

Then David crept forward again, very quietly. Saul did not hear him come. David went very near Saul. David took his sword and cut off a part of Saul's robe. With the piece of Saul's robe in his hand, David went back to his men.

The men said to David, "Why didn't you kill him? He wants to kill you."

David answered, "No, it would not be right. God made Saul king. I may not kill him."

After a little while Saul went away.

When Saul was gone, David went out and followed him. David called to Saul, "O King Saul!"

Saul looked around to see who called him. And there was David.

David held the piece of robe high, so Saul could see it.

"Look what I have," he called to Saul. "It is a piece of your robe. I cut it off while you were in the cave. I could have killed you, but I did not. Now you can see that I will not harm you."

Saul looked at the piece of his robe, and he was ashamed.

Saul said to David, "You are better than I am. I will hunt you no longer. I promise. You may come back home. You need not be afraid of me."

After that, Saul and his soldiers went back home. But David and his men still lived in the cave.

VII

Saul Hunts for David Again

(I Samuel 26)

After a while some people said to Saul, "David is hiding in the hills near our city. Why don't you come and find him?"

Then Saul called his men and went out to hunt for David again.

David heard that Saul was hunting for him. So David sent out spies to see where Saul was.

The spies came back. They told David just where Saul and his soldiers had their camp.

David said, "Who will go with me, right into the camp of Saul?"

One of David's men, Abishai, said, "I will go with you."

David and Abishai went at night. They found Saul's camp. There were wagons in a great big circle. Inside the circle were the soldiers.

David and Abishai went very quietly. They went through the circle of wagons. There they saw the soldiers fast asleep. David and Abishai walked past rows and rows of soldiers, all fast asleep. Then they found Saul. Saul was asleep, too. And Abner, Saul's general, was asleep. Saul's spear was stuck in the ground, beside Saul's bed. A jug of water stood beside his bed, too.

Nobody heard David and Abishai come. God made them all sleep very tight.

Abishai whispered to David, "Let me kill Saul."

But David whispered, "No. Saul will die when it is God's time. We will not harm him."

Then David said, "Take Saul's spear, and take the jug of water. And we will go away."

Abishai took Saul's spear and the jug of water. Very quietly they went away. No one heard them.

When they were outside the circle of wagons, David and Abishai climbed up a high hill. From the hilltop they could look down on the camp.

It was morning, then. David stood on the hill and called out, "Abner, O Abner!"

Abner awoke. He looked around to see who was calling him. He saw David standing on the hill.

David called out, "What a brave man you are, Abner! Why don't you keep better watch over your king? I might have killed your king this night!"

David held up the spear and the jug of water. "Look!" he called. "See what I have here. It is the king's spear and the king's water jug."

Then Abner knew that David had been by Saul's bed. Abner was ashamed that he had not watched.

Saul awoke, too. Saul saw the man on the hill and heard him. Saul called out, "Is that your voice, David?"

David answered, "Yes, O King, it is my voice. See, I took your spear and your water jug. But I did not harm you. Now why do you hunt me to kill me?"

Then Saul said, "My son David, I have sinned again. I will hunt you no longer. I see that you do not mean harm to me."

Saul sent one of his men to get the spear and the water jug.

Then Saul and his soldiers went home. But David still lived in the hills.

VIII

David Becomes King
(II Samuel 1; 4:4; 9)

After a while, the Philistines made war again. Saul and his soldiers had to fight against the Philistines. Jonathan was a captain in the army. They all went out to fight a big battle.

The Philistines were strong. They won the battle. Saul and Jonathan were killed.

The news went through the land, the awful news — King Saul is killed, and Jonathan, his son, is killed. People were afraid. They did not know what would happen next. They did not have a king to lead them.

In Jonathan's house, a nurse was taking care of Jonathan's little boy. The boy's name was Mephibosheth. The nurse did not know what to do. She picked up little Mephibosheth and started to run away. But she dropped him, and the fall hurt both his feet. After that, Mephibosheth could not walk well. But somebody took him and cared for him.

David heard about the battle, too. A messenger came and told him that Saul and Jonathan were dead.

See accompanying illustration
between pages 160 and 161

Then David was very sad. He had loved Jonathan very much.

After a while David asked God, "Shall I go back to my own country now?"

God told him to go.

David went back to his own country. And the people made him king in Saul's place. At last the little shepherd boy became a king.

The people loved David. He was a good king. He did what was right.

One day David said, "Is there anybody left of Saul's family? If there is anybody, I want to be kind to him."

They told David about Mephibosheth.

David told his men to find Mephibosheth. They brought him to David. Mephibosheth was a cripple. He came to David and fell on his face before David.

David said to him, "Do not be afraid. Jonathan, your father, was my friend. I will be kind to you."

David gave Mephibosheth some servants and some land. And Mephibosheth ate at the king's table every day.

David lived in Jerusalem. He built a beautiful house there. And God blessed David.

IX

David Sins Against God

(II Samuel 11)

The roof of David's beautiful house was flat. David liked to walk on the roof. He could look down upon the city. He could look down at the busy streets. He could see the houses of other people.

He walked on the roof one evening. And he looked down at a little house near-by. There he saw a beautiful woman.

David asked his servant, "Who is this woman?"

The servant said, "She is Bathsheba. Her husband is Uriah."

David said, "Send her to me."

Uriah was a soldier. He was gone to war. Bathsheba was alone. She came when the king sent for her.

The king loved Bathsheba. But he could not marry her. She had a husband.

Then King David sent a servant to the army. He said to Joab, the captain of the army, "Send Uriah home."

Uriah came to Jerusalem. He came to David. The king asked him about the war. Then the king sent him home to Bathsheba.

Uriah did not want to go home. He said, "The soldiers are fighting. I cannot go home while they are fighting."

Then David wrote a letter to Joab. He gave the letter to Uriah and sent Uriah back to the army. In the letter David said to Joab, "Put Uriah in the front lines of battle, so that he will surely be killed."

Uriah took the letter to Joab. Joab read the letter. And he put Uriah in the front lines of battle.

When the battle was over, Uriah was dead. That was how David killed Uriah.

Bathsheba was sad when she heard that Uriah was dead. But after a while David sent for her. Bathsheba became David's wife. And they had a baby boy. But God was not pleased with David.

X

A Little Lamb and a Little Boy

(II Samuel 12; Psalm 51)

Samuel had died many years before. But there was another prophet in Jerusalem. His name was Nathan.

God sent Nathan to David.

Nathan told David a story. He said, "There were two men in one city. One was rich; the other was poor. The rich man had very many sheep and lambs. The poor man had just one little lamb. The poor man loved his little lamb. His children played with the little lamb. They fed it from the table. They let it drink out of the cup. It slept in the house with them.

"One day a traveller came to visit the rich man. The rich man wanted to make a big dinner for his visitor. But he did not want to take any of his own sheep or lambs. He went to the poor man and took his little lamb. He killed the poor man's little lamb and made a big dinner for his visitor."

David listened to the story, and it made him angry.

David said, "That was very cruel! The rich man must be punished. He must give back four little lambs for the one he took away."

Then Nathan said to King David, "You are that man!"

Nathan said, "You have riches. You have wives and children. Yet you took Bathsheba. You took her away from Uriah. You had Uriah killed. You are like the rich man who stole the poor man's little lamb."

David knew that all this was true.

Nathan said, "God will punish you. Your baby boy will surely die."

Then David was very sorry for his sin. He told Nathan that he was sorry. He told God that he was sorry. He wrote a beautiful poem telling God how sorry he was (Psalm 51).

God forgave David his sin.

But after a little while the baby boy became sick. David loved the little boy. He prayed that God would make the baby well. All night long David prayed. He did not eat and he did not sleep.

For seven days the baby was sick. In all that time David would not eat and would not go to bed. But the baby died.

Then David washed himself and dressed himself. He went to the Tabernacle to worship God.

When he came home, he asked for something to eat.

The servants said, "How strange! When the baby was sick, King David would not eat. Now the baby is dead, and he will eat."

David said to them, "While the baby was alive, I prayed. I thought maybe God would make him well. But now he is gone. I will go to him when I die, but he will not come back to me."

For David knew that God had taken the baby to heaven.

After a while Bathsheba had another baby boy. They called him Solomon.

16

DAVID'S SON SOLOMON

I

A New King
(I Kings 1; 3:1-15)

Years went by. David became old. He knew that God would soon take him home to heaven.

One day David called the prophet Nathan.

He said to Nathan, "Take my son Solomon, and anoint him to be king. Let him ride on my best horse. Let a man blow a trumpet ahead of him. And call out in the streets, 'Long live the king!'"

They did as David said. They poured the oil on Solomon's head. They put him on the king's horse. They sent a man ahead to blow the trumpet. And they called out in the streets, "Long live the king!"

The people heard the noise. They came running out of their houses. They saw Solomon riding upon the king's horse. They heard the trumpet and the call, "Long live the king."

Then they knew that Solomon was their new king. They were happy. They all followed Solomon and Nathan and the king's men. They shouted and sang. They blew their horns. The singing and shouting filled the whole city.

After that, Solomon came back to his father David. David told Solomon that he would soon die.

David said to Solomon, "When you are king, you must serve God always. You must keep His commandments. Then God will bless you."

God soon took David home to heaven. And Solomon was king.

Solomon loved God. He went to Gibeon to make a special offering to God. At Gibeon he prayed to God and worshipped Him.

That night God came to Solomon in a dream.

God said to Solomon, "Ask anything that you wish. I will give it to you."

Solomon said, "Oh, my God, You have made me king. I must rule over all these people. It will be very hard, sometimes, to know just what to do. Please give me wisdom, so that I shall do the right."

Then God said, "You asked for wisdom. That is better than riches. I will give you wisdom. And I will give you riches, too. If you serve Me, I will also give you a long life."

Solomon awoke. He thought about his dream. He knew it was not just a dream. He knew that God had truly spoken to him.

Solomon became a very wise king and a very rich king. God made him the wisest man that ever lived.

II

Solomon is Very Wise

(I Kings 3:16-28)

One day two women came to Solomon. They brought two babies — a dead baby and a living baby.

One woman said to Solomon, "We two women live together. I had a baby and she had a baby. Last night her baby died. Then she put the dead baby in my bed, and she took my baby. Now she says the dead baby is my baby. But the living baby is really my baby."

The other woman said, "My baby did not die. The living baby is my baby."

One woman was telling a lie. But Solomon did not know which one. Solomon did not know which was the mother of the living baby.

Solomon thought a little. Then he said, "Go get a sword."

One of his servants went to get a sword — a big sharp sword.

"Now," said Solomon, "cut the living baby in two, and give each woman a half of it!"

The two women thought that Solomon really wanted the baby cut in two.

One said, "Oh no, no! Don't do that!"

The other said, "All right. Cut it in two. We'll each have half."

Then Solomon knew which was the real mother. The real mother did not want her baby cut in two!

Solomon gave the baby to its mother, and the mother went away happy.

Everybody in Israel heard about the two babies. They thought, "Solomon is a very wise king. God has given us a wise and good king."

The wise Solomon wrote many wise things. He said that to be really wise we must first of all know God and serve Him.

III

A New House for God

(I Kings 5, 6, 7, 8; II Chronicles 6, 7)

King David had saved very much gold and silver. He had saved it to build a house for God. But David did not build the house. David told Solomon to build it.

Solomon needed wood for the house, too. He sent men to a far-away country to cut wood. He sent other men to the hills to cut stone. They brought the wood and the stone to Jerusalem. They brought more gold and silver, too.

When David came near, Samuel
poured the oil on his head.

The people loved David;
he was a good king.

Then they began to build the house. They called it a Temple. In this Temple the people could worship God, as we worship Him in church.

But you have never seen a church as beautiful as the Temple. The men worked seven years to build the Temple. They used beautiful wood, and beautiful stones. Inside, the walls were covered with gold. The furniture was also covered with gold.

At last the Temple was finished. Then Solomon told the people to come to Jerusalem. There would be a great feast.

Many people came to the feast.

The priests took the Ark of God out of the old Tabernacle. They brought it to the Temple.

The people brought their gifts to God. They stood in the Temple yard. And the glory of God filled the Temple. The glory of God was like a bright shining cloud. So Solomon and all the people knew that God was there.

Solomon stood by the big altar. All the people could see him. They saw him kneel down. They saw him spread his hands toward heaven. And they heard him pray.

Solomon prayed a wonderful prayer. He asked God to live in this new house. He asked God to answer prayer when people prayed in this new house. He asked God to forgive their sins.

Then Solomon stood up. He stretched his hands over the heads of the people. He said, "God has blessed His people. He has kept all His promises to do good to us. Let us live for Him every day."

The feast lasted two whole weeks. Then all the people went home. They were very happy. They knew that God was very good to them.

17

ELIJAH, MAN OF GOD

I

God Feeds a Prophet

(I Kings 17:1-9)

Solomon was king for forty years. Then he was an old man. And he died.

There were other kings after Solomon. But there was never another king so rich and so wise as Solomon.

Some of the kings were bad. They did not serve God. They made idols of wood and stone. They prayed to these idols, and they told the people to pray to the idols.

Ahab was one of the bad kings. He made an altar for the god Baal, an idol.

God sent a prophet to Ahab. The prophet's name was Elijah.

Elijah said to Ahab, "Because you are very wicked, it shall not rain for a long, long time."

That was bad news. When it does not rain, corn and wheat cannot grow; our gardens dry up; there is no food to eat.

Ahab did not like to hear such bad news. But Elijah said that it was God's word. Then Ahab was angry with Elijah.

God told Elijah to hide away from Ahab. Elijah went to a little creek out in the country. There he had water to drink. He made himself a place to sleep on the ground.

In the morning, when Elijah awoke, he drank water from the creek. But he had nothing to eat. Then he saw a big black bird come flying over the hills. The bird had something in its bill. It flew to Elijah. Elijah saw that the bird was a raven. The raven had bread and meat in its bill, and dropped it beside Elijah. That was Elijah's breakfast.

At evening, the raven came again. It brought more bread and meat.

The next morning, the raven came to bring Elijah's breakfast again. And in the evening it brought supper. Every day the raven brought food to Elijah, for God sent the raven. And Elijah drank water from the creek.

But after a while the creek dried up. Then Elijah had no water to drink. We cannot live without water.

God told Elijah to go to a certain town not far away. He said that Elijah would find a widow lady there, and she would give him food and drink.

II

A Widow Lady

(I Kings 17:10-16)

Elijah walked away toward the city. By the gates of the city, he saw a woman. She was picking up little sticks.

Elijah said to the woman, "Will you please get me a little drink of water?"

When she went to get the water, Elijah called to her, "Please bring me a piece of bread, too."

But the woman said, "I have no bread. I have just a little flour and a little oil. I am going to make a fire with these sticks. Then I will bake a little bread of the flour and oil. That is all we have. When it is gone, my son and I will die."

Elijah said to her, "Do not be afraid. Make me a little biscuit first. Then make one for your son and one for you. And God will take care of you. The oil will not be all gone. And the flour will not be all gone."

The woman could hardly believe that. But she did as Elijah said. She made a little biscuit for Elijah first. Then she made one for her son and one for herself. And when she had them all made, there was oil left, and there was flour left.

Every day the woman used her little bit of oil and her little bit of flour. And every day there was some left.

So God took care of His prophet. And He took care of the woman who did what the prophet told her to do.

III

The Widow's Son

(I Kings 17:17-28)

One day the widow's son became sick. The woman was very sad. She had only this one son. She held the boy in her arms. After a while he died.

Then the woman called Elijah. She said to Elijah, "Why did you come to me? Now my son is dead!"

Elijah said, "Give him to me."

Elijah took the boy upstairs to his little room. He laid the boy on his own bed.

Then Elijah prayed. He said, "O God, I pray that the soul of this little boy may come back!"

Elijah laid himself down on the bed on top of the boy. Then he got up and prayed again. Then he lay down again.

God heard Elijah's prayer. God sent the soul of the little boy back. The little boy opened his eyes. He breathed again. He was well.

Elijah took him down to his mother.

How happy his mother was to see her boy alive and well! She reached out her arms to take him.

She said to Elijah, "Now I know that you are a prophet. Only a prophet, a man of God, could make my little boy live again."

IV

Who Is the True God?

(I Kings 18)

Every day the sky was blue. The sun shone hot. Rain did not come. The ground was hard and dry. Even the grass did not grow. There were no gardens at all. For three years it did not rain.

The people could not find enough food to eat.

But Ahab still served the idol, Baal. And the people served Baal, too.

God said to Elijah, "Go to Ahab now. Tell him, 'We shall see who is the true God.' "

Elijah went to Ahab.

Elijah said to Ahab, "We shall see today who is really God. Go call all the prophets of Baal. And call all the people of Israel."

Ahab called all the prophets of Baal — four hundred and fifty of them. And he called all the people of Israel — a great big crowd of people.

Elijah stood and talked to them. He said to them, "I am the only prophet of the Lord. There are four hundred and fifty prophets of Baal. Now we shall see who is truly God, Baal or the Lord."

Elijah said, "I will pray to the Lord. You will pray to Baal. The God who sends fire, He will be the true God."

The people said, "Yes, that is good. If Baal sends fire, he is the true God. If the Lord sends fire, He is the true God."

Elijah said, "Let the prophets of Baal pray first."

So the prophets of Baal made an altar. They put wood on the altar. They put an ox on it, to burn as a gift to Baal. Then they began to pray. They asked Baal to send fire from heaven. They asked Baal to send fire down on the altar to burn the ox.

But fire did not come.

They cried, "O Baal, hear us!" But Baal did not answer.

All morning long they prayed.

Elijah laughed at them. He said, "You must call louder. Maybe your god is sleeping."

Then they called louder and louder. They jumped up and down. They cut themselves. And still Baal did not answer. Baal did not send fire.

At last Elijah said, "Now it is my turn. Come near me and watch."

The people all came near. They stood around Elijah.

Elijah made an altar of stones. He dug a ditch around the altar. He put wood on the altar. And he put an ox on the altar as a gift to God.

Then Elijah said, "Get four barrels of water. Pour the water on the altar."

They poured four barrels of water on the altar.

He said, "Do it again." And they poured more water on the altar.

They made the altar all wet. The wood was wet. The ox was wet. The ditch was full of water. How could fire burn on such a wet altar?

Then Elijah prayed. He said, "O God, show us that Thou art truly God. Show these people that I am Thy prophet. Then they will serve Thee again."

And while Elijah prayed, the fire came. It came from heaven. It burned the wet wood; it burned the wet ox; it burned even the stones; and it dried up all the water in the ditch.

The people saw the fire. And they were afraid.

They said, "The Lord, He is God! He is truly God!"

V

Elijah Goes to Heaven

(I Kings 19; II Kings 2)

Elijah was a great prophet. He went all through the land, telling the people to serve God. He was not afraid of the wicked king.

But Elijah became old. Then God said to him, "Go find Elisha. Elisha will be my prophet when you are gone."

Elijah found Elisha in a field. Elisha was plowing. Elijah walked near Elisha, and threw his coat on Elisha.

Elisha knew what that meant. He knew that Elijah wanted him to be a prophet. So Elisha stopped plowing. He went to say good-bye to his mother and father. He went with Elijah.

After that, wherever Elijah went, Elisha went along. Elisha learned to be a prophet of God.

Elijah knew that God would soon take him away. He was an old man.

Elijah said to Elisha, "I must go to Bethel. Perhaps you should not go along."

But Elisha said, "I do not want you to go without me. I will go along."

At Bethel they met some young men. The young men said to Elisha, "God is going to take Elijah away today. Did you know that?"

"Yes, I know it," Elisha said.

Elijah and Elisha went on. After a while they came to Jericho. There they met more young men. The young men said to Elisha, "God is going to take Elijah away today. Did you know that?"

Elisha said, "Yes, I know it."

Elijah and Elisha went on. After a while they came to the river Jordan. Elijah took off his coat. He rolled it up. Then he hit the water with his coat. The water divided, so that there was a little dry path through the river. Elijah and Elisha walked across the river on this little path.

Then Elijah said to Elisha, "God will soon take me away. Is there something I can do for you?"

Elisha said, "Please let a double portion of your spirit fall on me."

The spirit of Elijah was the Spirit of God. Elisha wanted to be a good prophet, as Elijah had been.

Elijah said, "If you see me when God takes me, then you shall have a double portion of my spirit."

They walked on. They talked together.

And then they suddenly saw horses and a chariot in the sky. The horses came rushing down to them. The horses and the chariot were bright like fire.

The fiery horses and chariot rushed toward Elijah and Elisha. And a great whirlwind blew. And Elijah went up to heaven in the wind, with the horses and chariot. But Elijah dropped his coat on the ground.

Elisha watched him go. Elisha watched until he could not see Elijah and the horses and the chariot.

Then Elisha took Elijah's coat. He went back to the Jordan river. He hit the water with Elijah's coat.

Elisha said, "Is the God of Israel with me?"

And the water divided. It made a path for Elisha. Then Elisha knew that God was with him. And Elisha became a great prophet.

18

THE PROPHET ELISHA

I

The Widow's Oil

(II Kings 4:1-7)

One day a widow came to Elisha. She was in trouble. She owed money to a man, and she could not pay it. The man said he would take her sons away.

The widow loved her two boys. She did not want them to be slaves for the man. So she went to Elisha. She told her trouble to Elisha.

"The man is coming to get my boys," she said. "What shall I do?"

Elisha said, "Have you anything to sell?"

The widow said, "I am poor. I have only a little oil in a jar."

Elisha said, "Go to all your neighbors. Ask them for jars. Get all the empty jars you can find. Then go into your house. Shut the door. And pour your oil into the empty jars."

The widow sent her boys to the neighbors. They asked for empty jars. They brought the empty jars to their mother and set them in a row in the house. There was a long row of them.

Then the widow and her two boys closed the door. The boys brought the jars to their mother, one by one. She poured oil from her jar into the other jars. She filled one jar after another. She poured and poured, and her jar did not get empty.

When all the jars were full, she said, "Bring me another jar."

The boys said, "There are no more."

Then the widow ran to Elisha. She told him about the wonderful thing that had happened. Her little jar of oil had become very many jars of oil.

Elisha said, "Now go sell your oil. Then you will have money. Pay the man what you owe him. And you will still have enough to live on."

People used oil for baking and for many other things in those days. The widow soon sold all her oil. She paid the man all that she owed him. And she had money left to buy food for herself and her boys.

So God showed His love and His power through the prophet Elisha.

II

A Lady in Shunem

(II Kings 4:8-37)

Elisha went all through the land of Israel. He told the people how to serve God. The people had no Bible. They only had the prophets to tell them about God. So Elisha went from place to place. He was God's messenger to the people.

Many times Elisha went through a little city called Shunem. A lady in Shunem asked him into her house. She knew that he was a man of God, and she liked to have him come.

One day the lady of Shunem said to her husband, "The man of God comes through Shunem often. Let us build a little room for him. We can put a bed in it, and a chair, and a table, and a candle. Then he can live there when he comes to Shunem."

So they built the little room.

When Elisha came again, the little room was ready.

Elisha liked the little room. When he was tired, he could lie down there to rest.

Elisha wanted to do something for the lady of Shunem. He told her that she would have a baby.

After a while, the baby came. The lady of Shunem was very happy with her little boy. He grew up and played around the house. Sometimes he went with his father to the field.

One summer day the little boy went with his father. It was a warm day. The sun shone bright. The men in the field were cutting grain. It was fun to watch them.

But suddenly the little boy began to cry. He said his head hurt. Then his father sent one of the men to carry him home.

The little boy became very sick. At noon he died.

When the little boy was dead, the lady of Shunem laid him on Elisha's bed. Then she rode away to find Elisha. She fell on her knees at Elisha's feet.

"Oh!" she said, "I did not ask for a baby!"

Then Elisha knew that something was the matter with the boy.

Gehazi was with Elisha. Gehazi was a man-servant who went with Elisha everywhere, and helped him.

Elisha said to Gehazi, "Take my staff. Run to the lady's house, and lay the staff on the face of the boy."

Gehazi went away at a run. But the lady of Shunem would not go. She wanted Elisha to come with her.

Elisha went with her. They met Gehazi coming back. Gehazi said the staff did not help at all.

Elisha went to his room and found the little boy on his bed.

Elisha closed the door. He prayed. Then he lay down on the bed. He put his mouth on the boy's mouth. He put his hands on the boy's hands. After a while the boy sneezed. Then he opened his eyes. He was alive again.

Elisha sent Gehazi to call the mother. She came quickly. She took the boy in her arms and she was too happy to talk. She fell down at Elisha's feet to thank him. God had given her the little boy again.

See accompanying illustration between pages 192 and 193

III

A Little Slave Girl

(II Kings 5:1-19)

Elisha told the people about God. But many of the people still served idols. Sometimes God would send punishment upon them. Often other nations would come to fight against Israel. Sometimes they would steal sheep. Sometimes they would steal corn and wheat. Sometimes they would steal boys and girls, and even grown people.

One day the Syrians came. They stole a little girl. The little girl became a slave of a Syrian woman.

This Syrian woman was the wife of Captain Naaman. The captain was sick. He had a terrible sickness called leprosy. Naaman knew it would get worse and worse, and that at last he would die.

The little slave girl was sorry for Naaman. She said to her mistress, "I wish Naaman could go to our prophet. Our prophet could make him well."

The king of Syria heard what the little girl said. He sent Naaman to the prophet.

Naaman rode in a beautiful chariot with beautiful horses. He had gold and silver and some beautiful clothes with him. These were presents for the prophet, if the prophet made him well.

Naaman rode to Elisha's door. But Elisha did not go out to see him. He sent Gehazi out.

Gehazi said to Naaman, "Elisha says you must go and wash in the river Jordan seven times. Then you will be well."

That made Naaman angry. He said, "The prophet does not even come out to see me! I thought he would look at the spot, and pray with me, and I would be well. I will not go to the river Jordan. The rivers in my country are better than the Jordan."

He was very angry. He rode away.

But one of his men said, "Why not do what the prophet says? It is not a hard thing to do."

Naaman listened. Yes, it would be easy to go to the Jordan and wash seven times. Naaman went. He stepped down out of his chariot and dipped into the river Jordan. He dipped seven times. When he came out of the water, the leprosy spots were gone. He was well.

Then Naaman was very happy. He rode back to Elisha's house. He wanted to give Elisha the gold and silver and beautiful clothes.

But Elisha did not want presents. He would not take any of them.

Naaman said to him, "I will never serve idols again. I will worship only the true God."

And Elisha said to him, "Go in peace."

So the little slave girl was a great blessing to her master.

IV

Gehazi's Lie

(II Kings 5:20-27)

Gehazi watched Naaman ride away. Gehazi wished he had some of that silver, and some of the beautiful clothes.

Gehazi said to himself, "I will run after Naaman. Elisha would not take anything, but I can take something."

Naaman saw Gehazi coming. He stopped the chariot and waited. Gehazi came running.

"Is all well?" Naaman asked.

"Yes, all is well," said Gehazi. "But two young men came to my master, and my master would like something for them. He would like a piece of silver, and two of the beautiful suits of clothes."

"Take two pieces of silver," said Naaman. "My servants will carry the things for you."

Two servants carried the silver and the clothes as far as the city gate. Gehazi sent them back and hid the things in his house. Then he went to see Elisha.

Elisha said, "Where did you go, Gehazi?"

Gehazi said, "I did not go anywhere."

Elisha said, "I saw Naaman get down from the chariot to meet you."

Gehazi hung his head. He could not hide anything from Elisha. Elisha was God's prophet.

Elisha said, "Now you shall have the leprosy of Naaman."

Then Gehazi's skin became white as snow. He went away, a leper. Gehazi had to be punished because he lied to Elisha.

V

A Hungry City

(II Kings 6; 7:1, 2)

Again and again the people of Israel forgot God. They made idols of wood and stone, and they prayed to these idols.

God wanted His people to love Him. He wanted to be their God. When they served idols, He sent trouble to them to make them sorry for their sin.

So one day God sent the Syrians. The Syrians had a big army. The Syrian soldiers put their tents all around the big city of Samaria. They would not let anyone go in or out of the city.

For many, many days the army was around the city. The people inside the city ate all the food there was. And they could not go out to buy more. Then they were hungry. When there was nothing more to eat, they cried to the king for help. But the king could not help them.

The king said, "It is Elisha's fault. I will punish Elisha."

Then the king went to Elisha. A captain went with him.

Elisha knew that the king was coming. He waited for him. As soon as the king came, Elisha said, "Hear the word of the Lord. Tomorrow there will be plenty of fine flour and barley. It will be for sale at the gate of the city."

The captain would not believe that. He said, "If the Lord would make windows in heaven, even then how could this be?"

Elisha said to the captain, "You shall see it. But you shall not eat of it."

The king and the captain went away. They did not harm Elisha.

VI

God Feeds the Hungry City
(II Kings 7:3-20)

There were four men outside the city of Samaria. They were lepers. They had the awful disease called leprosy. That is why they had to live outside the city.

When the soldiers of Syria came, the lepers lived between the city and the big army around the city. But when the people in the city had no food, the lepers had no food, either. They were hungry, too.

That night, when the king had talked with Elisha, the lepers were very hungry. One leper said, "Let's go to the Syrian soldiers. They have food. Maybe they will give us something to eat."

They were all a little bit afraid to go, but they went just the same. The sun had set. It was almost dark.

The four lepers came to the nearest tent. Nobody was there. They looked inside. They did not see any soldiers. Then they went to the next tent. They did not see any soldiers there.

"How strange!" they said. "Where are the soldiers?"

They found food in the tents. They said, "Let's eat."

So they ate. They ate all they wanted.

But one of the lepers said, "This is not right. The people in the city are hungry, too. We must tell them that there is food here."

So they went to the city gate. A watchman was sitting in the tower. They called to him, "The soldiers are all gone! The camp is empty!"

The watchman sent the news to the king. And the king sent his men out to see if the soldiers were really gone.

The king's men did not find one soldier. They hunted carefully, for they thought perhaps the soldiers were hiding. But they could not find one.

Then the people of Samaria went out to get food. They hurried out the gate. They crowded and pushed. They were so hungry that they could not wait.

The king sent his captain to the gate to keep order — the captain who would not believe that God could feed the city. The captain tried to keep order, but the crowd was too big. They pushed him down, and stepped on him, and killed him. As Elisha had said — he saw the flour and the barley, but he did not eat of it.

The people hurried on to get the food. They found plenty, enough for everybody.

But what had become of the Syrian soldiers?

They had run away. God had made them hear a big noise. The noise sounded like horses and chariots, coming fast. The Syrians thought a great big army was coming. And they had all run away.

So God fed the big city of Samaria.

19

THREE KINGS AND A PROPHET

I

A Boy King

(II Kings 11; II Chronicles 23)

Athaliah was a wicked woman. She wanted to be queen. She told the soldiers to kill all the sons of the king. Only in this way could she become queen.

The sons of the king were David's grandchildren. God had promised that the Saviour, Jesus, would be born of them. But Athaliah wanted to kill them all.

One son of the king was a baby, just a year old. His aunt loved him. She did not want wicked Athaliah to kill him. So she ran away with the baby and hid him. She took care of little Joash and did not let Athaliah find him. They lived in the Temple with the high priest.

Athaliah did not know that the baby was still living. She made herself queen. She served idols. And the people served idols, too.

When Joash was seven years old, the high priest sent a messenger through the land of Israel. He told the people to come to Jerusalem. He called the soldiers, too.

A great crowd came. The high priest set the soldiers all in a row around the Temple. They stood tall and straight. Their spears shone in the sunshine. The priests were in the Temple. The people stood outside, wondering what was going to happen.

Then the high priest brought out the little Joash.

The high priest led little Joash to one of the big pillars of the Temple. Then he poured anointing oil on his head. And he put a crown of gold on his head.

The priest said, "God save the king!"

Then all the people clapped their hands. They shouted, "God save the king!"

The men blew trumpets. The people sang and shouted. More and more people came running to see the new king.

At last Athaliah heard the noise. She came to the Temple to see what all the noise was about. She saw the soldiers. She saw the little boy standing by a pillar, with a crown on his head. She heard the people shout, "God save the king!"

Then she knew that they did not want her to be queen. She was angry, and she was afraid. She took hold of her dress and tore it.

The high priest told the soldiers to take her away.

Then the high priest talked to all the people. They promised to serve God again. They broke their idols and threw them away. They worshipped God in His Temple.

II

A Letter for God to Read
(II Kings 18, 19; II Chronicles 32)

Israel had many kings. Some were bad. Some were good. Hezekiah was one of the good kings.

Hezekiah trusted the Lord. He taught the people to serve God.

But one day a very big army came to Jerusalem. The soldiers put up their tents all around the city. It was the army of Assyria.

The king of Assyria sent a messenger to Hezekiah. He said, "I will take your city. You may as well give up. You cannot fight against me."

The people of Jerusalem heard about it. They were afraid of the king of Assyria.

Hezekiah said to them, "Do not be afraid. Just trust in God."

Then the king of Assyria sent a letter to Hezekiah. In the letter he said, "Do you think that God can save Jerusalem? There were many other big cities. I took them all. They had gods, but their gods could not help them. Your God cannot help you, either."

Hezekiah read the letter. He knew that the king of Assyria had a very big army. He knew that he had taken other big cities.

Hezekiah went to the Temple to pray. He took the letter with him. He opened the letter and laid it out for God to read.

Then Hezekiah prayed. He said, "O Lord, Thou art the only God, the God of all the earth. See this letter that the king of Assyria sent me. He says that other gods could not save other cities. He says that our God cannot save Jerusalem. But, O God, save us!"

There was a prophet in Jerusalem at that time. His name was Isaiah.

God told Isaiah to go to Hezekiah.

Isaiah said to Hezekiah, "God says that He will save Jerusalem. He will chase away the armies of Assyria."

That night God sent an angel to the army of Assyria. The angel killed many of the soldiers of Assyria, and the others all ran away. Then the king of Assyria knew that the God of Jerusalem was the only true God. He learned that God can save His people.

III

A King Goes to Prison

(II Chronicles 33)

Hezekiah died. God took him home to heaven. His son, Manasseh, became king.

Hezekiah had told Manasseh how to serve God, but Manasseh did not want to serve God. He made idols. He prayed to the sun and stars. He did not keep God's laws.

One day Manasseh made a beautiful idol. He put it in the Temple of God. He told the people to worship that idol.

Then a prophet came to Manasseh. He told Manasseh and all the people that they must not sin against God. He told them that God would surely punish them.

But Manasseh would not listen to the prophet. The people would not listen, either. They still served the idol.

Soon after that, the king of Assyria came back. He came to Jerusalem with his big army. Manasseh was afraid, but he did not pray to God. He prayed to his idols. And his idols could not help him.

The king of Assyria took Manasseh. He tied Manasseh's hands with chains and took him away to Babylon. He put Manasseh in prison.

Manasseh was very sad, there in the dark prison. He thought of all his sin. And he began to pray. He asked God to forgive his sins. He asked God to bring him out of prison and back to Jerusalem.

God heard Manasseh's prayer. God forgave his sins. The king of Assyria let Manasseh go back to Jerusalem.

Manasseh was very happy then. He broke down the idols that were in Jerusalem. He took the idol out of the Temple of God. He told the people that they must throw away their idols and worship God.

Manasseh served God the rest of his life.

IV

God's Mercy to a Big City

(Jonah)

At this time there was a very big city called Nineveh. The people of Nineveh were wicked. God, looking down from heaven, saw how wicked they were.

Then God spoke to a prophet named Jonah. God said to Jonah, "Go to Nineveh and preach to these wicked people."

But Jonah did not want to go. Instead, he went down to the sea. There was a big ship just ready to sail away. Jonah paid his fare and went on the ship. Soon they sailed away on the big blue sea. They were not going to Nineveh. They were going the other way!

Jonah went into the ship and lay down. He fell asleep.

After a while the wind began to blow, and big clouds covered the sky. A great storm came up. The wind blew harder and harder. The waves grew big, and the ship rolled up and down.

Then all the men on the ship were afraid. They began to pray. They prayed to their gods of wood and stone. But their gods could not help. The storm grew worse and worse.

The men found Jonah asleep, and woke him up. They said to him, "Wake up and pray to your God! We are going to drown!"

They said to each other, "It must be that somebody has sinned. That is why God sent the storm."

And they asked Jonah, "Who are you? Where are you going?"

Then Jonah told them that he was running away from God.

He said, "The storm came because of me. God sent me to Nineveh, and I would not go."

The men said, "What can we do to stop the storm?"

Jonah said, "Throw me overboard, into the stormy water. Then the storm will stop."

The men did not want to do that. They tried and tried to row the ship. They tried to get to shore. But the storm grew worse and worse.

Then they took Jonah and threw him overboard into the stormy water.

And the storm stopped.

But Jonah went down, down, down into the deep water. He thought he was going to drown. Then God sent a big fish. The big fish opened its mouth wide, and swallowed Jonah. So Jonah did not drown.

Inside the fish Jonah prayed to God. And God spoke to the fish, so that the fish spit Jonah out on the shore.

Then God spoke to Jonah again. God told Jonah again to go to Nineveh and preach. God said, "Tell the people that they must be sorry for their sins. If they do not turn from their sins, I will destroy the city in forty days."

At last Jonah went to Nineveh. Jonah walked up and down the streets of the big city, preaching to the people. He said to them, "In forty days the Lord will destroy this city!"

When the people heard Jonah, they were afraid. Even the king was afraid when he heard what the prophet said. The king told all the people to put on sackcloth and to sit in ashes. That was their way of showing they were sorry. So they put on sackcloth and sat in ashes. And they did not eat or drink. They prayed to God, and said they were sorry for their sins.

When Jonah had preached in the whole city, he went out on the hillside and sat down. He wanted to watch God destroy the city. God caused a pretty vine to grow over Jonah's head, to give him shade.

But God heard the people of Nineveh pray and He saw how sorry they were. So God did not destroy the city.

Then Jonah was angry.

In the night, God sent a worm to eat the root of the vine that gave Jonah shade. So the vine died.

Jonah was sorry to see the vine dead.

God said to Jonah, "You are sorry about the vine. But think of all the people in the big city! Many of them are little children. Should I not take pity on them?"

So God showed mercy to the people of Nineveh when they were sorry for their sins.

20

IN A STRANGE LAND

I

Jeremiah's Book

(Jeremiah 36)

The people of Israel served idols again. God sent many prophets to them, but they would not listen.

Jeremiah was one of God's prophets. God said to Jeremiah, "Write a book. I will tell you what to write. Perhaps my people will listen to the book."

Jeremiah called Baruch. Baruch could write well.

God put words into Jeremiah's mouth. Jeremiah spoke the words. And Baruch wrote all the words in a book.

At last the book was done. Jeremiah said to Baruch, "Now go read the book to the people."

Baruch called the people together. They came to the Temple. Baruch read the book to them.

The book told them terrible things. It told how God would punish them for their sins. Jerusalem would be broken down. The beautiful Temple and all the beautiful houses would be broken down and burned. The people would be taken away to a strange country.

But the book said, "If you are sorry for your sin, if you turn now and serve God, then these terrible things will not happen."

The people told the king about the book.

The king said, "Bring the book here and read it to me."

They brought the book. The king sat in his house by the fireplace. His men stood around him.

One man began to read the book. He read one page; then he cut that page out and threw it into the fire.

Some said, "Oh, do not burn the book. It is the prophet's book."

But the man read on, and he burned the whole book in the fire, one page at a time.

Then the king said, "Go get Jeremiah and Baruch." He was angry at them for writing a book with such terrible things in it.

But the king's men could not find Jeremiah and Baruch. God had hid them.

God said to Jeremiah, "Write the book again. The terrible things of the book shall surely happen."

Jeremiah wrote the book again. But the king and the people would not listen. They went on living in sin.

II

The Punishment Comes
(Jeremiah 39, 52)

Far away, in Babylon, lived King Nebuchadnezzar. He had a very big army. He came to Jerusalem with his big army. The soldiers put their tents up all around Jerusalem.

Then Nebuchadnezzar took the city. He broke down the walls. He burned the king's beautiful house. He burned the beautiful Temple. He bound the king with chains and took him and many of the people to Babylon.

The people were sad. They cried as they walked the long, long road to Babylon. They looked back and saw the smoke. Their beautiful city was burning. Their homes were burning. The beautiful Temple was burning. And they were slaves.

See accompanying illustration between pages 192 and 193

Nebuchadnezzar let Jeremiah go free. Jeremiah trusted in God. And God took care of Jeremiah.

From His home in heaven, God looked down. He saw the people walk the long, long road to Babylon. He saw how they cried.

Then God said to Jeremiah, "I will bring my people back some day. I will bring them back to their own city and their homes. I will forgive their sins, and I will bless them."

III

A Strange Dream

(Daniel 2)

Nebuchadnezzar took many of the people of Israel to Babylon. He took Daniel and some other young men to live with him in his palace.

Daniel loved God and served Him. God made Daniel a wise man, and God talked to Daniel. But Daniel was a servant of King Nebuchadnezzar.

One night King Nebuchadnezzar had a dream. When he awoke, he could not remember the dream. But he felt afraid. He thought the dream must mean something.

King Nebuchadnezzar sent for some of his wise men. He said to them, "I had a strange dream last night. I want to know what the dream means."

The wise men said, "O King, tell us the dream. We will tell you what it means."

But King Nebuchadnezzar said, "I do not remember the dream. You must tell me the dream, and then tell me what it means."

The wise men shook their heads. "No, O King," they said, "we cannot tell you the dream. Only God knows the king's dream."

Then the king was angry. He said, "If you do not tell me the dream, I will have all the wise men killed."

They told Daniel about the king and his dream.

Then Daniel went to King Nebuchadnezzar. Daniel said to the king, "Give me time. I will ask God about the dream. Then I will tell the king the dream, and I will tell the king what the dream means."

Daniel went home. He called three of his friends, and they prayed to God. They asked God to show Daniel the dream.

God heard their prayer. In the night God showed Daniel the dream.

In the morning, Daniel and his friends thanked God for hearing their prayer. Then Daniel went to the king.

King Nebuchadnezzar said to Daniel, "Can you tell me my dream, and what it means?"

Daniel said, "Wise men cannot tell you the dream. But there is a God in heaven. He knows all things."

Then Daniel told the king his dream. He said, "In the dream you saw a very big image of a man. It was made of gold and silver and brass and iron and clay. Then you saw a great stone break away from the hillside. The stone rolled. It hit the image. The image fell flat. The image broke into small pieces like dust. The stone grew and grew until it became a big mountain and filled all the earth.

"And the meaning of the dream is this," said Daniel. "The image means the kingdoms of this world. Gold, silver, brass, iron, and clay — they mean many different kingdoms. The stone is the Kingdom of God. The Kingdom of God will break the kingdoms of earth. The Kingdom of God will grow stronger and stronger. God has shown the king what is going to happen."

Then King Nebuchadnezzar said, "Your God is great. He is King of kings."

And he made Daniel a great man.

IV

God Saves in the Fire

(Daniel 3)

One day King Nebuchadnezzar made a big image of gold. It stood as high as a house. He set it in a field. Then he sent a messenger through all his land. He told all his men to come to the image.

Daniel did not have to go. But the three friends of Daniel — Shadrach, Meshach, and Abednego — had to go.

A great crowd of men stood before the image.

The king's messenger called to them, "The king commands you all to kneel before the image and worship it. You will hear music. And when you hear the music, you must fall down upon your knees. If you do not kneel to the image, the king will throw you into a fiery furnace."

After a while the music began. Then all the men fell down before the image — all but three. Three men stood up, tall and straight.

The servants of the king saw the three men stand. They said, "Who are these three men? How dare they disobey the king?"

They were Daniel's three friends, Shadrach, Meshach, and Abednego.

The king's servants brought the three men to King Nebuchadnezzar. He was angry. He said to them, "How dare you disobey me? I will give you another chance. We will play the music again. When you hear the music, you must fall down and worship the image. If you do not, I will throw you into the fiery furnace."

The three men were not afraid of King Nebuchadnezzar. They said, "O King, our God can save us. We will not worship your image."

Then the king was very angry. He said to his servants, "Make the fire seven times hotter. Tie Shadrach, Meshach, and Abednego. Throw them into the fire!"

The servants of the king made the fire hotter and hotter. They took the three men and tied them. They threw them into the fire. The fire was very, very hot.

King Nebuchadnezzar looked through the door of the furnace. He could see the three men.

King Nebuchadnezzar thought the three men would fall down and die. But he saw them walking! Then he saw four men! He counted them — one, two, three, four!

He called his servants. He asked them, "Did you throw three men into the fire?"

They said, "Yes, O King. We threw three men into the fire."

The king said, "I see four men! One looks like the Son of God! They are walking in the fire! The fire does not hurt them!"

Then King Nebuchadnezzar called to the men in the fire, "Shadrach, Meshach, and Abednego, come out!"

The three men came out. They stood before the king. The fire had not hurt them at all!

Nebuchadnezzar said, "Your God sent His angel to take care of you. No other God could do that!"

And Nebuchadnezzar said to all the people, "Shadrach, Meshach, and Abednego were brave men. They went to the fire, rather than worship another god. And their God saved them. No one may say anything against the God of Shadrach, Meshach, and Abednego."

V

A Strange Hand

(Daniel 5)

After a while, Nebuchadnezzar died. Then Belshazzar was king.

One day Belshazzar made a great feast. All the lords and great men came to the feast. They used the gold cups from the Temple in Jerusalem. They drank wine. They sang songs. They laughed. They praised their gods — gods of gold and silver and brass and iron and wood and stone.

Then the king saw something on the wall. It was a hand. The hand moved slowly. It was writing something on the wall.

The king stared at it. Whose hand could that be? The king was afraid. He began to shiver.

The king could not read what the hand wrote. No one could read it. The king called all his wise men, but they could not read it.

"I must know what the hand wrote," said the king. "Find someone to read it. I will give him a chain of pure gold, and I will make him third ruler of the kingdom."

Then the queen thought of Daniel.

The queen said, "There is a man who has the wisdom of God. He was a wise man for King Nebuchadnezzar. His name is Daniel. He can read what the hand wrote."

So they called Daniel.

King Belshazzar said to Daniel, "None of my wise men can read what the hand wrote on the wall. If you can read it, I will give you a chain of pure gold. And I will make you third ruler of the kingdom."

Daniel said, "I do not want the chain of pure gold. But I will tell you what the hand wrote."

And Daniel said, "You know about God, the true God. But you do not serve Him. You serve idols. That is why God sent this hand. The writing says that God will take the kingdom away from you."

Belshazzar gave Daniel the chain of pure gold. He made Daniel third ruler in the kingdom.

But that night a big army came to the city. They took the kingdom away from Belshazzar.

VI

Daniel in the Lions' Den
(Daniel 6)

The new king was Darius.

Darius liked Daniel. He made him the greatest man in the kingdom.

But some other men hated Daniel. They wanted to be as great as Daniel.

These men said, "We must find something wrong with Daniel, to get rid of him."

Daniel was a good man and a wise man. They could not find anything wrong in Daniel's life.

At last they thought of a plan. They went to King Darius.

They said to King Darius, "O King, you are a very great king. We want to make a new law, to honor you. The law is this: Nobody may pray to any god for thirty days. People may only ask the king for things that they want. And if anybody does pray to a god, he must be thrown into the den of lions."

King Darius listened to the men. He thought, "That will make me like a god." And he thought that would be fine. So Darius wrote his name under the law.

But Daniel always prayed to God each day. Three times a day he would kneel and pray.

The men watched Daniel. They looked through the window and saw him kneel again, after the law was made. Then they hurried to the king.

They said to the king, "O King, you have made a law. Nobody may pray to any god for thirty days. They may only ask you for things that they want. Any man who disobeys must be thrown into the den of lions. You made the law, didn't you, O King?"

King Darius said, "Yes, I made the law."

Then the men said, "This man Daniel prays three times a day. He prays to the God of Israel."

The king was sorry when he heard that. He liked Daniel. He did not want to throw Daniel into the den of lions.

But the king had put his name on the law. He could not change it.

So he sent for Daniel.

The king said to Daniel, "Your God, whom you serve, can save you."

And they threw Daniel into the den of lions. They put a big stone across the door of the den.

The lions were hungry. They walked around Daniel. They sniffed at him . .

King Darius could not sleep that night. He lay awake, thinking about Daniel. As soon as morning light came, he got up and went to the door of the lions' den.

King Darius called to Daniel, "Daniel! Daniel! Did your God save you?" He listened for an answer.

And Daniel's voice came out of the dark den, "Yes, O King! The lions did not hurt me. My God sent His angel to shut the lions' mouths."

Then they took Daniel out of the lions' den. And King Darius was happy.

But they took the wicked men who wanted to kill Daniel. They put them in the lions' den. And God did not send His angel to save them.

After that, King Darius made another law. The new law said, "The God of Daniel is the living God. Let everybody fear Him."

She was too happy to talk. God had given her the little boy again.

*Nebuchadnezzar bound the king of
Judah with chains.*

21

GOD CARES FOR HIS PEOPLE

I

The King Chooses a Queen

(Esther 2:1-20)

Of all the many, many people in the world, God long ago chose the people of Israel to be His special people. He promised to take special care of them. He promised that Jesus the Saviour would come to them.

God did not forget His people. Even when they were in the far-away strange land, He took care of them.

In the far-away land of Persia, the people of Israel were called Jews. There were many Jews in Persia — older folks, and little children too. There was a pretty Jewish girl named Esther. Esther did not have a father or a mother. She lived with Mordecai, her cousin. Mordecai was like a father to her. Mordecai loved Esther, and Esther loved Mordecai.

Now the king of this far-away country was Ahasuerus. His kingdom was a great kingdom. For miles and miles and miles around, the people had to do just as Ahasuerus said.

One day Ahasuerus said to his servants, "I must choose me a new queen. Now go through all of my kingdom and find all the pretty young women. Bring them all to me. I will choose the prettiest to be my queen."

The servants went to do as the king said. They found very many pretty young women. They found Esther too. Esther had to go with them to the city of the king.

In the city of the king Esther lived in a big house with the other women until the king was ready to see her. The servants brought the young women to the king one by one.

After a while it was Esther's turn. They dressed her in beautiful clothes, and took her to the king's palace.

And when the king saw Esther, he loved her. He chose Esther to be his queen.

So Esther, the Jewish girl, became queen of the great King Ahasuerus. The king gave her beautiful clothes and sparkling jewels. And Esther lived in a beautiful palace.

Mordecai wanted to be near Esther. Every day he came to the palace, and sat down by the palace gate.

King Ahasuerus did not know that Mordecai and Esther were Jews.

II

A Wicked Plan

(Esther 3)

In the great kingdom of Ahasuerus there were many princes. The greatest of all the princes was Haman. The king made Haman rich. And the king told the people that they must all bow down when Haman passed by.

But the Jews did not want to bow down to Haman. The Jews knew they must bow down to worship God, and not man.

When Haman rode down the streets of the city, all the people bowed down to him. But one day Haman rode by the palace gate. Mordecai was sitting there. And Mordecai did not jump up and bow down to Haman.

The other people said to Mordecai, "Why do you not bow down to Haman? Don't you know that the king says we must all bow down to him?"

Mordecai told them that he was a Jew. He said he would not bow down to Haman.

So every day, when Haman rode past the palace gate, Mordecai just sat still.

When Haman saw that Mordecai did not bow down, he was angry. Haman said to his servants, "Who is this man that will not bow down to me?"

The servants said, "That is Mordecai, the Jew."

Every day Haman was more and more angry when he saw Mordecai sit by the gate. At last he was so angry that he said, "I will kill all the Jews!"

Then Haman went to the king. He said to the king, "There are some people in your kingdom who will not obey you. It would be well to kill all these people. If you wish me to, I will write a letter to have them all killed."

The king said to Haman, "You may do just as you think best."

So Haman wrote a letter. He made many copies of the letter, and he sent them to every corner of the great kingdom. In the letter he said that on a certain day — the thirteenth day of the twelfth month — all the Jews would be killed.

When the letters were sent away, Haman was happy. He would soon be rid of Mordecai, he thought.

III

Mordecai in Sackcloth

(Esther 4)

One day Esther's maids came to tell her strange news. They said, "Mordecai is sitting by the palace gate, as he always does. But he is wearing sackcloth and ashes!"

In those days people wore clothes made of sacks when they were sad. And they put ashes on their heads.

Esther said, "What can be the matter with Mordecai?"

She quickly sent good clothes to Mordecai, and told him to take off the sackcloth and ashes.

But Mordecai would not take the good clothes.

Then Esther sent a servant to ask Mordecai what was the matter.

Mordecai told the servant about Haman's letter. He gave the servant a copy of the letter to show Esther.

Mordecai said, "Tell Esther to go to the king. She must ask the king to save our people."

Esther read the letter. And she shook her head. No, no, she could not go to the king. She sent the servant back to Mordecai.

She said, "Tell Mordecai that I do not dare go to the king. I may not go to the king except when he calls me. If he does not want to see me, he will be angry. Then he will kill me."

Then Mordecai said to the servant, "Tell Esther that she, too, is a Jew. When the awful day comes, she too will be killed, even though she is queen."

Mordecai said, "Tell her: who knows — maybe that is why you became queen, so that you could save your people."

Then Esther said, "I will try. Tell all the Jews of the city to fast with me. For three days they must not eat or drink. Then, after the three days, I will go to the king."

So for three days the Jews fasted. They did not eat or drink. They bowed down before God. They knew that God could help them.

Would God let Haman kill His people?

IV

Esther Goes to the King
(Esther 5, 7, 8)

King Ahasuerus was sitting on his throne. In one hand he held a rod of gold. That was his sceptre.

In those days every king had a sceptre. The king used his sceptre to welcome his visitors. He would hold the sceptre out to the visitors he liked. If he did not want the visitor, he would not hold out the sceptre. Then the servants would hurry the unwelcome visitor away. Sometimes unwelcome visitors were killed.

Esther came in slowly. What if the king did not want to see her? Then the king looked up. He saw Esther standing near the door. And when he saw her he held out the golden sceptre.

Esther came near and touched the golden sceptre.

King Ahasuerus said to her, "What do you wish, Queen Esther? Ask whatever you wish. I will give it to you, even if it is half of my kingdom."

Queen Esther said, "I should like the King and Haman to come to my house tomorrow, for a banquet."

The king said to his servants, "Tell Haman to get ready. We will go to Queen Esther's banquet tomorrow."

Haman was very happy. Just think — he and the king would go to visit the queen!

The next day the king and Haman came to the banquet.

While they were eating, the king said to Esther, "What do you wish, Queen Esther? Ask whatever you wish. I will give it to you even if it is half of my kingdom."

The queen said, "I should like King Ahasuerus and Haman to come to my house again tomorrow, for another banquet."

How proud Haman was! Another banquet with the king and queen!

While they were eating the next day, the king said to Esther, "What do you wish, Queen Esther? Ask whatever you wish. I will give it to you, even if it is half of my kingdom."

Then Esther said, "O King, give me my life and the lives of my people. We are all going to be killed . . ."

The king said, "Who is the man that wants to kill all your people? Where is he?"

Esther said, "There he is!" and she pointed at Haman.

Then the king was very angry with Haman. He called his servants and said to them, "Take Haman away, and hang him."

The servants took Haman away and hanged him.

After that, the king called Mordecai. He made Mordecai a prince instead of Haman.

And the king told Mordecai to write another letter and send it to all the Jews. Mordecai wrote the letter in the name of the king. In the letter, Mordecai told the Jews they must not be afraid. When the awful day should come, they must stand and fight. For King Ahasuerus did not want them to be killed.

So when the awful day came — the thirteenth day of the twelfth month — the Jews were not afraid. Nobody dared to kill them. But the Jews did kill their enemies.

So God used Queen Esther to save His people.

22

BACK TO JERUSALEM

I

Building Jerusalem Again

(Nehemiah 1, 2, 4, 8)

For many, many years the people of Israel were in strange lands, far away from home. They were sorry for their sins. They cried to God to help them.

Nehemiah was one of the men of Israel. He was a servant of the king of Persia. But he loved Jerusalem. He wanted to go back to his own country, and to his own city Jerusalem.

One day a messenger came from the land of Israel. The messenger told Nehemiah that Jerusalem was all broken down. There was no wall left around the city. The beautiful Temple was gone. There were a few people in the city, but they were very poor.

Nehemiah prayed, "O Lord, have mercy upon us. We have sinned against Thee. We are sorry for our sins. Now bring us back to Jerusalem."

Every day Nehemiah brought wine to the king. That morning the king said to Nehemiah, "You look very sad this morning. What makes you so sad?"

Nehemiah said, "I am sad because our city is burned to ashes."

The king said, "Is there something you wish to ask me?"

Nehemiah did not dare to ask the king to let him go back to Jerusalem. He was afraid the king would be angry.

But Nehemiah prayed to God in his heart. Then he said to the king, "If the king would send me to Jerusalem, to build it again . . ."

And the king was not angry. God heard Nehemiah's prayer. The king told Nehemiah he could go. He wrote letters for Nehemiah to take along, and he gave him horses and servants.

So Nehemiah went back to Jerusalem.

Many other people of Israel went back to Jerusalem. They wanted to live in their old homes again. But they found Jerusalem all ruins.

Nehemiah told the people that the king of Persia had sent him. He called all the people together, and they began to build the wall.

There was a man named Sanballat. He did not like the people of Israel. He did not want them to build the wall of Jerusalem. He said he would fight against them.

Nehemiah said to the people, "Do not be afraid. Trust in God."

They all worked very hard. They built the wall little by little. Sanballat tried to stop them, but God helped them.

At last the wall was finished, all around Jerusalem.

Then the people had a feast. They made little tents of tree branches. They lived in these little tents for a whole week.

They made a wooden pulpit and set it up in the street. They called for Ezra, the priest. Ezra stood on the pulpit and read the Word of God to the people.

The people had not heard the Word of God for a long, long time. They listened very carefully. Then they all said, "Amen, Amen." And they praised God.

When the week was gone by, they all went to their homes. They were happy. And they never again made idols of wood or stone or gold or silver.

II

God's Promises

(Isaiah 9:6, 7; 49:6; 53:2-5; Daniel 2; 7:14; Micah 5:2; Zechariah 9:9)

God sent many prophets to His people. The prophets taught the people how to serve God. The prophets told the people God's promises.

God made a promise to Abraham, long, long ago. He promised that all the nations of the earth would be blessed in Abraham. The blessings would come through our Saviour, Jesus Christ.

God made that promise again and again. Many prophets told about it.

Isaiah told about the Saviour. He said that a Baby would be born, and would be King forever. He said that God would send salvation to all people. He said that the Saviour would take away our sins and our sorrows.

Daniel told about the promise, too. He told the meaning of the stone in Nebuchadnezzar's dream. That stone broke all other kingdoms. It grew big. So the Kingdom of Jesus will grow big and will be an everlasting Kingdom.

Micah was another prophet. He said that the Saviour would come from Bethlehem.

Zechariah was still another prophet. He said that the great King would bring salvation.

The people of Israel waited many, many years. God would surely keep His promise. Some day He would send the Saviour, the great King.

THE NEW TESTAMENT

For God so loved the world, that he gave his only begotten Son, that whosoever believeth on him should not perish, but have eternal life. —JOHN 3:16

Beloved, if God so loved us, we also ought to love one another. —I JOHN 4:11

1

I

GOD KEEPS HIS PROMISE

God Sends an Angel

(Jeremiah 23:5, 6; Isaiah 9:6, 7; 25:9)

Once upon a time, long, long ago, God made a promise. He said He would send a great King to His people. This King would be a very, very great King. He would be greater than any other king ever was. He would be greater than any other king ever can be. He would do wonderful things. He would give new eyes to the blind. He would make the deaf hear again. He would make sick people well. He would save His people from their sins.

At that time God's people were the Jews. They lived in Palestine. They had a big city called Jerusalem. And in Jerusalem was a beautiful Temple.

The Temple was the House of God. It was the Jews' Church. They could go to the Temple every day to worship God.

The Jews were very happy with God's promise. They were happy to think they would have such a great King some day.

Many years went by. The great King did not come. The people waited and waited for God to send Him. It seemed a long, long time to wait.

But God keeps His promises. God plans all things. He makes things happen when it is time for them to happen.

And at last it was time for the great King to come.

Then God sent an angel — a bright shining angel from heaven. He sent the angel down to earth, to make things ready for the great King.

II

How the Angel Came to Jerusalem
(Luke 1:5-25)

Every morning many of the Jews in Jerusalem went to the Temple to worship God. Then the priest would pray for them and bless them.

It was morning again. This was the morning when God sent the angel to make things ready for the great King.

On this special morning, Zacharias was priest. Zacharias was a good man. He loved God. His wife, Elizabeth, loved God too.

Zacharias and Elizabeth did not have any children. They often asked God for a baby. Now they were old, and still God had not sent them a baby. But they loved God just the same.

When the people came to worship in the morning, Zacharias went into the little Holy Room of the Temple. He went alone. The people stood outside. They waited for Zacharias to come out and bless them.

In the Holy Room was a little golden altar. Zacharias burned incense on the little golden altar. The incense was sweet perfume for God. Zacharias watched the incense burn. He watched the little cloud of smoke go up, and he sent his prayers up to God with the little cloud of incense smoke.

And then, suddenly God's bright shining angel stood by the altar.

Zacharias saw the angel, and he was afraid. He put his hands over his face.

But the angel said to Zacharias, "Do not be afraid. God has heard your prayer. You and Elizabeth shall have a baby!"

Zacharias could hardly believe that wonderful message. He said, "I am an old man. Can you give me a sign that this will really happen?"

The angel said, "I am Gabriel. I stand before God in heaven. He sent me to tell you this good news. But I will give you a sign. You shall not be able to talk until the baby comes."

Then the angel went away. Zacharias was alone again in the little Holy Room.

Outside of the Holy Room, the people waited and waited. They said to each other, "Why does Zacharias stay away so long?"

But at last they saw him come out. They stood very still, waiting for him to bless them.

Zacharias lifted his hands over the heads of the people to bless them. But he did not say a word. He could not talk. Then he touched his lips and shook his head, and the people knew that he could not talk. They all went home, wondering what had happened.

Zacharias finished his work in the Temple. Then he went home to Elizabeth.

But he could not talk to tell her about the angel. So he took paper and pencil. He wrote on the paper all about the angel and about the baby God would send.

Then Elizabeth was very happy. She knew God would do wonderful things. She knew this would be a wonderful baby.

III

The Angel Visits Nazareth
(Luke 1:26-56)

After a little while, God sent the angel Gabriel to another city one day — to the little city of Nazareth, to the house of Mary.

Mary was a young lady. She was good and sweet. She loved God. Mary was a cousin to Elizabeth. And she was going to marry a good man named Joseph.

The angel came into Mary's house. He came into the room where Mary was.

When Mary saw the bright shining angel, she did not know what to say. She was a little bit afraid. She looked and looked at the bright shining angel.

The angel said to Mary, "Do not be afraid. God is pleased with you."

Then he told her wonderful news. He told her that she would have a Baby. Her Baby would be Jesus, the great King. He would be the Son of God.

Mary said, "Oh, how can that be?"

The angel said, "God will work the wonder in you."

The angel told her that Elizabeth, her cousin, was going to have a baby, too.

Then the angel went away, and Mary was alone. Mary was very happy. She sang praises to God. She thanked God for all His goodness to her. How wonderful, that God should choose her to be the mother of the great King!

Mary said to herself, "I must go tell my cousin Elizabeth all about it."

So Mary went to visit Elizabeth. And they were happy together. They sang praises to God together.

IV

Baby John Is Born

(Luke 1:57-80)

When it was time, God sent a little baby boy to Zacharias and Elizabeth — the baby boy He had promised them.

The neighbors all came to see Elizabeth and the baby.

They asked Elizabeth, "What are you going to call him? Will you call him Zacharias?"

Elizabeth said, "No; his name shall be John."

Then the neighbors asked Zacharias, "What are you going to call the baby? Will you call him John?"

But Zacharias could not talk. So they brought him paper and pencil. Zacharias wrote: His name shall be John.

That was the name the angel had told him.

And then God loosed Zacharias' tongue. He could talk again.

As soon as Zacharias could talk, he began to praise God. He talked about the little baby John. He said, "This baby will be a prophet of God. He will make the way ready for the Lord to come. The Lord will come. He will save His people!"

The neighbors listened. They did not understand. They said to each other, "This is strange! This is a wonderful baby! What will happen when he grows up? Surely something wonderful will happen!"

V

How the Great King Came
(Luke 2:1-20)

Weeks and weeks went by. And then, one day, the great King came — the King whom God had promised long, long ago. He came to the little city of Bethlehem. He came as a tiny Baby, Mary's Baby Jesus.

It was night. All the earth was dark and still. Up in the sky the stars twinkled. And the little city of Bethlehem was asleep.

Around the little city of Bethlehem there were sheep on the hills. The sheep were asleep on the green grass.

But the shepherds were not asleep. They were awake. They kept watch over the sheep all night. They sat together on the dark hillside, around a little fire. They talked together softly.

*See accompanying illustration
between pages 224 and 225*

Then suddenly the shepherds saw a bright light in the sky. It was bright like the light of the sun. The light came down to earth. It shone around the shepherds.

The shepherds were afraid of this light from the sky. They did not know what it was. They all stood up.

And then they saw an angel standing in the light. The light was glory-light from heaven. When the shepherds saw the angel, they were more and more afraid.

But the angel said to the shepherds, "Do not be afraid! I have very happy news for you, and for everybody. The Saviour, Christ the Lord, was born today, in Bethlehem!"

Oh, that was wonderful news! The great King had come at last!

Then the angel said, "You may go see Him. He is a Baby. You will find Him in a manger, wrapped in swaddling clothes."

Then there was another bright light, all over the whole sky. The whole sky was filled with shining angels.

These angels began to sing. They sang, "Glory to God! Glory to God in the highest! Peace on earth! Good will to men!"

How sweetly they sang! Their music floated down from the sky. And the glory-light from heaven shone on the shepherds.

The shepherds stood very still. They listened and listened.

At last the angels stopped singing. They went away, back into heaven.

Then the sky was dark again. Only the stars twinkled. And the hills were dark, too, where the sheep lay sleeping.

The shepherds said to each other, "Let us go to Bethlehem. We must see the wonderful Baby!"

They hurried down the hill to Bethlehem. There they found Mary and Joseph, in a stable. There was no room anywhere else.

Mary and Joseph had to sleep in the stable, where sheep and donkeys slept.

And the shepherds saw the Baby lying in a manger — the box that the donkeys ate out of. There was no bed for the Baby. He slept in the manger, just as the angel said.

But the shepherds knew that this Baby was the Saviour. He was Christ, the Lord, the great King. And they kneeled down by the manger to worship Him.

Then they told Mary and Joseph about the angels, and about the wonderful music, and about the glory-light from heaven.

Mary listened. How wonderful it all was! Her Baby Jesus was the Son of God! And the angels sang for Him!

After a while the shepherds went back to their sheep. All along the way they praised God. They told people about the angels, and about the Baby. The great King that God had promised long, long ago had come at last!

2

THE WONDERFUL BOY JESUS

I

Two Old People See the Baby

(Luke 2:21-40)

In Jerusalem there were two old people who waited and waited for the great King to come. One was an old man, named Simeon. The other was an old lady, named Anna.

Simeon was a fine old man. He loved God. He knew all about God's promise to send the great King, the Saviour. And oh, how he wished he would live long enough to see the Saviour!

One day God spoke to Simeon's heart. God told Simeon that he would surely see the Saviour. So Simeon waited. He grew very, very old. But he knew he would not die till the Saviour came.

Simeon did not know about the angels that sang for the shepherds in Bethlehem. He did not know about the Baby in the manger.

But one day God spoke to Simeon again. God told Simeon to go to the Temple.

Simeon went. Perhaps at last the King was coming. And what would the King look like? Simeon sat down in the Temple and waited.

After a while a man and lady came into the Temple with a Baby. It was Mary and Joseph, with the Baby Jesus. They had come to the Temple to bring a gift to God.

Simeon saw them. And God told Simeon that this Baby was the great King, the Saviour!

Simeon stood up and hurried to Mary and Joseph. He took the little Baby in his arms. He held the Baby close and looked at Him. This Baby was the King he had waited for! The One who would bring salvation! Simeon was very happy.

Simeon looked up to heaven and said, "O Lord, now I am ready to die. Now I have seen the Saviour!"

Simeon blessed Mary and Joseph. He told them that wonderful things would happen when this Baby grew up.

Just then Anna came into the Temple. Anna came to the Temple every day, to pray. She served God all the time.

Anna saw Simeon holding a Baby in his arms. She saw Mary and Joseph standing with Simeon. And then God told Anna that this Baby was the Saviour.

Anna hurried to see the Baby. And when she saw the Baby, she praised God. She told other people around her that this Baby was the Saviour.

Mary and Joseph brought their gift to God. Then they went back to Bethlehem.

Simeon and Anna went home, praising God all the way. At last they had seen the Saviour, the Saviour they had waited and waited for.

II

Wise Men Follow His Star

(Matthew 2:1-11)

Far, far away, many, many miles from Bethlehem, lived some very wise men. These wise men studied the stars. Every night they looked at the sky. They tried to learn all about the stars.

One night, when they looked at the sky, they saw a new star. It was a beautiful star. They had never seen it before.

And the next night, when they looked at the sky, they saw the beautiful new star again.

The wise men said, "Surely, this new star means that there is a new King! It is a beautiful star. It must be the star of a very great King!"

Every night they saw the star.

At last they said to each other, "We must follow the star. We must find the great King. And we want to bring beautiful presents to Him."

The wise men took gold and frankincense and myrrh. These were presents fit for a king. Then one night they rode away on their camels. They followed the star.

The star went on and on. Each night the wise men saw it. They followed it farther and farther. After a long time, the star led the wise men to the land of the Jews.

The wise men said, "We will go to Jerusalem. Jerusalem is a big city. The great King will surely be in Jerusalem."

There was a king in Jerusalem. His name was Herod. He was a wicked king. But the wise men did not know that Herod was a wicked king. So they went to King Herod.

The wise men said to King Herod, "Where is the new King of the Jews? We saw His star. We came from the far East, to see the new King and worship Him."

Herod shook his head. He said he did not know about any new King at all!

The wise men said, "But we have seen His star. We followed His star."

Herod thought and thought. Then he remembered that God had made a promise long, long ago, to send a great King.

Herod called the teachers of the Jews. He said to them, "When the Christ comes, the Christ that God promised to send, where will He be born?"

The teachers of the Jews said, "He will be born in Bethlehem."

So Herod told the wise men to go to Bethlehem.

Herod said to the wise men, "When you find the King, come and tell me. I want to worship Him, too."

Then the wise men hurried away. Bethlehem was not very far.

After a while, night came. The stars began to twinkle in the sky. And there it was again — the beautiful big new star! The wise men said, "See! There it is!" And they were very happy.

The star moved on. The wise men followed it. And when they came to Bethlehem, the star stood still. Its light shone on a house in Bethlehem.

The wise men hurried to that house. And there they found Mary and Joseph and the Baby Jesus. He was the new King! They had found Him at last!

The wise men fell down on their knees by the Baby Jesus. They worshipped Him. Then they gave Him presents — the gold and frankincense and myrrh.

And they thanked God for the wonderful star that had led them to the great King.

III

Wicked King Herod Is Afraid of Him
(Matthew 2:12-23)

At night, when the wise men were asleep, God came to them. God said to them, "Do not go to King Herod, to tell him about the Baby."

God knew that Herod was a wicked king, and that he would try to harm the Baby Jesus.

So the wise men went back another way.

Then King Herod was angry. He was afraid that this Baby would grow up to be King in his place. So he said he would kill Jesus. He thought that if he killed all the baby boys of Bethlehem, he would surely kill Jesus, too.

But God spoke to Joseph in a dream. God told Joseph to take Mary and the Baby, and hurry away to Egypt.

Joseph awoke from the dream in the night. He woke Mary up and told her about the dream.

They hurried to get ready. They took the Baby out of His sleep. And in the dark night they went away. Mary rode on a donkey, with the Baby in her arms. Joseph walked. They went to far-away Egypt.

Soon after that, King Herod sent his soldiers to Bethlehem. The soldiers killed all the baby boys in Bethlehem.

That was a very, very sad day in Bethlehem.

But Jesus was safe. He was far away, in Egypt.

After a while wicked King Herod died. Then God spoke to Joseph again in a dream. He told Joseph that Herod was dead. He told Joseph to take Mary and the Baby back home.

So they went home again. They went to the little town of Nazareth.

Jesus grew up in Nazareth. He grew up as other boys grow up. He learned to read and to write. He played with other boys. He helped Joseph and Mary. He was a good boy.

Yet He was different from other boys. Jesus had a pure and sinless heart. He was always good and kind. He was never selfish or naughty or rude. The boys and girls of Nazareth loved Him. And the older people loved Him, too.

IV

Jesus in His Father's House
(Luke 2:41-52)

Jerusalem was far away from Nazareth. But once every year Joseph and Mary went to Jerusalem, for the Passover Feast. Then they worshipped God in the Temple.

When Jesus was twelve years old, they took Him along to Jerusalem. That was a happy time! Jesus was glad to go along. He wanted to see the beautiful Temple, God's house. And it was so much fun getting ready to go!

Very many people went. They all went together. They took lunch along to eat by the roadside. They walked all day long, and slept under the stars at night.

When they came near Jerusalem, they could see the beautiful houses and the beautiful Temple. Jerusalem was a beautiful city.

They stayed in Jerusalem for seven days. There was so much to see! The Temple was the best of all. All the people went to the Temple. Jesus went there, too. Jesus loved the Temple, because it was God's house.

But soon it was time to go home again. So, one morning, they started off, along the road to Nazareth.

It was a big crowd, walking along the road to Nazareth. The older people talked together as they walked. The children ran ahead and played. But they talked, too. They talked about the wonderful city, and the Temple, and the Feast.

At lunch time, they all sat down by the roadside to eat. Mary and Joseph did not see Jesus. They said, "He is eating with some friends."

All day long they walked on and on. Then evening came. The people made a cozy place to sleep, under the stars.

Then Mary and Joseph looked for Jesus. But they could not find Him! They called Him. They asked about Him. Nobody had seen Jesus all day long.

Mary and Joseph said, "He is surely lost. He is lost in Jerusalem. We must hurry back to Jerusalem and find Him."

They hurried back to Jerusalem. They did not know where to look. They walked up and down the streets of the big city. They could not find Jesus.

At last they went to the Temple. And there Jesus was! He was in God's house — in His Father's house!

There was a circle of men around Jesus. They were talking with Him. They asked Him questions. Jesus answered the questions. Sometimes He asked questions. Jesus and the men were talking about the wonderful things of God.

Joseph and Mary were surprised to find Jesus talking with these men.

But they said to Jesus, "Son, we have hunted and hunted for You. We have come all the way back to look for You. We thought You were lost."

Then Jesus said, "Why did you look for Me? Don't you know that I must do My Father's work?"

But Jesus went with Mary and Joseph, to Nazareth. And even though He was the Son of God, He obeyed Mary and Joseph.

3

JESUS BEGINS HIS WORK

I

By the River Jordan

(Matthew 3:13-17; Mark 1:9-11; John 1:19-34)

Do you remember the baby John, the baby that God gave to Zacharias and Elizabeth? John grew up to be a man. And then he went to the country. He wanted to live alone — alone with God. God had called him to be a prophet.

John lived very close to God. Sometimes God talked to John.

After a while God sent John to the river Jordan. God told John to preach.

John went to the river Jordan. People came to him there. And he preached to the people. John told the people they must be sorry for their sins. They must not sin anymore. And when they were sorry for their sins, John baptized them in the river Jordan.

John was a wonderful preacher. The people came every day to hear him.

The people said, "Who is this John? Is he a prophet of God?"

John said, "I am only a voice. I tell you to be sorry for your sins. I tell you to get ready. For a great Man is coming. This great Man will baptize you with the Holy Spirit."

John did not know who this great Man was.

But one day God said to John, "The Spirit of God will come down from heaven, like a dove. It will rest on the head of a man. That man is the Son of God."

Every day John preached by the river. And he baptized the people who were sorry for their sins.

And then, one day, Jesus came to John. Jesus was a young man now. Jesus did not have sins. But He wanted John to baptize Him.

So they went into the river together — John and Jesus. And John baptized Jesus.

When they came out of the water, John looked up to the sky. He saw the heavens open. And he saw the Holy Spirit, like a dove, come down. The Holy Spirit came upon Jesus' head.

At the same time a voice came from heaven. It was God's voice. God said, "This is my beloved Son. Hear Him!"

Then John knew that Jesus was the Son of God.

But the Holy Spirit took Jesus away, into a lonely country.

II

Jesus and Satan

(Matthew 4:1-11; Luke 4:1-13)

Jesus was in the lonely country for forty days, all alone. There was no food for Him. After a while He was hungry.

Then Satan came to Jesus. Satan wanted to make Jesus sin. He wanted Jesus to do whatever he told Him to do.

Satan had seen the Holy Spirit come down from heaven like a dove, and rest on Jesus' head. Satan had heard God's voice, too, when God said, "This is my beloved Son." And Satan knew that Jesus was hungry.

So Satan said to Jesus, "If you are really the Son of God, You can turn stones into bread."

But Jesus would not do what Satan told Him to do. Jesus said, "The Word of God tells us that man does not need only bread to eat. Man lives by the Word of God."

Then Satan took Jesus to Jerusalem. He took Jesus up on a tower of the Temple. Satan stood there with Jesus, high up above the street. Down below, they could see people walking.

Satan said to Jesus, "If You are really the Son of God, throw Yourself down. God will send His angels to catch You. You will not be hurt."

Jesus shook His head. "No," He said. "The Word of God tells us that we may not tempt God."

Satan tried again. He took Jesus to a very high mountain. He told Jesus to look all around. Jesus could see all the beautiful countries of the world, all the big cities, all the gold and silver and riches.

Satan said to Jesus, "I will give all this to You. Just fall down and worship me. Then it will all be Yours."

But Jesus said to Satan, "Go away! The Word of God says that we must worship only God. We may not worship anyone else."

Satan had to go away then. He could not make Jesus sin.

When Satan was gone, angels came from heaven. They brought Jesus all that He needed.

III

Two Men Visit Jesus

(John 1:35-42)

One day John the Baptist stood by the river Jordan with two men. They were talking together. After a while they saw Jesus walking down the path by the river.

John said to the two men, "See! There is the Lamb of God!"

Then the two men began to follow Jesus.

Jesus turned around. He saw the two men following Him.

Jesus said, "What are you looking for?"

The two men said, "Master, where do You live?"

Jesus said to them, "Come and see where I live."

So the two men went along with Jesus and they visited with Jesus all that day.

What a wonderful visit that was! Jesus talked with them. He told them about the Kingdom of God. He told them wonderful things. Then they were sure that Jesus must be the Christ, the great King.

When the sun set, they said goodbye to Jesus. They went home.

One of the two men was Andrew. He hurried home to tell his brother Simon about Jesus.

Then Simon wanted to see Jesus, too. So the next day Andrew and Simon went together.

Jesus saw Andrew and Simon come.

Jesus said to Simon, "You are Simon. But after this your name shall be Peter."

Simon was surprised. How could Jesus know his name?

Jesus talked to Simon and Andrew for a long time. Then Simon, too, knew that Jesus must be the Christ, the Son of God.

IV

Jesus Calls His Disciples

(Matthew 4:18-22; Mark 1:16-20; John 1:43-51)

One day when Jesus was walking down the road, He saw a man named Philip. Jesus said to Philip, "Follow Me!"

Philip looked at Jesus. Philip did not ask, "Why must I follow you?" He just put his work away. He followed Jesus.

Philip had a friend named Nathaniel. Philip told Nathaniel about Jesus. Then Nathaniel came to Jesus. He followed Jesus, too.

After a while, Jesus went to the Sea of Galilee. Simon and Andrew were in a little boat, out on the water. They were fishing.

Jesus stood on the shore. Jesus called to them, "Follow Me, and I will make you fishers of men!"

Then Simon and Andrew rowed the little boat to shore. They pulled the boat up on shore. And they went to follow Jesus.

There was another little boat near shore. Three men were in it — Zebedee, and his two sons, James and John.

Jesus called to James and John. They looked up and saw Him on the shore.

Jesus said to them, "Come and follow Me!"

James and John put their nets down. They said goodbye to Zebedee, their father. And they went to follow Jesus.

Jesus found more men. He called them. And they followed Him. These men were Jesus' disciples. After a while Jesus had twelve disciples.

The twelve disciples followed Jesus wherever He went. Jesus told them about God, and about all the wonders of the Kingdom of God.

4

JESUS SHOWS HIS GREATNESS

I

Jesus at a Wedding

(John 2:1-11)

One day Jesus went to a wedding. It was in the little city of Cana, near Nazareth. Jesus took His disciples along.

Jesus' mother, Mary, was at the wedding. And many other people were there. There was a happy wedding feast, with good things to eat and drink.

But there was not enough wine for all these people. After a while the wine was all gone. They had nothing to drink.

Mary told Jesus about it.

And then Mary said to the servants, "If Jesus tells you what to do, you must do it."

Six big water jugs were standing by the well. The Jews always had jugs of water for drinking and washing.

Jesus said to the servants, "Fill the jugs with water."

The servants took the jugs to the well. They filled them with fresh clean water.

Then Jesus said, "Now pour some in a cup, and bring it to the ruler of the feast."

The servants were surprised. Why should they bring water to the ruler of the feast? But they poured some in a cup. And then they saw that it was not water. It had turned into wine!

The servants hurried to bring the new wine to the ruler of the feast. He had to taste it first of all.

224

The angel said to the shepherds,
"Do not be afraid!"

*Nicodemus came at night, to talk
with Jesus alone.*

The ruler of the feast did not know where the new wine came from. He did not know that Jesus had turned water into wine. He drank it.

"This is very good wine," he said. "It is better than the other wine we had!"

This was the first wonder that Jesus did. We call such wonders miracles. After this Jesus did many more miracles.

II

Jesus Teaches a Teacher

(John 3)

It was night. Jesus was at home. He was tired. He had been very busy all day. He had helped many sick people. He had made them well and told them about God.

Jesus was alone when He heard a knock. A man was there to ask if he could talk with Jesus. So he had come at night when Jesus was alone.

This man was a teacher of the Jews. His name was Nicodemus.

Nicodemus said to Jesus, "We know that You surely came from God. You could not do miracles, if You did not come from God."

Jesus said, "If you want to see the Kingdom of God, then you must be born again."

Nicodemus said, "How can I be born again? Can an old man be born again?"

Jesus said, "You must be born of the Holy Spirit. You must become a child of God."

Nicodemus did not know how to become a child of God. He asked Jesus many questions.

Jesus said to him, "Do you know the story of the snake in the desert?"

Yes, Nicodemus knew the story: Long, long ago the people of Israel were in a desert. There they sinned against God. And God sent snakes. The snakes bit the people. Many people died. Then the people cried to God. And God told Moses to make a snake of shining brass, to put it on a pole, and to lift it up high. If the people looked at the shining snake on the pole, they did not die.

Jesus said, "The Son of man must be lifted up that way. And anyone who believes on Him will live forever. For God so loved the world that He gave his only begotten Son, that whosoever believeth on Him should not perish but have everlasting life."

Jesus and Nicodemus talked for a long, long time. Then Nicodemus went home.

Nicodemus thought and thought about the words of Jesus. And after a while he believed on Jesus. He believed that Jesus is the Son of God, the Saviour.

III

Jesus in the Temple

(John 2:13-17)

Every year there was a big feast in Jerusalem — the Passover feast. Every year many Jews came to Jerusalem for the feast. Then they worshipped God in the Temple. And they ate the Passover supper.

It was time for the Passover feast again. Jesus went to Jerusalem. All His disciples went along.

Jesus and His disciples went to the Temple to worship God.

When Jesus came to the Temple, He saw a crowd of people in the Temple yard. But He saw cows there, too, and sheep. And He saw doves in big cages. Men were sitting by big tables, with heaps of money. The men were selling sheep and cows and doves in the Temple yard.

The cows said, "Moo." The sheep said, "Baa, baa!" The doves cooed. The men talked loud. The Temple yard was very noisy.

Then Jesus was angry. The Temple was God's house. It was a place to worship God. It was not a place to buy and sell cows and sheep and doves!

Jesus found some rope. He tied little pieces of rope together, to make a whip.

Then Jesus went to the men who sold the cows and sheep and doves. Jesus said, "Take these things out of here! How dare you make my Father's house a market! Take them all out!"

Jesus swung the whip. He chased the cows and sheep out. He chased out the men with the cages of doves. He turned the tables upside down, so that the money rolled all over the floor.

The men picked up the money as fast as they could. They ran to catch the sheep and cows. They were angry. They were angry with Jesus.

But they were afraid of Jesus, too.

Jesus would not let them make God's house a market place.

IV

Jesus Heals a Nobleman's Son

(John 4:46-54)

One day Jesus went to the little city of Cana again. That is where He turned water into wine, at the wedding. The people were happy to see Jesus. They told the news to everybody: "Jesus is here!"

Twenty miles away was the big city of Capernaum. The news came to Capernaum, too. People said, "Jesus is in Cana!"

There was a nobleman in Capernaum. His son was very sick. He was sure the boy would die.

The nobleman heard that Jesus was in Cana. He said, "I will go to Cana and ask Jesus to come to my son. He can make my son well."

The nobleman had servants. He could send a servant to Cana. But he did not send a servant. He went himself. He went as fast as he could go, because he was afraid the boy would soon die.

The nobleman found Jesus. He said to Jesus, "Please, come to Capernaum. My son is very sick."

Jesus said to the nobleman, "Do you want a sign, so that you can believe on Me?"

The nobleman said, "No, I do not need a sign. Just come! Please come before my boy dies!" The nobleman believed that Jesus could make the boy well.

Then Jesus said, "You can go back home. Your son is alive. He is not dying."

The nobleman believed Jesus. He went back home with a happy heart. He was sure the boy would be well now.

On the way, he met his servants. They came to meet him. When they saw him, they called to him, "Your son is well!"

The nobleman said, "Oh, that is fine! When did he begin to get well?"

They said, "Yesterday, at one o'clock, the fever went away."

At one o'clock! That was just when Jesus had said that the boy would live.

The nobleman praised God, and hurried home to see his son.

V

Jesus Helps Four Fishermen
(Luke 5:1-11)

Peter and Andrew went fishing one day, in a little boat, on the Sea of Galilee.

James and John went fishing, too, in another little boat.

They threw out their nets to catch fish. Then they pulled the nets back in again. But there were no fish in the nets.

They threw their nets out again, and again. But they did not catch any fish. All night long they were on the lake, fishing. But they did not catch even one fish.

In the morning they gave up. They rowed the boats to shore. They pulled their boats up on the sand, and washed their nets.

After a while Jesus came to the lake. Many other people came, too. The people came to Jesus, to hear Him talk. More and more people came.

Then Jesus said to Peter, "Please push your boat into the water a little way."

Jesus sat down in Peter's boat. And Peter pushed the boat into the water a little way. Then all the people on the shore could see Jesus. And Jesus talked to them from the boat.

Jesus told them about God. There was so much to tell! And the people were glad to listen to Jesus.

At last Jesus finished talking. The people went away. Then Jesus said to Peter, "Let us go far out now, into deep water, and go fishing."

Peter said, "We were out fishing all night. We did not catch even one fish. But if You say so, we will try again."

So Peter and Andrew rowed the little boat out into deep water. There they let the net down. Then they pulled it up. And this time the net was full of fishes! The net was so full that Peter and Andrew could not pull it up. And the net began to tear.

James and John were on shore. Peter and Andrew called to James and John, "Come and help!"

James and John pushed their little boat off quickly, and rowed to the other boat. All together they pulled the net up. They took the fish out of the net and put them into the boats. And both boats were full of fish.

Then Peter was afraid. He fell down on his knees before Jesus. "Oh Lord," he said, "I am a sinful man!"

But Jesus said to Peter, "Do not be afraid. After this you will go fishing for men."

They rowed the two boats to shore. They pulled the boats up on shore, and left them there. Then they went away with Jesus. Other people could have the fish. Peter and Andrew and James and John wanted to be with Jesus.

5

JESUS HEALS MANY SICK

I

At Peter's House

(Matthew 8:14-17; Luke 4:38-44; Mark 1:29-39)

One day Jesus went to Peter's house. Andrew and James and John went along.

There was someone sick at Peter's house. It was an old lady, the mother of Peter's wife. She was very sick with fever. Her friends did not know what to do for her.

Peter told Jesus about her. Jesus went to her room to see her. He stood by her bed and took hold of her hand. Then He told the fever to go away.

At once the fever was gone! The old lady was well! How happy she was! She got up and went to the kitchen, to make dinner for them all. She was glad to do something for Jesus.

At night, when they were all in the house, someone knocked at Peter's door. Peter went to open the door. He saw a crowd of people. They all wanted to see Jesus. They had many sick people with them — men and women, boys and girls, and even little babies that were sick.

Jesus went outdoors to the people. He touched all the sick ones. He made them all well. Some had evil spirits. Jesus sent the evil spirits away.

At last it was late, and all the people went home. Jesus and His disciples went to bed.

But very early in the morning, before the sun came peeping over the edge of the world, Jesus awoke. He got up and quietly went away.

Peter and Andrew and James and John heard Him go. They got up too. They followed Jesus.

Jesus went out to the country, to a lonely place, to pray.

When daylight came, the people went to Peter's house again, to see Jesus. But Jesus was gone. Then they went out to the country to find Him.

When they found Jesus, they said, "Please do not go away. Please stay with us, in our city."

But Jesus said, "I must go tell other people about God, too."

II

A Leper

(Matthew 8:1-4; Mark 1:40-45; Luke 5:12-15)

A leper is a person who has leprosy. Leprosy is a very bad sickness. It eats the skin and the flesh. It makes big sores. The leper slowly dies little by little. He can walk around, but he cannot live like other people. He is very sick. Doctors cannot help him.

A leper must live alone. In the land of Israel, the priest would send the leper away, out in the country, to live alone. He could not come near other people. And other people were afraid to come near him. They were afraid they would get sick, too.

No one would touch a leper. No one would take care of him. So the lepers were very unhappy.

One day, as Jesus walked along the road, a leper came to meet Him.

There were many people with Jesus. They saw the leper come. They saw his bad sores. And they did not want him to come near.

So the people stood still. They called to the leper to go away. But Jesus did not tell the leper to go away.

The leper came nearer and nearer. He had heard about Jesus. He knew that Jesus could make sick people well. The leper thought, "Maybe Jesus can make me well, too."

The people began to back away when the leper came near. But Jesus waited for him.

The leper came to Jesus and fell down on his knees.

"Oh!" he said, "if You would only make me well! If You want to, You can!"

Then Jesus put out His hand and touched the leper. He touched the leper's awful sores.

Jesus said, "I do want to. Be clean."

And when Jesus said that, the leprosy was gone! The sores were all gone. The man was well, from head to foot.

Oh, he did not know how to thank Jesus. He was so happy.

The people stared at him. They saw that the sores were all gone. They could hardly believe their eyes.

Jesus said to the leper, "Go to the priest. Let him see that you are really well. But do not tell who made you well."

So the leper went away. He sang for joy. He *had* to tell! He was so happy, he had to tell everybody about the wonderful Jesus.

III

A Roman Soldier's Servant

(Matthew 8:5-13; Luke 7:1-10)

There were very many Roman soldiers in the land of the Jews. The Jews did not like the Roman soldiers. Most of the Roman soldiers were hard, cruel men.

But in Capernaum there was a good Roman soldier. He was a captain. He built a church for the Jews. He did other good things.

This captain had many servants. His servants all obeyed him.

But one day one of the servants became sick. He was very sick. The doctor could not help him. He was going to die. The captain was sorry. He loved his servants.

The Jews said to the captain, "Jesus is coming to Capernaum. He can make your servant well."

Then the captain said, "Please go to meet Jesus. Ask Him to come and make my servant well."

The Jews hurried away, to meet Jesus. They told Jesus about the captain.

They said, "The captain is a Roman soldier, but he is a good man. He built a church for us. He does many good things. Please come and make his servant well."

So Jesus went with the Jews. Many people went along.

But the captain came to meet Jesus.

The captain said to Jesus, "Lord, do not come to my house. I am not good enough. If You will just say the word, my servant will be well. I know You can make him well."

Jesus turned around to look at the people. He said, "See how this man believes on Me! He is a Roman soldier, but he believes on Me more than the Jews do!"

Then Jesus said to the captain, "Because you believe, your servant is well."

The captain thanked Jesus and hurried home. And he found that his servant was well. At the very minute when Jesus had said the word, he had become well.

IV

A Man Who Could Not Walk
(Mark 2:1-12; Luke 5:18-26)

In the city of Capernaum there was a very sick man. He lay on his bed all the time. He could not get up and walk.

This sick man wanted very, very much to see Jesus. But he could not go to Jesus.

One day four friends came to see the sick man. They said to him, "We will carry you to Jesus!"

Each took hold of a corner of the sick man's bed. They lifted him up, bed and all. And away they went. They carried him down the street, to the house where Jesus was.

There were people outdoors by the house where Jesus was. And there were people in the doorway. The men peeked, and they saw that the house was full of people.

"We cannot get in," they said. "What shall we do?"

They did not want to take the sick man back home.

They thought and thought. At last they said, "We can go up on the roof. We can let the sick man down through the roof!"

The house was little. It had a flat roof. And there were steps to go up to the roof.

Up they went, with the bed, and the sick man on it.

The four men set the bed down on the roof. Then they made a hole in the roof. They looked down through the hole and saw Jesus.

Very carefully they let the bed down through the hole, with the sick man on it. Down, down, down, right in front of Jesus.

The people were surprised. A bed coming down through the roof, with a sick man on it!

But Jesus was not surprised.

Jesus said to the sick man, "Your sins are forgiven."

The people were surprised again. They said, "Only God can forgive sins."

They did not know that Jesus is the Son of God

Jesus said to the sick man, "You may get up. Pick up your bed. You can walk now."

The sick man sat up. Then he stood up. And he was all better.

How happy he was! He said "thank you" to Jesus again and again.

Then he rolled up his bed and took it under his arm. He went away. His face was all smiles.

The people in the house praised God. They said, "We never saw such wonderful things before!"

V

A Man with a Withered Hand

(Mark 3:1-10; Luke 6:6-12)

It was the Sabbath day. The people put on their best clothes and went to the synagogue, to worship God and listen to His Word.

Many Pharisees went. Jesus went, too. Jesus sat down in front of all the people, to teach them.

In the crowd of people there was a man with a withered hand. His right hand was thin and twisted and dried, so that he could not use it.

The Pharisees saw this man, and saw his withered hand. They thought, "If Jesus sees this man, and sees his withered hand, He will want to heal him. And this is the Sabbath day."

For the Pharisees were very careful on the Sabbath day. They would not do any work at all. They thought it very sinful to do even a very little work on the Sabbath day.

So they watched Jesus.

Soon Jesus saw the man with the withered hand. And Jesus knew what the Pharisees were thinking.

Jesus said to the man with the withered hand, "Stand up, and come to the front."

The man stood up and came to the front, where the Pharisees and all the other people could see him.

Jesus looked around at all the people and at the Pharisees. Jesus was sad. The Pharisees were so hard. They did not feel sorry for the man with the withered hand. They just wanted to see if Jesus would dare heal him on the Sabbath.

Jesus said to the Pharisees, "Now tell me—is it right to do good on the Sabbath day? If you have a sheep, and it falls into a pit on the Sabbath day, would you not take it out?"

But they did not answer.

Then Jesus said to the man with the withered hand, "Stretch out your arm."

The man did stretch out his arm. And see—the hand was well, strong and straight as his other hand.

Then the Pharisees grumbled.

But the man was very happy.

And Jesus went away. He healed very many people, as many as would come to Him.

VI

The Widow's Son

(Luke 7:11-17)

Nain was a little city near Nazareth.

There was a poor widow lady in Nain. She lived with her son. He was a young man. He was all the family that the poor widow lady had. And one day this son died.

Then the poor widow lady was alone. She was very sad. All the people of Nain were sad, too. They felt sorry for the poor widow lady.

The young man had to be buried outside the city. Some friends carried his body on an open coffin — the way they always did at funerals in those days. The widow lady walked by the coffin. All her friends walked with her. They went out the city gate, to go to the cemetery. It was a sad funeral.

But on that very same day Jesus was coming to Nain. He walked down the road with His disciples, to the city gate.

When Jesus and His disciples came near the city gate, they saw the funeral. The funeral came nearer and nearer. Then Jesus saw the poor widow. She was weeping. Her friends were weeping, too.

Jesus felt sorry for the widow. He said, "Do not weep."

Then Jesus touched the coffin. And the men who carried the coffin stood still.

Jesus looked at the young man lying there. Jesus said to him, "Young man, I say to thee, arise!"

The young man heard Jesus. He sat up. He was alive. He began to talk!

Jesus gave the young man to his mother. He could get up and walk home with her!

How happy the poor widow was! And all the people were happy with her.

They said, "This Jesus is a great prophet from God! For only God can make dead people alive!"

6

JESUS THE TEACHER

I

A Foolish Rich Man

(Luke 12:16-20)

Sometimes Jesus told stories to the people. One day He told them this story:

Once upon a time there was a rich man. He had a very, very big farm. He had very big barns on his farm. Every year he cut the wheat and hay and corn on his farm, and put it all into his barns.

One summer he had very much wheat and hay and corn. He put it into his barns till they were full. And then he had a great deal left. He had never been so rich before.

The rich man said to himself, "What shall I do with all the wheat and hay and corn? I shall build more barns, and bigger barns. Then I can put all my wheat and hay and corn into my barns, and keep it."

The rich man thought how fine it would be to have so much. He said to himself, "When my barns are all full, I shall be happy. I will not have to work. I can eat and drink and be happy all day long. I will be happy for many, many years."

But in the night God came to the rich man. God said to the rich man, "How foolish you are! Tonight I shall take your soul away. You shall die. Then who will have your wheat and hay and corn?"

So the foolish man died. God took his soul away in the night.

And then he was not rich at all. For he did not have a home in heaven.

He was a very foolish rich man.

A really rich man is one who is rich in God. He has a home in heaven.

II

The Lilies and the Birds

(Luke 12:22-32)

Jesus walked along the dusty road again. His friends walked with Him. Many people walked with Him.

Up on the hillside, the grass was green. And in the green grass the pretty white lilies were growing.

Jesus stood still to look at the birds and the lilies.

Jesus said, "Look at the birds. They do not put food away in barns. They do not worry. God takes care of them. God feeds them."

Then Jesus pointed to the white lilies growing in the green grass.

Jesus said, "Look at the lilies. See how pretty they are. The lily petals are more beautiful than any silk or satin. Even Solomon, the rich King Solomon, did not have clothes as pretty as the petals of a lily. But the lilies do not work hard to make their pretty petals. They just grow. God gives them their pretty petals."

The people looked at the birds, flying and singing in the blue sky. They looked at the white lilies growing in the green grass.

Jesus said, "Your Father in heaven takes care of them. He will take care of you, too. He knows what you need. You must love Him and live for Him. And He will take care of you."

The little birds in the sky, and the lilies in the grass — they tell us that God cares for us.

*See accompanying illustration
between pages 256 and 257*

III

A Story About Seeds
(Matthew 13:1-23; Mark 4:1-20; Luke 8:4-15)

It was a beautiful day. Jesus sat by the Sea of Galilee. The little blue waves sparkled in the sunshine. Little birds sang in the trees.

Many people came to Jesus, by the Sea of Galilee. They sat in the sunshine and listened to Him.

Jesus went into a little boat. He pushed the boat out on the water a little way, and sat in it. The people sat on the shore. And then Jesus told them a story about seeds.

Jesus said: "Once upon a time a man went out to his farm, to sow seed. He had a bagful of seed over his shoulder. He walked up and down, up and down, on his farm. He threw a handful of seed this way; he threw a handful of seed that way. He threw seed all over.

"Some of the seed fell on the hard path. It could not grow there. The birds saw it on the path. They flew down and ate it up.

"Some of the seed fell on the stony ground. It began to grow. Little roots went down into the ground. Little green leaves came up. But the roots could not get through the stones. They could not reach the water under the stones. After a while the sun shone hot. Then the little plants dried up. They died.

"Some seed fell by the weeds and thorns. The seed began to grow. Little roots went down into the ground. Little green leaves came up. But the weeds and thorns grew, too. The weeds and thorns grew very fast. They choked out the good little plants. The good little plants all died.

"Some seed fell on good ground. It began to grow. The little roots went down deeper and deeper. The little green leaves came up. The plants grew bigger and bigger. Soon flowers came. Then the fruit came. And last of all the new seeds grew on the plants.

Each plant grew many new seeds. Some grew a hundred seeds, some sixty, and some thirty."

The people listened to Jesus' story. But when it was finished they did not understand it.

Then the disciples said to Jesus, "Please tell us what the story means."

Jesus said, "The seed is the Word of God. The ground is the hearts of people who hear the Word of God.

"Some people have hard hearts — like the hard path. The Word of God does not grow in their hearts. Satan comes and takes it away.

"Some people have hearts like the stony ground. They are glad to hear the Word of God. But the Word of God does not grow deep into their hearts. When it is hard to live for Jesus, the Word of God dies in their hearts.

"Some people have hearts like the ground where weeds and thorns grow. These people have so many other things to do. They are so very busy. They have no time for God. All the other things choke out the Word of God.

"But some people keep the Word of God in their hearts. The Word of God grows there. Its roots go deeper and deeper. These people love God and serve Him. The Word of God in their hearts is like a plant that grows big and has many, many seeds."

IV

Good Seed and Bad Seed

(Matthew 13:24-30, 36-43)

While Jesus sat in the little boat, and all the people sat on the shore, Jesus told another story.

Jesus said: "Another man went out on his farm, to sow seed. This man had a good farm. And he put good seed into the ground.

"When the man had put the seed into the ground, he went home.

"After a while the seed began to grow. Little roots went down into the ground. Little green leaves came peeking out of the ground.

"The servants of the man went to see the little plants. They saw how nicely the little plants were growing. But they found many little weeds growing, too.

"The servants went to the farmer. They said, 'Did you put good seed into the ground? There are weeds growing with the good little plants.'

"The farmer said, 'I did put good seed into the ground. But when I was gone a bad man came. He sowed weeds.'

"Then the servants said, 'Shall we go and pull up the weeds?'

"But the farmer said, 'No. Do not pull up the weeds. You might pull up some of the good plants, too. Just let them all grow together. When harvest time comes, we will pull them all up. Then we will put the good plants in our barns. And we will burn up the weeds.' "

The disciples listened to the story. But they did not know what the story could mean.

After a while Jesus went home. Then the disciples asked Him, "What did the story mean, the story of the good seeds and the bad seeds?"

Jesus said, "The farm is the world. The good little plants are God's children. But Satan put the bad seeds in the world. The weeds are Satan's children. God's children and Satan's children all live together in the world. Someday the harvest time will come. Then God will send His angels. The angels will take God's children to heaven. But they will put Satan's children in the fire."

7

JESUS IS MASTER OF ALL

I

Wind and Water Obey Jesus
(Matthew 8:23-27; Mark 4:35-41; Luke 8:22-25)

One day Jesus talked to the people by the Sea of Galilee. He told them many stories about the Kingdom of God.

Then the people went home. And Jesus was tired.

Jesus said to His disciples. "Let us row across to the other side of the lake."

So the disciples got into the little boat with Jesus. They took the oars and began to row. Jesus lay down. He went to sleep.

After a while, when they were in the middle of the lake, the wind began to blow. It blew harder and harder. Big waves began to splash into the boat. The boat rolled up and down on the big waves.

It was a bad storm. The disciples were afraid. The little boat was almost full of water. And they could not row it any more.

But Jesus was asleep.

The disciples said to each other, "Soon the boat will be full of water. We will all drown!"

At last they woke Jesus up.

They said to Jesus, "Lord, save us! We will all drown! Look at the storm!"

Jesus opened His eyes. He saw the big waves. He heard the wind roar.

Jesus said to the disciples, "Why are you afraid?"

Jesus was not afraid. He stood up in the boat. The wind blew hard and the waves rolled the boat. But Jesus stood up.

Jesus looked at the stormy waves.

Then He told the wind to stop blowing. And He told the waves to lie still.

At once the wind did stop blowing. And at once the waves did lie still. Then the lake was very, very quiet.

The disciples looked at each other. They whispered to each other, "What a wonderful Man this Jesus is! The wind obeys Him! And the water obeys Him!"

Why did the wind and the water obey Jesus? Because Jesus is the Son of God. Jesus made the wind and the water.

The disciples took the oars. They began to row again. They rowed to the other shore. And all the way they thought, "What a wonderful Man this Jesus is!"

II

Evil Spirits Obey Jesus
(Matthew 8:28-34; Mark 5:1-20; Luke 8:26-39)

Jesus and His disciples were on the Sea of Galilee. The disciples rowed the little boat. They looked at the pretty green hills along the shore.

After a while they came to shore. They pulled the boat up on the sand.

And then they saw a man come running down the hill. This man was a wild man. He tore his clothes. He screamed. Sometimes he cut himself.

Satan had put evil spirits into this man. The evil spirits made him wild. All the people of the country were afraid of him.

The wild man ran to Jesus. He fell on his knees. He said, "Jesus, Son of God, do not hurt me!"

Jesus knew that there were evil spirits in the man. Jesus knew that the evil spirits made the man wild. So He told the evil spirits to go out of him.

The evil spirits said, "Oh, do not send us away!"

Up on the green hills there were some pigs. The evil spirits said to Jesus, "Please let us go into the pigs."

Jesus said to them, "Go!"

Then the evil spirits went out of the man. They went into the pigs. The pigs became wild. They ran down the hill. They ran into the lake and they all drowned.

But the wild man was not wild any more. He sat down by Jesus. He was happy. He was very glad that the evil spirits were gone.

Other people came to see Jesus, too. And they saw the man sitting by Jesus.

They said, "Look! This is the wild man! Now he is not wild any more!"

And they knew that Jesus had made him well.

Then they heard about the pigs. They heard how the evil spirits went into the pigs, and the pigs all drowned.

They said, "What kind of man is this Jesus? Even the evil spirits obey Him!" And they were afraid of Jesus.

They all begged Jesus to go away.

So Jesus and His disciples got into the little boat again.

Then the man who had been a wild man wanted to go along. He said, "Please let me go with You."

But Jesus said to him, "No, you must not go along. You must go home. Tell all the people about Me. Tell them what God did for you."

So the wild man said goodbye to Jesus. He went home. He told the people about Jesus, the Son of God. He said, "Even the evil spirits obey Him!"

III

Jesus Stops a Bleeding

(Matthew 9:18-22; Mark 5:22-34; Luke 8:40-48)

It was morning. In the city of Capernaum the people woke up. They ate breakfast, and went to their work.

Somebody went down to the shore of the pretty blue lake — the Sea of Galilee. And he saw a little boat out on the lake.

He thought, "Maybe that is Jesus' boat!"

And it was Jesus' boat! Jesus was coming to Capernaum again.

Soon everybody heard the news: Jesus is coming!

People came running to the lake. They were very glad to have Jesus come again. They sat down to wait for Him — a big crowd of people.

In the big crowd there was a sick woman. She had been sick a long, long time. She was bleeding, and the doctors could not stop the bleeding.

The sick woman said to herself, "Jesus can stop the bleeding. I know He can. If only I can get near Him and ask Him."

But there was such a big crowd! When the little boat came to shore, all the people tried to get near to Jesus.

The sick woman was weak and tired. She could not hurry. She could not push through the crowd. And she was afraid of all those people.

She could not get near Jesus, to ask Him to make her well.

And Jesus did not look at her at all.

Then a rich man came. That was Jairus. Jairus wanted to see Jesus, and the crowd let him go through. When he came to Jesus, he fell on his knees.

Jairus said, "Please come to my house. I have a little girl. She is twelve years old, and she is very, very sick. Please come and make her well."

Jesus said, "I will come."

So Jesus followed Jairus. And all the people followed Jesus.

The little sick woman thought, "I must stay near Him." So she followed Jesus, too.

After a while she said to herself, "If I could only touch Him, I would be better. If I could just touch His coat, I would be better!"

Then she began to squeeze through the crowd. She came nearer and nearer to Jesus. At last she put out her hand between the people. And she touched Jesus' coat.

And at once she was better! The bleeding stopped. She felt strong and well! Oh, how good she felt! And how happy! And nobody knew about it!

But Jesus stopped. He turned around to look at the crowd. He said, "Who touched Me?"

And he looked right at the little woman.

All the people looked at her, too.

Then she was afraid. She fell down in front of Jesus. She told Him all about it.

Jesus spoke kind words to her. He said, "You believed. Because you believed, you are well."

Then she was very happy. She went back home, praising God.

IV

Jesus Raises a Little Girl to Life
(Matthew 9:23-26; Mark 5:35-43; Luke 8:49-56)

Jairus stood still. But oh, he did not want to stand still. He wanted to hurry home. His little girl was so very, very sick. If only Jesus would come! It was so hard to wait.

But Jesus was talking to the little woman — the little woman who had touched His coat to make the bleeding stop.

A man came running down the street. He went to Jairus. He said to Jairus, "Never mind. Don't bother Jesus. It's too late. Your little girl is dead."

Poor Jairus felt very sad then. Too late. There was no use waiting for Jesus any longer.

But Jesus heard what the man said.

Jesus turned to Jairus. He said to Jairus, "Do not be afraid. Just believe."

Then the little woman went home. And Jesus went with Jairus.

There were many people in Jairus' house. They were all weeping very loud. They said, "Oh, the little girl is dead! She is dead!"

Jesus told them not to weep. He said, "She is asleep."

Then Jesus took three of His disciples — Peter, James, and John. And He took the mother and father of the little girl. They went into the little girl's room. All the others had to stay out.

The little girl lay on her bed, still and cold. She was dead.

Jesus took hold of her little cold hand. He held it in His warm hand.

Then Jesus said, "Little girl, get up!"

The little girl opened her eyes. She sat up. She got out of bed. She talked. She was alive!

The mother took her little girl in her arms and held her close. Jairus looked and looked at her. How could she be alive? A moment ago she was dead!

All the people heard about it. And when they saw the little girl, they said, "What a wonderful Man this Jesus is!"

V

A Little Boy's Lunch Grows Big

(Matthew 14:13-21; Mark 6:30-44; Luke 9:10-17; John 6:1-13)

One day Jesus was tired.

Jesus said to His disciples, "Let us go away, to a quiet place. Then we can rest a while."

They went in the little boat, and they rowed away on the blue lake.

The people watched them go. The people did not want Jesus to go away. They wanted to be with Him.

So they said, "We will follow Jesus. We will walk on shore, and see where the boat goes."

They began to walk. They walked and walked, along the shore. Some carried sick folk. They watched the little boat. And when the little boat came to shore, all the people were right there.

Jesus came out of the boat. He sat down on the green hill. And all the people sat around Him. They laid the sick by His feet. And He made them all well.

Then He talked to the people. He told them how they must love God and serve Him.

All day long Jesus was busy, helping the people and talking to them.

Then the disciples said, "It will soon be supper time. You should send the people home. They have walked a long, long way. They are hungry."

Jesus said, "Why don't you give them supper?"

The disciples said, "Oh, how can we? It is such a big crowd. There are hundreds and hundreds of people."

There was a little boy standing near Jesus. The little boy had a lunch with him.

Andrew saw the little boy. Andrew said, "Look, here is a little boy who has a lunch with him. He has five little loaves of bread, and two little fishes. But that is nothing for so many people!"

Jesus said, "Tell all the people to sit down."

The disciples told all the people to sit down. Soon they were all sitting on the grass. The green hill was covered with people.

The little boy gave Jesus the five little loaves and the two little fishes.

Jesus folded His hands and looked up to heaven. He said "thank you," to God for the bread and the fishes.

The little loaves of bread were like big biscuits. Jesus broke them. He gave the pieces to the disciples. The disciples passed the bread to the people.

Then they came to Jesus for more, and more, and more. They passed bread to all the people, till all the people had enough.

Jesus broke the fishes, too. He gave the pieces of fish to the disciples. The disciples passed the fish to the people.

They came to Jesus for more, and more, and more fish. They passed fish to all the people, till all the people had enough.

There were more than five thousand people. But the five little loaves of bread and the two little fishes were enough for all. The disciples picked up the pieces that were left — twelve small baskets full.

For Jesus had made the little boy's lunch grow big — big enough for hundreds and hundreds of people.

VI

Jesus Walks on the Waves

(Matthew 14:22-33; Mark 6:45-51; John 6:16-21)

It was evening. Far away in the west the sun was going down behind the hills. But on the green hills by the lake, the people still sat to listen to Jesus. They had been with Jesus almost all day.

Jesus said to His disciples, "It is almost night. You get into the ship and row away. Then I will send the people home."

The disciples went into the little ship. They rowed away, out on the blue water.

Then Jesus sent the people home. They walked away slowly, along the shore of the lake.

At last Jesus was alone. The sun went down in the west. And Jesus kneeled in the grass on the green hill by the lake. Jesus looked up to heaven. He prayed. He talked with God for a long time.

After a while Jesus stood up. He looked away across the lake. It was dark. But Jesus can see in the dark. He saw the disciples on the lake, in the little ship.

The lake was stormy. The wind was blowing hard, and the waves were very big. The little ship rocked on the big waves. The wind blew so hard, and the waves were so big, that the disciples could hardly row the ship.

Then Jesus went down the hill to the water. And Jesus walked right out on the water to go to the little ship.

Jesus did not sink in the water. He walked on the tops of the waves.

The disciples saw Jesus come, but they did not know it was Jesus. It was something white. It came nearer and nearer to them in the dark. And they were afraid.

At last Jesus called to them, "Do not be afraid! It is I!"

They knew Jesus' voice. But how could Jesus be there, on the water?

Peter said, "O Lord, is it really You? Then let me come to meet You, on the water."

Jesus said to Peter, "Come."

Peter quickly climbed over the side of the little ship. He stood on the water. He looked at Jesus, and he walked on the tops of the waves, just as Jesus did!

But a big wave came. Peter saw the big wave come, and he was afraid. Then he began to sink down into the water.

Peter cried, "O Lord, help me!"

Jesus quickly took hold of Peter's hand, and held him up.

Jesus said to Peter, "Why were you afraid?"

Why should Peter be afraid, when Jesus was with him?

Then Peter and Jesus walked together on the waves. They walked to the little ship.

When they were in the little ship, the wind stopped blowing. The big waves became small again. The disciples could row very easily.

Then the disciples fell down at Jesus' feet.

They said, "Thou art the Son of God!"

And they worshipped Him.

8

THE GLORY OF JESUS

I

Peter's Confession

(Matthew 16:13:28; Mark 8:27-33; Luke 9:18-22)

Jesus went from city to city to tell the people about God. The people were happy when Jesus came. They brought the sick to Him, and He made all the sick well.

The people said, "What a wonderful Man this Jesus is!"

But they did not know that Jesus is the Son of God.

One day Jesus took His twelve disciples to a quiet place. In that quiet place Jesus and the disciples prayed.

After that, they walked together down the road.

Jesus said to the disciples, "What do people say about Me? What do they call Me?"

The disciples said, "Some say You are John the Baptist. Some say You are Elias, the great prophet. Some say You are some other great prophet."

Then Jesus said, "And what do you think? Who am I?"

Peter had his answer all ready. Peter said, "You are the Christ; You are the Son of God."

Peter knew.

Jesus said to Peter, "It is God who told you that. But you must not tell anyone else."

Then Jesus told His disciples what would happen by and by. He told them that He must die. The Jews would kill Him. He told them that afterwards He would rise from the grave.

The disciples could not believe that Jesus would die. How could the Son of God die?

Peter said to Jesus, "That can never happen!"

But Jesus knew better than Peter. Jesus knew He must die, to be our Saviour.

Jesus said to Peter, "You do not know the things of God."

Peter had much more to learn.

II

Glory Shines from Heaven
(Matthew 17:1-8; Mark 9:2-10; Luke 9:28-36)

One day Jesus took Peter, James, and John, and went up a high hill. They went up, and up, and up, to the top of the high hill. And there, on the top of the high hill, they prayed.

While Jesus prayed, His face began to shine. It became bright like the sun. Peter, James, and John saw Jesus' face shine. Then His clothes began to shine, too. His clothes became white like sparkling snow.

It was the glory-light from heaven that made Jesus' face and clothes shine. Peter, James, and John could hardly look at the shining glory-light.

And then they saw two more men on the hill. These two men stood with Jesus. They talked with Jesus. The glory-light from heaven shone on them, too.

These two men were Moses and Elijah. Long, long ago, God took Moses and Elijah to heaven. Now they came down from heaven to talk with Jesus on the hill.

It was wonderful to be on the hill, in the glory-light from heaven.

Peter said, "O Lord, let us make three little tents — one for You, and one for Moses, and one for Elijah. Then we can stay here."

But just then a shining cloud came down on the hill. The cloud came down on their heads, and covered them all.

A voice came out of the cloud. It was the voice of God. The voice said, "This is my beloved Son. Hear Him!"

Peter, James, and John were afraid in the cloud. And they were afraid when they heard the voice of God. They fell down. They hid their faces in their hands.

After a while Jesus came and touched Peter, and James, and John.

"Come," said Jesus. "Do not be afraid."

Peter and James and John looked up and saw Jesus. He was alone. Moses and Elijah were gone. The cloud was gone. The glory-light from heaven was gone. They were alone with Jesus.

Peter, James, and John stood up. Then they went down the hill with Jesus.

Peter, James, and John thought and thought about the wonderful things they had seen on the hill. They had seen the glory-light shining from heaven. They had seen Moses and Elijah. And they had heard the voice of God!

Jesus taught the people lessons
from the lilies and the birds.

Jesus' face and clothes shone with
heavenly glory-light.

9

JESUS TEACHES MANY THINGS

I

We Must Believe
(Matthew 17:14-21; Mark 9:14-29; Luke 9:37-42)

Jesus came walking down the hill, with Peter, James, and John. The other disciples were waiting. There was a crowd of other people waiting, too. They all wanted to see Jesus.

A man came running out of the crowd. He ran to Jesus and fell on his knees at Jesus' feet.

"O Lord!" he said, "Look at my poor little boy! He is very sick! An evil spirit throws him down. Sometimes it throws him in the fire. And he cannot talk. He is very sick."

Jesus said, "Bring the boy to Me."

The father brought the boy to Jesus. And the evil spirit threw the boy on the ground at Jesus' feet.

Jesus looked at the boy, and He felt sorry for him.

Jesus said to the father, "How long has he been so sick?"

The father's eyes were full of tears. He said, "He has been sick since he was very little. Sometimes he falls into the water. Sometimes he falls into the fire. Please, help him if You can!"

Jesus looked at the father. Jesus said, "If you believe that I can . . ."

The man said, "Oh! I do believe! Help me to believe even more!"

Then Jesus told the evil spirit to go out of the boy.

Evil spirits come from Satan. They are afraid of Jesus. They must obey Jesus. So the evil spirit went out of the boy.

257

Then Jesus took hold of the boy's hand. The boy stood up. He was well. He could talk, and walk, and run, and play.

The boy and his father went home happy.

Jesus can do wonderful things. If we believe, He will do wonderful things for us, too.

II

Peter Asks a Question
(Matthew 18:21-35)

One day Peter said to Jesus, "When my brother does something wrong to me, I know I must forgive him. And if he does it again, I must forgive him again. But if he does it again, must I forgive him again? Must I forgive him seven times?"

Jesus shook His head. He said, "You must not forgive him just seven times. You must forgive him seventy times seven times."

Seventy times seven times is very many times! It is hard to forgive so many times.

That is what Peter thought.

Jesus said, "I will tell you a story:

"Once upon a time there was a servant who had to pay money to the king. He owed the king very much money, thousands of dollars. And he could not pay it.

"The king said to the servant, 'We will sell your house and we will sell you; we will sell your wife and your children. We will sell everything you have, to get the money.'

"The servant begged, 'Oh, please don't do that! Please don't sell me, and my wife, and my children! I will work hard. I will pay the money as soon as I can!'

"The king was sorry for the servant. He knew that the servant could never pay all that money, even if he worked very, very hard.

"So the king said, 'Well, we will let you go free. You need not pay the money at all! We will forgive you all of it!'

"Then the servant was glad.

"But there was a poor man who owed money to the servant. He owed just a little bit. The servant found this poor man. He said to the man, 'You must pay me the money you owe me.'

"The poor man said, 'I will pay you as soon as I can. I will pay it all.'

"But the servant said, 'I will not wait for you to pay it. You must pay it now, or I will put you in prison.'

"And the servant put the poor man in prison.

"The king heard about the poor man in prison. Then the king was angry. He called the servant.

"The king said to the servant. 'You owed me a lot of money. I forgave you all of it. This man owed you just a little money. And you put him in prison. I forgave you so much! Why did you not forgive this man that little bit?'

"And the king put the servant in prison. He told him he must pay all that he owed."

Jesus said, "That is like the Kingdom of Heaven. God forgives us all our sins — our very, very many sins. Then we ought to forgive the little wrong things that people do to us. If you do not forgive other people, God will not forgive you."

III

Something to Be Happy About
(Luke 9:1-6; 10:1-20)

Jesus' twelve disciples were Peter, Andrew, James, John, Philip, Bartholomew, Thomas, Matthew, another James, Thaddeus, Simon, and Judas. These twelve men followed Jesus wherever Jesus went.

One day Jesus called the twelve around Him. He said, "You must go and preach now. Go to all the cities near by. Tell the people about God. And make the sick people well."

Then Jesus gave them power, so that they could make sick people well. And He sent them away.

The disciples went away two by two. They began to preach. They told the people about God and about Jesus. The people were glad to hear them. The people brought the sick, and the disciples made all the sick well. It was wonderful to work for Jesus. The disciples were very happy.

One day Jesus chose seventy other men. He told them to go out and preach, too. He gave them all power to make sick people well. And they went away two by two.

After a while they came back to Jesus. They told Jesus all about their work — how they preached, and how they made the sick people well.

They said, "Even the evil spirits obey us, when we send them away in Your name." And they were very happy.

Jesus was happy, too.

Jesus said, "Yes, I gave you power over evil spirits. That is something to be happy about. But there is something else even better. Be happy because your names are in the book of heaven."

Everyone who loves Jesus has his name in that book.

IV

One Thankful Leper
(Luke 17:11-19)

One day ten lepers were sitting by the roadside, out in the country. They could not go into the city, because they were lepers. They had the sickness which doctors cannot heal. And they had to live alone. They could not live with other people in the city.

The lepers sat together. They were sad. They wished they were not sick.

After a while the lepers saw a crowd of people coming. There was one man in the middle of the crowd. This man was talking. All the others were listening to Him. They came walking slowly to the city.

The ten lepers watched the crowd come nearer and nearer.

One leper said, "Who is that man in the middle of the crowd?"

Another leper said, "Maybe it is Jesus!"

Then another leper said, "Yes, it surely is Jesus!"

The ten lepers had heard about Jesus. They knew that Jesus can make even a leper well.

They said to each other, "Let us ask Him to make us well!"

They did not dare to go near the crowd. But they began to call Jesus. They called as loud as they could, "Jesus, Master, have mercy on us!"

Jesus heard them. He stopped, and looked at them. Then He said, "Go to the priest. Let him look at you. Let him see if you have leprosy."

The ten lepers all turned around and hurried away to find the priest.

They hurried away together. And then they looked at each other. And they saw that the sores were all gone. They were well! They were not lepers any more!

One leper stood still. The nine others hurried on, to see the priest.

But the one leper said, "I must thank Jesus first!"

He turned back. He ran to Jesus, and fell on his knees.

"Oh! See what God has done!" he said. "See! I am well! See what God has done!"

All the people heard him praise God and thank Jesus.

Then Jesus said, "Where are the other lepers? There were ten. Did only one come back to thank Me, and to praise God?"

Yes. Only one came back. He was the most thankful of all. And surely he was the happiest of all, too.

V

How We Must Love Each Other
(Luke 10:25-37)

One day a lawyer came to Jesus. A lawyer knows all about law. He knows what we must do and what we must not do.

This lawyer said to Jesus, "What must I do to go to heaven?"

Jesus said, "What does God's law say?"

The lawyer said, "God's law tells us that we must love God best of all. And we must love our neighbors just as much as we love ourselves."

"Yes, that is right," said Jesus. "If you do that, you will go to heaven."

The lawyer knew he could not do that.

So he said to Jesus, "Who is my neighbor?"

Then Jesus told him a story. Jesus said:

"Once upon a time a man went to Jericho alone. The road to Jericho was a lonely road. Some bad men saw the man on the road. They caught him. They knocked him down and hit him. They took his money and his clothes. And they left him lying in the road. Then they ran away.

The poor man could not get up. He was hurt and bleeding.

"After a while a priest came along. He saw the poor man lying in the road. But he did not stop to help him. He rode around him.

"Then a Levite came along. He saw the poor man lying in the road. He went to look at the poor man. But he did not help him. He rode away.

"Next, a Samaritan came along. He saw the poor man lying in the road. And he was sorry for the poor man. He gave the poor man a drink. He tried to stop the bleeding. He put the poor man on his donkey and brought him to the nearest house. He did all he could for the poor man."

Then Jesus said to the lawyer, "Now who was a good neighbor to the poor man?"

The lawyer said, "The last one, he was a good neighbor."

Jesus said, "You must be a good neighbor just like that. You must help anybody that needs you."

That is God's law: we must love others just as much as we love ourselves.

10

JESUS IN THE HOME OF FRIENDS

I

Two Sisters Who Love Jesus
(Luke 10:38-42)

Mary and Martha lived in Bethany. They lived with Lazarus, their brother. Jesus often went to Bethany to visit Mary and Martha and Lazarus. Mary and Martha and Lazarus loved Jesus very much. He was their best Friend.

One day Jesus went to Bethany again, to visit Mary and Martha and Lazarus. They were very glad to have Jesus come.

Martha hurried to make dinner for Jesus. She worked hard. She was very busy in the kitchen.

Mary did not help Martha. Mary sat by Jesus. She wanted to hear all that Jesus said. Jesus always talked about God and about the wonderful Kingdom of God. Mary loved to listen to Jesus.

So Martha did the work alone.

Martha did not like to do the work alone.

At last Martha went to Jesus. Martha said, "I have so much to do! Mary does not help me at all. Tell Mary that she must help me."

Jesus looked at Martha. And He looked at Mary. And He shook His head.

Jesus said to Martha, "You are very busy. You have many little things to do. But Mary does better things. She sits by Me and listens to Me. That is better than being busy with little things."

And Jesus did not send Mary away to the kitchen.

II

Jesus' Friend Lazarus Dies
(John 11:1-46)

It was very quiet in the little house in Bethany, the house where Mary and Martha and Lazarus lived. Mary and Martha were sad because Lazarus was sick.

Mary and Martha loved their brother Lazarus very much. They took care of him. They did all they could for him. But he did not get well.

Martha said, "If only Jesus were here. He would make Lazarus well."

And Mary said, "Yes, if only Jesus were here. He would make Lazarus well."

But Jesus was far away.

Then they said, "We will send for Jesus. We will ask Him to come. Jesus loves Lazarus. He will come right away if we tell Him that Lazarus is sick."

So they sent somebody to tell Jesus.

But Jesus did not come right away.

And Lazarus died.

They buried Lazarus in a stone cave. Then Mary and Martha went home again. They were very sad.

Jesus knew that Lazarus was dead, even though He was far away.

Jesus said to His disciples, "Lazarus is dead. Now we will go to him."

When Jesus came near Bethany, Martha came to meet Him. She said to Jesus, "Oh, if only You had been here. Then Lazarus would not have died!"

Mary came, too. Mary was weeping. And Mary said to Jesus, "Oh, if only You had been here! Then Lazarus would not have died."

Then they all went to the cave, where they had buried Lazarus. Many people went along. They were all weeping. Jesus wept, too.

There was a big stone in front of the cave.

Jesus said, "Take the stone away."

Some men took the stone away. Then they could see Lazarus lying there, in the grave.

Jesus looked up to heaven, to pray.

Then, with a loud voice, Jesus said, "Lazarus, come out!"

And Lazarus heard the voice of Jesus. He stood up. He came out of the cave. He was alive!

Oh, how happy Mary and Martha were!

And all the other people were happy with Mary and Martha.

They all walked home together.

All the way home the people talked about Jesus. Some said, "Jesus is the Son of God." Some would not believe that. But Mary and Martha and Lazarus loved Jesus more than ever.

11

JESUS TELLS BEAUTIFUL STORIES

I

The Shepherd Finds His Sheep

(Luke 15:1-7)

Every day people came to Jesus. Pharisees came. Publicans and sinners came, too.

The Pharisees thought they were very, very good. They thought they were just as good as Jesus — or maybe even better. The Pharisees did not like the publicans and sinners. They would not stand near them. And they did not love Jesus.

But the publicans and sinners loved Jesus.

Sometimes Jesus went to dinner with publicans and sinners.

Then the Pharisees were angry. The Pharisees said, "Jesus cannot be a good man. He eats with publicans and sinners. A good man would not eat with publicans and sinners!"

Jesus heard them say that.

Jesus said, "I will tell you a story:

"There was a shepherd who had one hundred sheep. Every night he counted his sheep — one, two, three . . . — one hundred of them. Then one night, when he counted his sheep, there were only ninety-nine. One sheep was lost. It was lost out in the dark.

"The shepherd hurried over to find the lost sheep. He hunted for it, over the hills and in the woods. And at last he found the poor little sheep.

"The shepherd was happy when he found the sheep. He put it on his shoulder and carried it home.

"Then the shepherd called his neighbors. He had to tell his neighbors how happy he was, because he had found the little lost sheep. And the neighbors were all happy with the shepherd."

Jesus said: "Sinners are like lost sheep. I came to find sinners. And the angels in heaven are happy when one sinner comes back to God. He is like a lost sheep that is found again."

II

The Boy Who Went Away from Home
(Luke 15:11-24)

One day Jesus told a story about a boy who ran away.

Jesus said: "There was a boy who did not want to stay at home. He had a beautiful home. But he just did not want to be a good boy.

"So one day the boy asked his father for some money. And then he went away. He went to a far-away country.

"In that far-away country the boy had a good time. He did just what he wanted to do. He had fun all day long and every day. He spent the money to buy just what he wanted.

"But after a while the money was all gone. Then the boy did not know what to do. He was hungry, and he could not buy anything to eat. Soon his clothes were all rags. His shoes were all worn out. And nobody would help him. Nobody cared.

"The boy said to himself, 'Oh, why did I go away from my good home!'

"He did not dare to go back. He had been a bad boy. He was sure his father would not want such a bad boy to come back.

"Then, one day, he sat down to think. He said to himself, 'My father has enough to eat, and I am very hungry. I will go to my father. I will tell him that I am very sorry. I will tell him I am not good enough to be his son. Then I will ask him to let me work for him. I will be his servant.'

"So the boy went home.

"It was a long, long way to go. And the boy was afraid. Maybe his father would be angry, and would send him away.

"Far away, in the home country, the father thought of the boy every day. He loved his boy. He wanted his boy to come home. And every day he looked down the road, to see if the boy was coming.

"And at last, one day, the father looked down the road and saw him coming!

"Then the father ran to meet the boy. He threw his arms around the boy and kissed him. He was so happy that he cried.

"The boy cried, too. He said, 'Oh, father, I am not good enough to be your boy! Let me be your servant. I will work for you!'

"The father said, 'No, no! You are my boy! I am so glad that you came back home!'

"The father gave the boy beautiful clothes to put on. He gave him new shoes. He put a beautiful gold ring on his finger. And he made a big supper for him. He was very happy to have his boy home."

Then Jesus said, "Our Father in heaven is happy, too, when a sinner comes back to Him."

III

Two Men Go to Pray

(Luke 18:9-14)

Jesus lived very close to God. He prayed very, very often. Sometimes He went to the woods or to a high hill, to be alone with God. Sometimes He took the disciples along. Sometimes Jesus and His disciples prayed together.

Jesus told the people that they should pray, too. He told them they must pray every day. They must ask God for help, and He would surely help them.

And then, one day, Jesus told a story about two men who went to pray.

He said: "Two men went to the Temple to pray.

"One was a Pharisee. He thought he was a very good man. He thought he was not a sinner at all. He stood where everybody could see him. He looked up to heaven and began to pray.

"The Pharisee said, 'God, I thank Thee that I am not a sinner, like other men. I am very good. I do not lie. I do not steal. I give God a tenth part of everything I have . . .'

"The other man was a publican. He knew that he was a sinner. He knew that he was not always good. And he was sorry for his sin. He hid in a corner. He did not dare look up to heaven.

"The publican said, 'O God, I am a sinner. Have mercy on me!'

"Then the two men went away.

"The Pharisee was not really happy. God did not forgive his sins. The Pharisee did not ask God to forgive his sins. He did not even know he was a sinner!

"But the publican went away happy. God forgave the sins of the publican, because the publican was sorry for his sins."

12

JESUS MEETS ALL KINDS OF PEOPLE

I

Jesus and the Little Children
(Matthew 19:13-15; Mark 10:13-16; Luke 18:15-17)

It was wonderful to be near Jesus, to see His face, to listen to Him. Every day the people came. Mothers and fathers came. Sometimes the mothers took their little children along — little boys and girls, and little babies too.

One day the mothers thought, "How wonderful it would be, if Jesus would bless our little children."

So they tried to bring the children near to Jesus.

The disciples saw the mothers come. They pushed the mothers back. They said, "You must not bother Jesus. Jesus does not have time for little children."

But Jesus saw what the disciples did. Jesus said to the disciples, "No, no! Do not send the little children away!"

Jesus put out His arms. He said, "Let the little children come. Let them come to Me."

Then the children came. Jesus put his arms around the bigger ones. He took the little ones on His knee. He put His hand on their heads. He looked up to heaven to pray. And He blessed all the little children.

Jesus loved those little children. He loves little children today, too.

II

A Sad Rich Young Man

(Matthew 19:16-24; Mark 10:17-27; Luke 18:18-25)

One day Jesus was walking along the road. He was talking with His disciples. And a young man came a-running down the road.

The young man ran to Jesus. Then he kneeled down before Jesus.

He was a rich young man. He had beautiful clothes. He had very much money. But he was not happy.

The young man said to Jesus, "Good Master, what must I do to go to heaven, to live for ever and ever?"

Jesus said to him, "You know what God says in His law: Do not steal. Do not tell lies. Love your father and your mother . . ."

"Oh, yes," said the rich young man. "I know that. And I have always done that. But what else must I do?"

Jesus loved this young man. He felt sorry for him.

Jesus said, "There is one thing you must do. You must give all your money away. Give it to poor people. Then come to Me, and follow Me."

But the rich young man shook his head. He could not do that! He could not give all his money away. He loved his money. He loved his money more than he loved Jesus.

So the rich young man shook his head, and went away. He was not happy. He was a sad rich young man.

III

Blind Bartimaeus

(Mark 10:46-52; Luke 18:35-43)

In Jericho there was a man named Bartimaeus. Bartimaeus was blind. He could not see the sunshine and the birds. He could not see the flowers. He could not see at all.

Because Bartimaeus could not see, he had to beg. He sat by the side of the road. When people came by, he would hold out his hand. He would ask for something.

Some people gave him food to eat. Some people gave him money. But oh, how Bartimaeus wished that he could see!

Every day Bartimaeus sat by the side of the road.

One day Bartimaeus heard many people come down the road. He heard the noise of their feet on the hard ground. He heard them talk. He knew it was a big crowd of people.

Bartimaeus asked somebody, "Why is there a crowd of people on the road?"

Somebody answered, "They are walking with Jesus. They are all coming this way."

Bartimaeus had heard about Jesus. He had heard that Jesus could do wonderful things.

Bartimaeus thought, "Jesus can open my eyes! He can make me see!" Bartimaeus really believed that Jesus could do that.

So Bartimaeus began to call Jesus. He called loudly, "Jesus, Son of David, have mercy on me!"

The people near-by said, "Hush! Be still! Don't make so much noise."

But Bartimaeus called again, "Jesus, Son of David, have mercy on me!"

He called louder and louder. He could not see Jesus, but he called as loud as he could. Oh, if only Jesus would hear him! If only Jesus would open his eyes!

Jesus did hear. Jesus said, "Bring that man to Me."

Somebody ran to Bartimaeus and said, "Jesus is calling you!"

Then Bartimaeus jumped up. But he could not see where to go. Somebody took his hand. And he stumbled along to Jesus as fast as he could go.

Jesus said to Bartimaeus, "What would you like Me to do?"

Bartimaeus said, "Oh, I wish I could see!"

Jesus said, "Because you have believed, you may see!"

See accompanying illustration between pages 288 and 289

Then Bartimaeus opened his eyes, and he could see! He saw Jesus first of all. Then he saw the hills and the trees and the city. He saw the people, too. But best of all, he saw Jesus.

Oh, how happy he was!

He could not say "thank you" enough. He praised God. And all the people praised God, too.

IV

A Little Man in a Tree

(Luke 19:1-10)

Zacchaeus lived in Jericho. He was a rich man.

But Zacchaeus was not a good man. He was not honest. He cheated the people. That is how he became rich.

One day Zacchaeus heard that Jesus was coming to Jericho. Zacchaeus wanted to see Jesus — he just wanted to see Jesus go by. So he stood in the street to wait for Jesus.

The big crowd of people came down the street. Jesus was in the middle of the crowd. Zacchaeus was a little man. And when he tried to see Jesus, he could not see Him at all. He could not see over all the people.

Then Zacchaeus ran ahead, and climbed up in a tree. Now Zacchaeus could look right down and see Jesus when He came.

Zacchaeus waited. Soon the crowd came near, right under the tree. And Zacchaeus saw Jesus.

But suddenly Jesus looked up, and looked right at Zacchaeus up in the tree.

Jesus said, "Zacchaeus, come down out of the tree. I must go to your house today."

Zacchaeus was surprised! How did Jesus know he was up there in the tree? And how did Jesus know his name? And why must Jesus come to his house?

But he climbed down as fast as he could, and he took Jesus to his house.

The Pharisees said, "This Zacchaeus is a bad man. He is not honest. How can Jesus go to his house?"

But Zacchaeus was happy. He said to Jesus, "Lord, I will give half my goods to the poor. And if I have not been honest, I will give back four times as much as I took."

Then Jesus said, "Today salvation has come to this house."

Zacchaeus was a lost sheep. And Jesus found him.

V

Greeks Come to Jesus
(John 12:20-36)

The Passover Feast was for the Jews, first of all. But sometimes Greeks and Romans heard about God and came to the feast. They, too, wanted to worship the true God.

While Jesus was in Jerusalem, some Greek men came to the feast. They heard about Jesus. And they wanted to see Him.

These Greeks went to Philip. They said to Philip, "We want to see Jesus."

Philip told Andrew about it.

Then Philip and Andrew told Jesus.

Jesus said, "Now it is time for the Son of man to be glorified. . . . If anyone wants to serve Me, let him follow Me."

Then Jesus looked up to heaven and spoke to His Father. He said: "Father, glorify Thy Name."

And a voice from heaven answered Jesus. The voice said, "I have glorified it, and I will glorify it again!"

The people heard the voice — a voice from heaven! They said, "An angel answered Him!"

But Jesus said, "That voice came for you." The voice came to show the people that Jesus was truly the Son of God.

Jesus began to teach them again. He said, "When I am lifted up, I will draw all men unto Me."

For Jesus knew He would be lifted up on a cross, to die. And He knew that many would believe on Him. Jews would believe on Him, and Greeks, and many others.

Jesus draws all men to His cross, to love Him and believe on Him. For He first loved us.

13

JESUS GOES TO JERUSALEM

I

Mary's Love Gift
(Matthew 26:6-13; Mark 14:3-9; John 12:1-8)

Once more Jesus and His disciples went to Jerusalem. On the way, they stopped at Bethany. They went to the house of Simon for supper. Lazarus was there, and many other friends were there.

Mary knew that Jesus was at Simon's house. Mary loved Jesus very much, and she wanted to show Jesus how much she loved Him. She wanted to give Him something.

The very best thing Mary had was a jar of wonderful perfume. It was like oil, and smelled very sweet.

Mary took the perfume to Simon's house to give to Jesus.

Jesus was at the table, with many other men. Mary went behind Jesus at the table. She broke open the jar of perfume, and she poured the perfume-oil on Jesus' head. Some of it she poured on His feet. Then she kneeled down by Jesus to wipe His feet with her hair.

Everybody at the table saw what Mary did. And they smelled the wonderful perfume. They knew the perfume cost very much money.

Some of the men were angry. They said, "What a shame, to pour that perfume on Jesus! If we had the perfume, we could sell it. And we could give the money to poor people."

They thought Mary was very foolish. They thought she had wasted the wonderful perfume. And they looked at her with angry faces.

But Jesus said, "Do not be angry with Mary. Do not make her feel sad. Mary did a very good deed. People everywhere will hear about it. People everywhere will know how Mary loved Me."

And so today we still tell the story about Mary's love gift to Jesus.

II

A King Rides Into the City
(Matthew 21:1-11; Mark 11:1-11; Luke 19:29-40)

Jesus walked along the dusty road. He was going to Jerusalem. His disciples were with Him, and many other people, too.

After a while Jesus stood still. He said to two of the disciples, "Go to the little town ahead of us. You will find a little donkey there. He is tied. Untie him, and bring him to Me."

The two disciples went to the little town. They found the little donkey. They untied him and brought him to Jesus.

The disciples took off their coats. They put their coats on the little donkey's back, and Jesus sat on the little donkey.

Then the people said, "Jesus is going to ride to Jerusalem. Jesus is our King!"

And they took their coats off, too. They laid their coats in the road, to make a carpet for the King. Some ran to the trees and cut branches. They put the branches on the road to make a carpet of leaves.

Then the people began to sing about their King. And they called to each other, "Hosanna! Hosanna to the Son of David!"

They praised God. They were very happy. They said, "Our King is coming!"

After a while they were near to Jerusalem. The people in Jerusalem heard the singing, and they came to meet Jesus. Then the whole big crowd sang about the new King. All the way to Jerusalem they sang, "Hosanna! Hosanna to our King!"

When they came to Jerusalem, Jesus went to the Temple. There the little children sang to Him. They sang, "Hosanna to the Son of David!"

So they all praised Jesus, the great King.

III

A Poor Widow Brings Her Gift

(Mark 12:41-44; Luke 21:1-4)

One day Jesus sat in the Temple. He watched the people come to the Temple to worship God. Jesus sat near the door, by the money box. When people came in, they put money into the money box. That is how they gave money to God. Jesus watched the people put money into the box.

Some people gave much money to God. Some gave just a little.

A rich man came in. He wore beautiful clothes. Jesus watched the rich man. And Jesus saw him put much money into the box.

Another rich man came in. He put much money into the box, too.

After a while a lady came in. She did not wear beautiful clothes. She was a poor widow. Jesus knew she was a poor widow. He watched her go to the money box. And He saw her put two little pennies in.

Then Jesus called His disciples.

Jesus said to His disciples, "Did you see that poor widow lady? She put more into the box than anyone else. She put more into the box than all the rich men did."

The disciples thought, "How can that be?" And they did not know what to say.

Jesus said, "The rich men put much money into the box. But they had much more money left. The poor lady put only two little pennies in. But she did not have any left. She put all that she had into the box. She gave her all to God."

IV

A Story About Hired Men

(Matthew 21:33-41; Mark 12:1-9; Luke 20:9-16)

One day Jesus said to the people, "I will tell you another story, another parable." And he told the story of hired men:

"There was a rich man who planted grape vines. He planted them carefully, in long rows. Then he put a fence around the vineyard. And he put a watchtower in the center of the vineyard.

"When all was ready, the rich man hired men to take care of his vineyard. He went away, to a far country.

"The grape vines grew, and after a while there were many ripe grapes. So the rich man sent a servant to get some of the fruit.

"But when the servant came to the vineyard, the hired men would not give him the grapes. They beat him with a stick, and sent him away.

"Then the owner of the vineyard sent another servant. But the hired men would not give him the grapes. They threw stones at him, and sent him away.

"After that the owner sent other servants. But the hired men sent each one away without fruit. They would not give the owner the fruit of his own vineyard. They even killed some of the servants.

"At last the owner said, 'I will send my son. Surely they will listen to him.'

"The wicked men saw the son coming. They said, 'Let's kill the rich man's son. Then the vineyard will be ours.'

"So they did kill him.

"But then the rich man came. He punished the wicked hired men. And he gave the vineyard to others."

When Jesus finished telling the story, the Pharisees were ashamed. They knew they were like the wicked hired men. God had put them in His beautiful vineyard to take care of it. But they would not give God the fruits. They would not serve Him. They would not listen to His prophets, or listen to Jesus. And they were thinking of killing Jesus, God's own Son.

But Jesus told them plainly, in the story, that God would take the vineyard away from them. God would give it to others, to all who believe in Jesus.

V

A Story About Ten Girls
(Matthew 24:3, 36; 25:1-13)

One day Jesus told His disciples that He was going to heaven. And He told them that He would come back.

The disciples said to Jesus, "Tell us more about the Kingdom of Heaven. Tell us when You will come back."

Jesus said, "Nobody but God knows just when I will come back. So you must watch for Me. You must always be ready."

Then Jesus told them a story. He said:

"The Kingdom of Heaven is like ten girls who went to a wedding.

"It was night. The streets were dark. So each girl took a little oil lamp to light the way.

"Five of the girls were wise. They took extra oil to put in their lamps, to keep their lamps burning a long time.

"Five of the girls were foolish. They did not take extra oil for their lamps.

"The ten girls had to wait a long time for the bridegroom. They sat down on the street corner. And soon they all fell asleep.

"After a while a man came down the street. He called in a loud voice, 'The bridegroom is coming! The bridegroom is coming!'

"The ten girls jumped up. They rubbed their eyes. Then they looked at their lamps. The lamps were going out!

"The five wise girls quickly put the extra oil in their lamps. Then their lamps burned bright again.

"But the five foolish girls did not have extra oil. Their lamps went out. They had to run to the store to buy more oil.

"The five wise girls went to the wedding.

"After a while the five foolish girls came. But they were late. And they could not go in. Then they were very sad."

Jesus said, "You do not know when I will come back. You must be ready all the time, like the five wise girls."

VI

A Story About Three Servants
(Matthew 25:14-30)

Jesus told another story about the Kingdom of Heaven. He said:

"The Kingdom of Heaven is like a man who went far away, to a far country. This man had three servants. Before he went away, he gave his servants money. He gave the first servant five talents. He gave the second servant two talents. And he gave the third servant one talent. Then he went away.

"When the master was gone, the first servant went to work. He used the five talents. After a while he earned five more talents. Then he had ten.

"The second servant went to work, too. He used his two talents. After a while he earned two more talents. Then he had four.

"But the third servant did not go to work. He dug a hole in the ground. He buried his one talent in the hole.

"After a long, long time the master came back.

"He called his servants.

"The first servant came, and gave his master ten talents.

"The master said, 'That is fine! You are a good servant. Come in and be happy with me in my house.'

"The second servant came, and gave his master four talents.

"The master said, 'That is fine! You are a good servant. Come in and be happy with me in my house.'

"Then the third servant came. He gave his master the one talent.

"He said to his master, 'I was afraid. So I hid the talent in the ground. Here it is.'

"The master said, 'You wicked and lazy servant! You should have worked for me. I gave you the talent to use!'

"Then the master took the one talent away. And he would not let the servant come into his house. He put him out in the dark."

Jesus is coming again. And we must work for Him until He comes.

14

JUDAS HAS A WICKED PLAN

I

Satan Whispers to Judas

(Matthew 26:14-16; Mark 14:10, 11; Luke 22:3-6)

Judas was one of Jesus' disciples. He carried the money bag. When somebody gave Jesus money, Judas put it in the money bag and took care of it.

Judas loved money.

Judas went everywhere with Jesus. He saw all the wonderful things Jesus did. He heard all the wonderful words that Jesus spoke. He saw Jesus heal the sick and blind and lame. But Judas did not love Jesus. Judas loved money.

Some other people did not love Jesus. The chief priests hated Him. Jesus sometimes told the chief priests that they were sinners. That made them angry. That is why they hated Jesus.

One day Satan came to Judas. He whispered in Judas' heart. He told Judas to sell Jesus to the chief priests.

Then Judas went to the chief priests. He said to them, "I want to sell Jesus to you. How much money will you give me?"

The chief priests were glad that Judas would sell Jesus. They said, "We will give you thirty pieces of silver."

Judas said that was all right. He would sell Jesus for thirty pieces of silver.

"I will do it as soon as I can," he said.

Then he went back to Jesus. He did not tell anybody where he had been. He walked with Jesus again, just like all the other disciples.

Judas thought nobody knew. But Jesus knew all about Judas' wicked plan.

II

A Man with a Jug

(Matthew 26:17-19; Mark 14:12-17; Luke 22:7-14)

It was time for the Passover feast again. Jesus and His disciples were in Bethany. They must go to Jerusalem for the feast.

Jesus said to Peter and John. "Go to Jerusalem and make the Passover supper ready for us."

Peter and John said, "Where shall we make the supper ready?"

Then Jesus said, "Go to the city. When you are in the city, you will see a man with a jug of water. Follow that man. Go into the house that he goes into. And ask the man of the house to show you a room. He will have a room ready for us."

So Peter and John went to Jerusalem. When they came inside the city of Jerusalem, they looked around.

"There he is," said Peter.

And sure enough, there was a man walking down the street, carrying a jug of water, just as Jesus had said.

Peter and John followed that man. He went into a house, and they went in, too. Then they asked the man of the house for a room for Jesus.

The man took them upstairs, and showed them a room. It was all ready — just as Jesus had said. There was a table, and there were couches to sit on.

Peter and John made the Passover supper in that room. After a while Jesus came, with the other disciples. And the supper was all ready.

III

Serve One Another

(John 13:1-17)

Jesus and His disciples walked a long, long way on the dusty road. At last they came to Jerusalem. They went to the upstairs room, where Peter and John had supper ready. They were tired, and their feet were dusty from the dusty road.

In that upstairs room Jesus and His disciples saw a jar of water and a basin, and a towel. These were for washing dusty feet.

But in those days people had servants to wash their feet. And there was not a servant in the room. So Jesus and His disciples sat down to supper without washing the dust off their feet.

But after supper Jesus stood up. He took the towel and tied it around Himself. He poured some water into the basin. And then He began to wash the feet of the disciples.

First He went to one disciple. He washed that disciple's feet and dried them with the towel.

Then He went to the next disciple.

The disciples did not know what to say. They did not want Jesus to wash their feet. That was work for a servant! But they did not dare tell Him to stop.

After a while it was Peter's turn.

Peter said to Jesus, "Are You going to wash my feet?"

Jesus said, "You do not understand this now. Sometime you will understand what I am doing."

But Peter pulled his feet away. Peter said, "No, I will never let You wash my feet."

Jesus said, "If I do not wash your feet, then you do not belong to Me."

Peter loved Jesus very much. He wanted to belong to Jesus. He wanted that more than anything else.

So Peter said, "Oh, then wash my feet, and wash my hands and my head, too!"

Jesus said, "No, just your feet need to be washed now."

Then Jesus washed Peter's feet. He washed the feet of all the disciples.

When the work was all done, Jesus sat down again.

The disciples thought, "Why did Jesus do that? He is our Master. He is the Lord. Why did He wash our feet?"

Jesus said to them, "You call Me Master and Lord. That is good. I am your Master and Lord. But I washed your feet, like a servant. I did it to show you how you must love each other and serve each other."

For if we serve each other, we will be happy.

IV

Jesus Sends Judas Away

(Matthew 26:20-25; Mark 14:18-21; John 13:18-30)

Jesus sat down again at the table. And He was very sad. He knew that He would soon die.

Then Jesus said to the disciples, "One of you is going to sell Me."

The disciples thought, "Oh, no! Who would do that?"

Peter said, "Surely, it is not I!"

John and Thomas and the others said, "Surely, it is not I!"

Even Judas said, "Surely, it is not I!"

Peter sat next to John, and John sat next to Jesus. So Peter whispered to John, "You ask Him who it is."

Then John put his head on Jesus' shoulder and whispered, "Who is it, Lord?"

Jesus said softly, "I will show you who it is. I will dip a piece of bread in the sauce. I will give it to the man who is going to sell Me."

Jesus took a piece of bread. He dipped it into the sauce. And He gave it to Judas.

Then Satan came into Judas' heart.

And Jesus said to Judas, "Go quickly now, and do what you are going to do."

Judas quickly stood up. He hurried away, out into the dark night. He went to the chief priests, to sell Jesus.

Jesus said, "Because you have
believed, you may see."

*They took Jesus to Pilate, who was
the ruler of the Jews.*

15

JESUS' LAST NIGHT

I

The Lord's Supper
(Matthew 26:26-29; Luke 22:18-20; I Corinthians 11:23-26)

Judas was gone. Jesus was alone with the eleven disciples who loved Him.

Then Jesus took the bread in His hands. He looked up to heaven to thank God for the bread. He broke it in little pieces. And He gave each disciple a piece.

Jesus said, "Take it, and eat it. This is My body that is broken for you."

Each of the disciples slowly ate a piece of the bread.

Then Jesus took a cup of wine. He looked up to heaven to thank God for the wine. Then He said to the disciples, "All of you drink a little wine from the cup. The wine is My blood, which I will give for you, for your sins."

The disciples took the cup. They passed it around. Each one drank a little of the wine.

That was the first "Lord's Supper."

Jesus said to the disciples, "When I am gone, you must break the bread and drink the wine together again and again, to remember me. Do it again and again, until I come back."

So even today we break the bread and drink the wine of the Lord's Supper. We will do it again and again, until Jesus comes back to us. We will always remember that Jesus gave His body and His blood for our sins.

II

Jesus Says Good-bye to His Disciples
(John 13:36; 14, 15, 16, 17)

Jesus and His disciples sat at the table. Jesus had so much to tell them.

Jesus said, "I am going away soon. Then you will not see Me for a long, long time."

Peter said to Jesus, "Where are You going?"

Jesus said, "I am going to My Father's house. I will make a place ready for you there. And then I shall come again, and take you there to live with Me. You know the way to go."

Thomas said, "Lord, we do not know where You are going. How can we know the way?"

Then Jesus said, "I am the Way. You can come to God the Father through Me. There is no other way to come to the Father."

Philip said, "Lord, show us the Father."

Jesus said, "If you love Me, the Father will come and live with you. He will love you. He will hear you when you pray."

Then Jesus told His disciples that we must pray to God in Jesus' name.

Jesus said, "If you pray in My name, the Father will surely hear you. I tell you this, because I am going away."

The disciples were very sad. How lonely they would be without Jesus!

But Jesus said, "Do not feel sad. And do not be afraid."

Then Jesus looked up to heaven and prayed for His disciples. He said, "Father, take care of them. Keep them from evil. Make them pure and good through Thy truth. And take them to live with Me by and by."

Then Jesus and His disciples sang a song together. And after that they went outdoors.

III

In the Moonlight

(Matthew 26:30-35; Luke 22:31-34)

It was night. There was a big round moon in the sky. Jesus and His disciples walked down a little path, in the moonlight. They went over a little creek, to the Garden of Gethsemane.

Jesus said to His disciples, "Tonight you will all run away from Me."

All the disciples said, "Oh, no! We will not do that!"

And Peter said, "Even if all the others run away from You, I will never run away from You."

Jesus looked at Peter sadly. He said, "Peter, Peter, Satan wants to get hold of you. But I prayed to the Father, and He will take care of you."

Peter said, "Lord, even if You go to prison, I will go to prison with You. I will even die with You."

Jesus shook His head. He said, "Before the rooster crows in the morning, you will deny Me three times. Three times you will say that you do not know Me."

Peter said, "No, no, no! I will never do that!"

But Peter did not know what was going to happen.

IV

Under the Garden Trees

(Matthew 26:36-46; Mark 14:32-42; Luke 22:39-46)

Jesus and His disciples came to the garden. It was dark there, under the trees.

Jesus said to Peter, James, and John, "You come with Me." And He told the others to sit down and wait.

Jesus went into the Garden with Peter, James, and John. After a while He said to them, "You stay here. Watch and pray. I will go a little farther and pray."

The three disciples sat down. Jesus went on alone.

Jesus was very sad. He knew that He must soon die. He knew that God would punish Him for our sins. He knew that God's punishment would be very, very hard to bear.

So Jesus fell down on the ground. He prayed to His Father in heaven. He prayed that His Father would take the punishment away. He prayed, "Not My will, but Thine, be done."

Then Jesus went back to the three disciples. And He found them asleep.

Three times Jesus prayed. And the disciples slept while Jesus prayed.

Then God sent an angel down from heaven. The angel talked with Jesus. He made Jesus feel strong again.

After a while Jesus went back to the three disciples. They were still sleeping.

Jesus woke them up. He said to them, "Wake up now. My time is come."

Then they all opened their eyes. And they were ashamed, because they did not stay awake to watch and pray with Jesus.

16

JESUS GOES TO THE CROSS

I

Judas Comes to the Garden
(Matthew 26:47-56; Mark 14:43-50; Luke 22:47-54; John 18:1-14)

When Jesus woke the disciples in the garden, they saw lights. The lights were coming near. The lights were torches, burning bright. Soon the disciples saw that soldiers were carrying the torches.

And then they saw Judas. Judas was with the soldiers. Judas brought the soldiers to Jesus.

When they came near, Judas kissed Jesus. He said, "Hail, Master!"

Judas kissed Jesus so that the soldiers would know which one was Jesus.

Then Jesus said to the soldiers, "Who is it that you want?"

The soldiers said, "We want Jesus of Nazareth."

Jesus was not afraid. He said to the soldiers, "I am He."

But the soldiers were afraid of Jesus. They stepped backwards. And they fell to the ground.

Jesus said again, "Who is it that you want?"

They said again, "We want Jesus of Nazareth."

Then the soldiers were going to take hold of Jesus. But Peter did not want them to take Jesus. Peter had a sword. He took his sword and swung it hard. He cut a man's ear.

Jesus said to Peter, "Put your sword away. We do not need the sword. If I ask my Father, He will send a whole army of angels to help us."

Then Jesus touched the man's ear and made it well.

Jesus said to the soldiers, "Take Me. But let these others go."

So the soldiers took Jesus. And the disciples were afraid. They all ran away.

II

Jesus in the Palace of the High Priest

(Matthew 26:57-68; Mark 14:53-65; Luke 22:63-71; John 18:12-24)

When the soldiers took Jesus, all the disciples ran away. Peter and John ran away, too.

But after a while Peter and John stopped.

They said, "We must follow the soldiers. We must see what they do with Jesus."

So they followed, far behind.

The soldiers took Jesus to the palace of the high priest. Peter and John saw them go into the palace. Then Peter and John went in, too. They stood with some soldiers, near the door. There they could watch, to see what would happen to Jesus. The soldiers made a little fire, because it was cold. And Peter stood with them, by the fire.

In the big palace room, the high priest was waiting for Jesus. There were many other priests with him, all sitting in a circle. The soldiers brought Jesus in the middle of the circle.

The men asked Jesus many questions. They tried to think of some very wicked thing to say against Jesus. But Jesus never did any wicked thing. They could not find even a little sin against Him.

At last the high priest said to Jesus, "Tell me, are You the Christ, the Son of God?"

Jesus said, "Yes, I am."

Then the high priest was very angry. He said to the other men, "Did you hear that? This man says He is the Son of God! He must surely die, because He says He is the Son of God!"

And all the other men said, "Yes, He must surely die."

Then they began to hit Jesus. And they spit at Him. And they made fun of Him.

III

Peter Denies Jesus

(Matthew 26:69-75; Mark 14:66-72; Luke 22:54-62; John 18:15-27)

Peter stood by the fire, with the soldiers. He saw all that happened to Jesus. He saw the men hit Jesus, and spit at Him, and laugh at Him.

Peter felt very sorry. And Peter was afraid. These men wanted to kill Jesus. Maybe they would kill His disciples, too.

After a while a maid saw Peter. She said to him, "Are you a disciple of Jesus?"

Peter felt his heart beat very fast. But he quickly said to the maid, "Oh, no! I do not even know the man!"

Then Peter went out on the porch. He stood with some soldiers.

But another maid saw Peter on the porch. She said to the soldiers, "This is one of the disciples of Jesus."

Peter quickly said, "I am not! I do not even know Him!"

One of the soldiers looked at Peter and said, "You are one of the disciples. I saw you in the garden with Him."

"No, no, no!" said Peter. "I do not know Him at all! I tell you I never saw Him before!"

And then Peter heard a rooster crow.

And Peter remembered what Jesus had said. Jesus had told Peter, "Before the rooster crows, you will deny Me three times. Three times you will say that you do not know Me."

Peter turned around and looked at Jesus.

Jesus turned around and looked at Peter.

Then Peter was very, very sorry. He did love Jesus, very, very much. But he had denied Him three times.

Peter's eyes filled with tears. He went outdoors. He covered his face with his hands, and then he cried, and cried, and cried.

IV

"Crucify Him!"

(Matthew 27:22-26; Mark 15:1-15; Luke 23:13-25; John 19:1-16)

It was Friday morning. The priests and the soldiers hurried through the streets of Jerusalem. They took Jesus to Pilate. A crowd of people followed, to see what Pilate would do.

Pilate was the governor. He was ruler of the Jews. The Jews had to do as Pilate said.

The chief priests said to Pilate, "This is a bad man. We think He must die."

Pilate said, "What bad thing did He do?"

The chief priests could not think of one bad thing that Jesus had ever done.

So they said, "He says He is a King. That is why He must die."

Pilate looked at Jesus. Jesus' hands were tied. He did not look like a king.

Pilate said to Jesus, "Are you a King?"

Jesus said, "Yes, I am a King. But My Kingdom is not of this world!"

And Pilate saw that Jesus' face was like a King's face. Then Pilate was afraid of Jesus.

Pilate said to the chief priests, "This man has not done anything wrong. I will let Him go."

But the chief priests said, "No, no! You must not let Him go! We want to crucify Him!"

See accompanying illustration between pages 288 and 289

All the chief priests began to shout, "Crucify Him! Crucify Him!"

And all the people began to shout, "Crucify Him! Crucify Him!"

Pilate did not want to crucify Jesus.

Pilate said, "I have a bad man in prison. He is a thief. His name is Barabbas. You may crucify Barabbas."

But the chief priests and the people shouted louder and louder, "Not Barabbas! Not Barabbas! Crucify Jesus! Crucify Him! Crucify Him!"

Pilate saw how angry the people were. And Pilate was afraid of the people. So Pilate said, "All right. You take Jesus and crucify Him."

V

Jesus Is Crucified

(Matthew 27:31-37; Mark 15:20-26; Luke 23:26-34)

The soldiers made a big wooden cross. They laid the cross on Jesus' shoulder. Jesus had to carry it.

Then the soldiers led Jesus away. The chief priests and all the people followed. They went down the streets of Jerusalem. They went through the city gate, out into the country. And then they came to a little hill.

But Jesus was tired. And the cross was heavy. Jesus could not carry the cross up the little hill.

The soldiers did not want to carry the cross. The chief priests did not want to carry the cross.

Then they saw a man coming down the road. He came from the country. His name was Simon. The soldiers stopped Simon. They made Simon carry the cross for Jesus.

Up the hill they went. More and more people came to follow Jesus and the soldiers. Some of Jesus' friends came, too. They were very sad.

At last they were at the top of the hill. Simon put the cross on the ground. The soldiers laid Jesus on the cross, and nailed Him to the cross. They put nails through His hands and through His feet.

The nails hurt Jesus' hands and feet. But Jesus prayed for the soldiers. Jesus prayed, "Father, forgive them, for they do not know what they are doing."

The soldiers did not know that Jesus was the Son of God. They did not know that He was the great King who came from God.

The soldiers dug a hole in the ground. They set the cross in the hole. And all the people saw Jesus, hanging there on the cross.

VI

Three Crosses on the Hill
(Luke 23:32-43)

Two other men were crucified with Jesus. These were bad men.

The soldiers put one of the bad men on one side of Jesus. They put the other bad man on the other side of Jesus.

Then there were three crosses on the hill.

The chief priests began to make fun of Jesus. They said, "If you are the Son of God, come down from the cross!"

But Jesus did not come down. Jesus stayed on the cross. He stayed on the cross to pay for our sins.

The two bad men heard the chief priests laugh. They looked at Jesus. They saw a sign above Jesus' head. Pilate had put a sign on the cross. The sign said, "This is the King of the Jews."

One bad man laughed. He said to Jesus, "If You are Christ, the king, save Yourself and save us, too. Take us all down from these three crosses." And he made fun of Jesus.

The other bad man believed on Jesus. He said to Jesus, "Lord, when You come into Your Kingdom, please remember me."

Then Jesus said to that man, "Today you will be with Me in Paradise." And that man was happy.

VII

The King Dies

(Matthew 27:45-54; Mark 15:33-39; Luke 23:44-49; John 19:28-30)

It was Friday noon. The sun was high in the sky. It shone down on the three crosses on the little hill.

Then something strange happened. The sun, shining way up in the sky, became dark. God took the light of the sun away. All the sky became dark. On the little hill the day turned into night. The people could hardly see the three crosses. And they were afraid. They did not dare make fun of Jesus any more.

For three hours God kept the light away.

Out of the darkness, Jesus cried to God. The people heard Him, and they shivered.

Then at last the light came back.

And Jesus said, "It is finished." His work was done. He had paid for all our sin.

Then Jesus died. He gave His soul to God.

A soldier thrust his spear into Jesus' side. Blood and water came out.

But when Jesus died, God shook the city of Jerusalem. And He shook the little hill where the three crosses stood. The people felt the ground shake under their feet. They saw stones come tumbling down the hill. And they were afraid. They hurried home. They said, "Oh, oh! What kind of man was this Jesus?"

The captain of the soldiers said, "Surely, this man was the Son of God."

VIII

Jesus Is Buried in a Garden

(Matthew 27:57-66; Mark 15:42-47; Luke 23:50-56; John 19:38-42)

It was evening. The sun went down in the west. Night began to creep up the little hill. Jesus was on the cross. He was dead.

Then a man hurried away to Pilate. This man was Joseph of Arimathea. Joseph loved Jesus.

Joseph of Arimathea said to Pilate, "Please let me take the body of Jesus from the cross. Let me bury Jesus."

Pilate said, "Is He dead already?"

And the captain of the soldiers said, "Yes, He is dead."

Then Pilate told Joseph to take the body of Jesus down.

Nicodemus came to help Joseph. Nicodemus loved Jesus, too. They took Jesus' body down carefully.

Joseph had a garden near the little hill. In the garden was a grave. The grave was cut into the stone of the hill. Joseph and Nicodemus carried Jesus' body to the grave. They laid it down carefully. They put linen cloth all around it. Then they put a big stone in front of the grave.

Mary Magdalene and some other friends watched. They said, "We will come on Sunday, and bring oil and spices for Jesus' body." They loved Jesus, too.

Then it was night, and they all went home.

But the Jews set soldiers by the grave, to watch it. They said, "Maybe the disciples will come and try to steal the body of Jesus."

17

JESUS LIVES AGAIN

I

Early Easter Morning
(Matthew 28:1-10; Mark 16:1-8; Luke 24:1-12)

It was very, very quiet in Joseph's garden. All night long the soldiers sat by Jesus' grave. They heard the wind whisper in the treetops. They saw the moon climb slowly across the sky.

Sometimes they talked together.

They were glad when the night was almost gone.

Then suddenly they felt the ground shake. And they saw a bright light up in the sky. The bright light came down to the garden. It came straight to Jesus' grave. It was a shining angel!

The soldiers were afraid. They fell down on their faces. They did not dare look at the angel.

But after a while they looked. Then they saw that the grave of Jesus was open. The big stone was rolled away. And the angel was sitting on it!

Then the soldiers jumped up and ran. They ran as fast as they could, to get away from the angel.

It was very, very quiet in the garden again. Slowly the daylight came, and chased the dark night away.

Then some women came up the hill to the garden. Mary Magdalene was one of them. They were all friends of Jesus. They came to bring oil and spices for Jesus' body.

The women talked together softly. One said, "Joseph and Nicodemus put a big stone in front of the grave. Do you think we can roll it away?"

They knew the stone was very big.

When they came near, they saw the stone. And they said, "Look! The stone is rolled away already!"

Then they ran to look. And they saw that the grave was empty!

Mary Magdalene said, "Oh, oh! Somebody came and took Jesus away! I will run and tell Peter and John!"

And she ran back to Jerusalem.

The other women went close to the grave. They looked into it carefully. And there they saw a shining angel. His clothes were white as snow. His face was shining like lightning. And they were afraid.

The angel said to them, "Do not be afraid. I know you are looking for Jesus. He is not here. He is risen. He is alive!"

The women looked at each other, and looked at the angel, and looked at the empty grave. Could it really be true? Was Jesus really alive again?

The angel said, "Go tell the disciples that Jesus is alive. Tell them that Jesus will see them in Galilee."

Then the women ran back to Jerusalem. They ran as fast as they could, to tell the good news. Jesus was alive! Jesus was not in the grave! He was alive!

II

Mary Magdalene Sees Jesus

(John 20:1-18)

Mary Magdalene did not see the angel. She saw only the empty grave. And she ran back to tell Peter and John.

She kept saying, "Oh, somebody took Jesus away. Somebody stole Him!"

She found Peter and John. She said to them, "Oh, come to the garden, quick! The grave is empty! Somebody took Jesus away!"

Peter and John were ready in a minute. They ran to the garden. Mary ran, too. But Peter and John ran faster.

Peter and John ran up the hill. They ran to the grave. They looked in — and it was empty. Then they walked right into the cave. But Jesus was not there. And they did not see the angel. They saw only the cloths that had been around Jesus' body.

"Something wonderful has happened," John thought.

Slowly Peter and John went back home.

But Mary Magdalene sat down by the grave. She did not know what to do. She wanted to find the body of Jesus. Big tears rolled down her cheeks.

After a while Mary looked around. And she saw a man standing near by.

The man said to Mary, "Why are you crying? Who is it you are looking for?"

Mary thought, "This must be the gardener. He will know where they put Jesus."

So Mary said, "Did you take Jesus away? Please tell me where you put Him!"

The man said, "Mary!"

Then Mary saw that it was Jesus!

Mary fell at Jesus' feet. "My Master! My Master!" she said.

Jesus said to her, "Now go tell My disciples that I am going to heaven, to My Father and your Father."

Then Mary hurried back to Jerusalem. How happy she was! She ran to tell the disciples, "I saw Jesus. He is alive!"

See accompanying illustration between pages 320 and 321

III

Two Men Walk with Jesus

(Luke 24:13-32)

It was afternoon, on Easter day. Two disciples went for a walk to Emmaus. On the way, they talked and talked. They talked about Jesus.

After a while a strange man came to walk with them.

This man said, "What are you talking about?"

They said, "Oh, we are talking about all the things that have happened."

The strange man said, "What things?"

The disciples said, "Don't you know? Didn't you hear about Jesus? We thought He was a great prophet. We thought He would be our King. But the chief priests took Him, and He died on the cross. We thought surely He would be the Saviour."

And they had more to tell. They said, "This morning some friends went to His grave. They came running back. They said the grave was empty. They said they saw angels by the grave, and the angels said Jesus is alive."

Then the strange man said, "Don't you understand? The Saviour had to die on the cross. Long, long ago, the prophets said that He would come, and that He would die on the cross, and that He would live again."

The strange man told them all about the prophets of long, long ago. The disciples listened. They thought, "What a wonderful man this strange man is!"

After a while they came to Emmaus. The disciples stopped at their house.

The strange man was going to walk on. But the disciples said, "Come in and eat supper with us."

They went into the house. All three sat down to eat supper.

Then the strange man took bread. He looked up to heaven and asked God to bless the bread. And He broke a piece for each of the two disciples.

When they saw the man break the bread, they suddenly knew who it was. It was Jesus!

But at that very moment Jesus was gone.

The two disciples looked at each other with shining eyes. They said, "No wonder we thought He was a wonderful Man!"

IV

Jesus Comes Through a Closed Door

(Luke 24:33-48; John 20:19, 20, 24)

The two disciples in Emmaus could not eat their supper. They were too happy to eat. They had seen Jesus!

They said to each other, "We must tell the other disciples! Let us go back to Jerusalem right now!"

Jerusalem was far away, and night was coming. But they went just the same. They could not wait to tell the good news.

They hurried to the house of the disciples in Jerusalem. They knocked at the door.

Somebody opened the door and said, "Jesus is alive! Peter saw Him!"

"Oh!" said the men from Emmaus, "we saw Him, too!"

Then they closed the door tight, and began to talk. They told how Jesus walked with them and talked with them. They told how He broke the bread.

And then — there Jesus was, right in the room. He did not open the door. He just stood there, in the middle of the room. All the disciples looked at Him with big wondering eyes.

Jesus said, "Peace be unto you."

But they were afraid. They could not believe that it was Jesus.

See accompanying illustration
between pages 320 and 321

Jesus said, "Do not be afraid. It is really I. Look at My hands, and look at My feet."

He showed them His hands and His feet. They saw the holes of the big nails. But still they could not believe that Jesus was alive.

Jesus said, "Have you something here to eat?"

Yes, they had a piece of fish. They gave it to Jesus, and He ate it. Then they knew that He was really alive.

Jesus talked with them a long time. He told them that He had to die on the cross. He told them that He took our sins to the cross.

Then Jesus went away again.

But the disciples were very happy. Now they were sure. They knew Jesus was alive. They knew He was the Saviour, the Son of God.

But Thomas was not there.

V

Jesus Comes to the Disciples Again

(John 20:26-31)

When Jesus was gone, the disciples talked and talked. How wonderful, that Jesus died on the cross, and then lived again!

After a while Thomas came in.

The disciples said to Thomas, "We have seen Jesus! He is alive!"

Thomas said, "That cannot be. I do not believe it."

They told Thomas all about it. Peter had seen Jesus. Mary Magdalene had seen Jesus. Jesus walked to Emmaus. And Jesus even came into the room, when the door was shut tight.

But Thomas shook his head.

Thomas said, "I will not believe it, unless I put my finger in the nail holes, and put my hand in the spear hole in His side."

A whole week went by. Nobody saw Jesus. Thomas was sure that Jesus was dead.

It was Sunday night again. All the disciples were in the room again. Thomas was there, too.

They talked about Jesus. The door was closed tight.

And suddenly Jesus was there, in the middle of the room.

Jesus said, "Peace be unto you."

Then Jesus looked at Thomas.

Jesus said, "Look at My hands. Come put your finger in the nail holes. Put your hand in My side. And believe."

But Thomas did not need to put his finger in the nail holes. He knew it was Jesus. He believed.

Thomas said, "My Lord and my God." He knew Jesus was the Son of God, the Saviour.

Then Jesus said, "You see Me, and you believe. Many people will not see Me, but they will believe. Blessed are those who will not see Me, and yet believe."

That means you and me. We do not see Jesus. But we do believe that He is the Son of God, our Saviour.

VI

Meeting by the Sea of Galilee
(John 21:1-14)

One day Peter and John, and some other disciples, went to the lake — to the Sea of Galilee. They did not know where Jesus was. They had not seen Jesus for a long time.

Peter said, "I want to go fishing."

The others said, "Let's all go fishing."

They took a big net to catch the fish in. They went into a little boat. And they rowed out on the lake.

The disciples let the big net down into the water. After a while they pulled it up. But there was not one fish in the net.

They let the net down into the water again. They pulled it up. Again there was not one fish in the net. They tried again and again. They did not catch one fish.

After a while the sun went down. But the disciples did not stop fishing. In the dark, under the stars, they put the net down into the water again. But when they pulled the net up, it was empty.

All night long they tried to catch fish.

At last morning came. The stars faded away. The sun came peeking over the edge of the earth. There was no use trying any more. They began to row to shore.

Then they saw a man standing on the shore.

The man called to them, "Did you catch any? Have you some to eat?"

The disciples called to the man, "No!"

The man said, "Put the net down on the other side of the boat! Then you will catch some."

The disciples put the net down into the water on the other side of the boat. And when they pulled it up, it was full of fishes!

John whispered to Peter, "That is Jesus!"

Peter thought so, too.

Peter jumped out of the boat, into the water. The water was not deep. Peter hurried to get to Jesus.

The others rowed the boat, and pulled the net full of fishes. When they came to shore, Peter helped pull the net. Then they counted the fishes — one hundred and fifty three.

There was a little fire on shore. There were some fishes frying on the fire. There was some bread beside the fire. Jesus had breakfast ready for the disciples.

So Jesus and the disciples ate breakfast beside the lake. And Jesus talked with His disciples again.

VII

Jesus Goes to Heaven

(Luke 24:50, 51; Acts 1:4-12)

Jesus came to His disciples again and again, very many times. But at last it was time for Jesus to go to heaven.

Jesus took the disciples to a little hill, near Jerusalem. There He talked to them. He told them that they must go all over the world. They must tell people everywhere about Jesus, the Saviour. They must tell people everywhere to believe on Jesus.

He said to them, "The Holy Spirit will come. He will make you strong. He will tell you what to do and where to go. You must wait in Jerusalem until the Holy Spirit comes."

Then Jesus lifted His hands over the heads of the disciples. He blessed them.

And while Jesus blessed the disciples, He was lifted up from the ground. He began to go up, slowly, higher and higher, up into the sky.

When He was up high, a cloud came. The cloud hid Jesus. Then the disciples could not see Him anymore.

But the disciples stood there, looking and looking up into the sky.

Then two men came along. They were dressed in white. They were angels.

The angels said, "Why do you stand looking up into the sky? Jesus is gone to heaven. But He will come again, in just the same way."

Then the disciples went back to Jerusalem. They were happy, because they knew Jesus was in heaven, watching over them.

Jesus is still in heaven. He has not yet come back. But He will come, some day. What a wonderful day that will be!

18

THE WORK OF THE HOLY SPIRIT

I

The Holy Spirit Comes

(Acts 1:12-14; 2:1-42)

When Jesus was gone to heaven, the disciples went back to Jerusalem. There they waited for Jesus to send the Holy Spirit.

The disciples waited many days. Every day they prayed to God. And every day they sang praises to God together.

One day they were all in a big room, and they heard a strange noise. It was a rushing noise, like the noise of a rushing wind.

The disciples looked around, and they saw little tongues of fire, like little flames. The little tongues came on the heads of the disciples. One little tongue came on each disciple.

Then a wonderful feeling came into their hearts. The Holy Spirit filled their hearts. They felt strong and brave. They felt they must go tell everybody about Jesus.

The noise like a rushing wind, and the little tongues like flames of fire, these were signs that the Holy Spirit had come.

Soon many people came running to the house. They wanted to see what made the noise. When they saw the little tongues like flames of fire, they said, "Oh, what has happened?"

Peter stood up and began to talk to them.

Peter said, "The Holy Spirit has come. That is what you see and hear."

Then Peter told the story of Jesus. He said, "Jesus came from heaven. God sent Him. He did many, many good things for you.

But you nailed Him to the cross. He died. And He was buried. But He arose from the grave. We all saw Him. He went up to heaven. And now He sent the Holy Spirit from heaven. This Jesus is the Son of God. He is Christ, the Saviour."

Then the people were afraid. Jesus is the Son of God! And they nailed Him to the cross!

The people said, "Oh, what must we do?"

Peter said, "You must be sorry for your sins. You must believe on Jesus. Then you will be saved."

Many, many people believed on Jesus that day. The Holy Spirit came into their hearts. They were baptized. And they were happy with Peter and all the other disciples.

II

A Lame Man Walks

(Acts 3)

There was a lame man in Jerusalem. He could not walk. When he was a little boy, his feet did not grow strong. Now he was a man, but still he could not walk.

Every day his friends brought the lame man to the Temple. They set him down by the Temple door. There he sat, on the floor. He waited for people to come to the Temple. When people came, the lame man put out his hand. And kind people gave him some money.

One day, early in the morning, Peter and John came to the Temple. The lame man saw them come, and he put out his hand.

Peter and John stopped by the lame man. But they did not put any money into his hand.

Peter said to him, "Look at us."

The lame man looked up at Peter and John. He thought they would give him money.

Peter said, "I do not have money to give you. But I have something else."

Then Peter took hold of the lame man's hand.

Peter said, "In the name of Jesus Christ, stand up and walk!"

The lame man felt his feet grow strong. He jumped up. And he could walk!

He went into the Temple with Peter and John. He skipped and jumped and hopped. And he kept saying, "Oh, praise God, I can walk! Praise God, I can walk!"

There were many people in the Temple. They heard the lame man praise God. They saw him skip and jump and hop. And they said, "Why, this is the lame man, the man that sat by the door!"

They looked at the lame man. They looked at Peter and John. They could not understand how the lame man could walk.

At last Peter said, "Do not look at us so! Do you think we can make a lame man walk? We did not make the lame man walk. Jesus did that!"

Then Peter told them all about Jesus, the Son of God, the Saviour.

Peter said, "Jesus made the lame man walk. And Jesus saves us from sin."

Then many more people believed on Jesus.

III

Peter and John Are Not Afraid
(Acts 4:1-31)

All day long Peter and John talked to the people in the Temple. Then the priests were angry. They took Peter and John away and put them in prison.

Peter and John were in prison all night. In the morning a soldier came to get them. He took Peter and John to the house of the high priest.

Many great men were at the house of the high priest. They sat in a circle. They put Peter and John in the middle of the circle.

Then the high priest said, "Now tell us — how did you make that lame man walk?"

Peter and John were not afraid. The Holy Spirit made them strong and brave.

Peter said, "We did it in the name of Jesus. You nailed Jesus to the cross. But God made Him alive again. And Jesus made the lame man walk."

Then the high priest and the others said, "You must not talk about this Jesus any more."

Peter and John said, "God sent us to tell everybody about Jesus. Must we obey God? Or must we obey you? You know that we must obey God."

But they said, "You must not talk about Jesus."

Then they let Peter and John go.

Peter and John went to the other disciples. They all prayed together. They said, "O God, make us strong and brave, so that we are not afraid. And let us do more wonderful things in Jesus' name."

And the Holy Spirit made them strong and brave. They went out to preach about Jesus again, every day. And they made many sick people well.

IV

An Angel Opens Prison Doors
(Acts 5:12-42)

Many, many people came to hear the disciples. Some came from far away. Many sick people came, too. The disciples made all the sick well, and told them about Jesus.

Then the high priest became angry. He said, "We must not let these men talk about Jesus. We must stop them."

So the high priest put the disciples in prison again. He locked the prison door tight. And he put keepers by the door to keep watch.

But at night an angel came to the prison. The angel opened the door of the prison. He led the disciples out. The keepers did not hear them at all, and did not see them go.

The angel said to the disciples, "Go to the Temple, and tell about Jesus again."

So the disciples went to the Temple.

Early in the morning the people came to the temple. And there they saw the disciples! They were glad to hear more about Jesus.

But the high priest did not know that the disciples were in the Temple. He though they were in prison. The high priest called a meeting of all the great men. Then he sent soldiers to get the disciples out of prison.

The soldiers went to the prison. The keepers were by the door. They opened the door for the soldiers. But the prison was empty! The disciples were not there!

Then the soldiers hurried back to the high priest. They told him, "The prison was locked, and the keepers were by the door. But the disciples are gone!"

The high priest did not know what to think of that.

But someone came running. He said, "The disciples are in the Temple! They are telling about Jesus again!"

Then the soldiers hurried to the Temple. They found the disciples. And they brought them to the high priest.

The high priest said to the disciples, "We told you not to talk about this Jesus. You are making trouble in all Jerusalem."

But Peter said, "We must obey God. He sent Jesus to be the Saviour. We must go and tell everyone about Jesus."

Then the high priest was very angry. All the other big men were angry, too.

They said to each other, "We must kill these disciples of Jesus."

But they were afraid to kill the disciples. So they only gave them a whipping. Then they let them go.

The disciples were happy. They went all through Jerusalem. They told everyone about Jesus.

V

Stephen Sees Jesus

(Acts 6, 7)

At first there were only twelve disciples. But later there were many more. One of the new disciples was Stephen.

Stephen was a good young man. The Holy Spirit filled his heart. The Holy Spirit made Stephen strong and brave to preach about Jesus. And the people liked to hear Stephen.

But some men hated Stephen. They took Stephen to the high priest. They said to the high priest, "Stephen talks against God. He says very bad things."

The high priest looked at Stephen. And he saw Stephen's face begin to shine, like the face of an angel. All the men stood around. They all saw Stephen's face shine.

But the high priest said to Stephen, "Is that true? Do you talk against God?"

Then Stephen told the high priest all about God, and about Jesus. He told how God sent Jesus to be the Saviour.

Stephen said, "Long, long ago God said He would send the Saviour. At last He did send Jesus. But you killed Him on the cross."

That made the men very angry. They shook their fists at Stephen.

Stephen looked up to the sky. He saw the heavens open. He saw the shining glory of God. And he saw Jesus there.

Stephen looked and looked. His face shone with joy. He said, "I see heaven open, and I see Jesus standing at the right hand of God."

Then the men were very, very angry. They took hold of Stephen. They dragged him out of Jerusalem. They took off their coats and threw them on the ground. Then they picked up stones, and threw the stones at Stephen.

Stephen kneeled down to pray. He prayed God to forgive the men who threw the stones. He prayed Jesus to take his soul to heaven.

The angry men threw stones until they killed Stephen.

And Jesus took Stephen to heaven.

VI

Riding with a Black Man

(Acts 8:26-40)

Far, far away from Jerusalem, across the big desert, is the land where the black people live.

Once upon a time the black people had a rich queen. And the rich queen had many good men to help her.

One day one of the queen's black men came to Jerusalem. He rode in a beautiful chariot. Beautiful horses pulled the chariot. And a servant drove the horses.

The black man went to Jerusalem to worship God. He did not know about Jesus. He worshipped God in the Temple. After that, he rode away, to go back to his own country.

At that time, Philip was preaching about Jesus. God sent an angel to Philip. The angel told Philip to go walk along the road to Gaza.

Philip did not know why he must walk along the road to Gaza. But Philip went.

While Philip walked along the road, he saw a chariot with horses. The chariot came near, and Philip saw a black man riding in it.

Then the Spirit of God whispered to Philip, "Go talk to that man in the chariot."

Philip ran to the chariot. The black man was reading. Philip heard him read aloud.

Philip said to the black man, "Do you understand what you are reading?"

The black man shook his head. "I cannot understand it. I need somebody to help me. Will you sit with me and help me?"

The driver stopped the chariot. Philip climbed in and sat with the black man.

The black man showed Philip what he was reading. It was something a prophet wrote about Jesus, long, long ago, before Jesus came.

The black man said, "Who is it the prophet wrote about?"

Philip said, "It is Jesus. The prophet told, long, long ago, that Jesus would come. Now Jesus did come. And He died for us."

Then Philip told the black man all about Jesus.

The black man listened and listened. And he believed.

After a while the black man saw some water near the road. He said to Philip, "Look, there is water. I should like to be baptized."

Philip said, "If you really believe on Jesus, you may be baptized."

The black man said, "I really believe that Jesus is the Son of God."

Then he told the driver to stop.

Philip and the black man got down from the chariot. They went into the water, and Philip baptized the black man.

When they came out of the water, God took Philip away. The black man did not see him any more.

But the black man was happy. He rode on home. And his heart was full of joy, because he found Jesus.

19

SAUL'S CONVERSION

I

Jesus Calls Saul

(Acts 9:1-9; 26:9-19; 22:1-11)

In Jerusalem was a young man named Saul. Saul wanted to serve God. He wanted to do just what God says. But Saul would not believe in Jesus. He would not believe that Jesus is the Son of God.

Saul hated Jesus. And he hated the Christians, all the disciples of Jesus. He tried to put them all in prison.

One day Saul went to the high priest. He said to the high priest, "Give me letters to take to Damascus. Then I will go find all the Christians there. I will bring them to Jerusalem and put them in prison."

So the high priest wrote letters for Saul. And Saul rode away to Damascus. He took men along to help him.

Damascus was far away. Saul and his men rode on and on.

At last, one day, they were near Damascus. The sun shone bright, high in the sky.

Then suddenly there was another light in the sky. It was brighter than the sun. It shone on Saul and his men.

The light was so bright that they were afraid. They all fell down. They hid their faces.

Then Saul heard a voice. The voice called, "Saul! Saul! Why do you persecute me?"

Saul did not know who was talking to him. He said, "Who are You?"

The voice said, "I am Jesus!"

Then Saul knew that Jesus is really the Son of God. Then he knew that Jesus was in heaven.

Saul was afraid. He cried, "Lord, what must I do?"

Jesus said, "Go to Damascus. And I will show you what you must do."

Saul stood up. But he could not see. The light had made him blind. Everything was dark now. Somebody took Saul's hand and led him to Damascus.

There Saul sat alone. Everything was dark. But Saul waited for Jesus to tell him what to do. And he prayed.

II

Saul Becomes a Christian

(Acts 9:10-21)

The Christians in Damascus were afraid. They had heard that Saul was coming. They knew Saul would take them to Jerusalem, and put them in prison.

There was a man in Damascus called Ananias. Ananias was a Christian. He was afraid of Saul, too.

Then, one day, Jesus called to him, "Ananias!"

Ananias said, "Here I am, Lord."

Jesus said to him, "Go to Straight Street. Go to the house of Judas, and ask for Saul. He is praying. And I have told him that you will come."

Ananias said, "Oh, but this Saul hates the Christians. He came to Damascus to get the Christians, and put them in prison."

Mary ran to the disciples, "I saw Jesus. He is alive!"

Saul was afraid. He cried, "Lord, what must I do?"

Jesus said, "Go to him. He belongs to Me. I am going to use him. He will tell many, many people about Me."

Then Ananias went to Straight Street, to the house of Judas. And he found Saul.

Saul sat in a chair with his eyes shut. He was blind.

Ananias put his hands on Saul's head. He said, "Brother Saul, Jesus sent me to you."

Then scales fell off Saul's eyes. He opened his eyes, and he could see.

Saul told Ananias about the bright light from heaven. Saul believed in Jesus now. So he was baptized. Then he went to the churches in Damascus, and told all the people about Jesus.

The people said, "Is this Saul? He came to take the Christians to Jerusalem, to put them in prison. Now he is a Christian. He preaches that Jesus is the Son of God."

And they were all surprised.

III

Saul Goes Back to Jerusalem

(Acts 9:22-28; 13:9)

Every day Saul preached about Jesus in Damascus. The Holy Spirit filled Saul's heart. He loved Jesus very much. He wanted others to love Jesus, too.

But some men hated Saul. They said they would catch Saul, and kill him. They tried to find him, and they set men to watch the gates of the city, so that he could not get away.

But all the Christians were Saul's friends. They said they would help Saul get away. So they took a great big basket, and a rope, and they went to the top of the city wall. There was a big high wall all around the city.

They tied the rope to the basket. They told Saul to sit in the basket. And they let the basket down over the wall.

Down, down, down Saul went, in the basket. At last he was on the ground, outside of the city. Then he climbed out of the basket. He waved goodbye to his friends up on the wall. And he went away.

Saul went to Jerusalem. In Jerusalem Saul preached about Jesus, too. At first the Christians in Jerusalem were afraid of Saul. They thought he would put them in prison. But he told them about the bright light on the way to Damascus. He told them how Jesus talked to him from heaven. Then they knew he was a Christian.

Many people believed on Jesus when they heard Saul preach.

After this Saul was called Paul.

20

HOW THE HOLY SPIRIT USED PETER

I

When Dorcas Died

(Acts 9:36-42)

In that long ago time, there lived a woman named Dorcas. Dorcas was a Christian. And she was a very good woman. She was very kind to everybody. She liked to help people. Sometimes she made clothes for the poor people. She made coats and dresses for little girls. She made coats and suits for little boys.

But one day Dorcas was sick. She was very sick. Her friends came to take care of her, but they could not make her well. After a while Dorcas died.

All the people were very sad. They all loved Dorcas so much.

They had to have a funeral, to bury Dorcas. Somebody said, "Maybe Peter will come for the funeral. Peter is not far away."

So they sent to get Peter. And Peter came.

They took Peter to the room where Dorcas lay on her bed. All the friends of Dorcas stood around. They were crying. They told Peter all about Dorcas. They showed Peter the little dresses and coats and suits Dorcas had made. Peter was sad, too.

After a while Peter told them all to go out of the room. When Peter was alone with Dorcas, he kneeled down to pray. Then he looked at Dorcas and he said, "Dorcas, arise!"

Dorcas opened her eyes. She saw Peter, and she sat up. Peter took hold of her hand, and she stood up. She was alive.

Then Peter called her friends. They came to the room, and they saw Dorcas standing there alive! How happy they were!

All the people in the city heard the wonderful story — how Dorcas was dead, and then came alive again. And many of them believed on Jesus. For it was Jesus — not Peter — who made Dorcas to live again.

II

A Roman Soldier Calls Peter

(Acts 10)

In that long ago Bible time there was a Roman soldier named Cornelius. Cornelius was a captain — a captain of a band of soldiers.

Most of the Romans were hard men. They did not love God. They were often wicked.

But Cornelius was a good man. He prayed to God every day. And he helped the poor people. He tried to do right.

One day, when Cornelius was praying, an angel came to him. The angel called his name, "Cornelius!"

Cornelius was afraid when he saw the angel. He said, "What is it, Lord?"

The angel said, "God heard your prayer. Now send somebody to Joppa, to get Peter. Peter will tell you what you must do."

Then the angel went away.

Cornelius did not know Peter. But he called two servants and an old soldier. He sent them to Joppa to find Peter.

The next morning the two servants and the old soldier came to Joppa. Peter was up on the top of his house. He was praying. And he heard somebody call, "Does Peter live here?"

The Holy Spirit said to Peter, "Three men are looking for you. I have sent them. Go along with them, and do not be afraid."

So Peter went down to the men.

They said to Peter, "Cornelius, the Roman captain, saw an angel. The angel told Cornelius to send for you. So we have come to get you."

Peter took the three men into the house. They stayed all night. In the morning Peter went with them to Cornelius.

Cornelius was waiting for them. He had his house full of people. They were all waiting to see Peter, and to hear Peter.

Cornelius was very glad to see Peter.

Peter asked, "Why did you send for me?"

Cornelius told Peter about the angel. And Cornelius said, "Now we are waiting to hear what you can tell us about God."

Then Peter told them about Jesus, the Son of God. Peter told them that God forgives us our sins through Jesus' name.

And while Peter was talking, the Holy Spirit came on Cornelius and on the others. They were happy. They believed in Jesus the Saviour, too.

Then Peter baptized Cornelius and the other people. And Peter was glad that even a Roman soldier can love Jesus.

III

King Herod Takes Peter

(Acts 12:1-11)

Herod was king of the Jews. He was a wicked king. He did many, many wicked things. He did not serve God at all.

One day King Herod sent his soldiers to take James, one of the disciples. Herod killed James.

Then King Herod sent his soldiers to take Peter. He put Peter in prison. He said he would kill Peter, too.

King Herod set soldiers to keep watch over Peter in prison. There was a big iron gate. Herod set two soldiers to watch the gate. Then he set two more soldiers inside the prison with Peter. Peter was tied to these two soldiers with chains.

Herod thought, "Peter cannot get out of prison this time!"

But the Christians prayed for Peter all the time.

One day Herod said, "Tomorrow I will take Peter out of prison and kill him."

Peter's friends heard about it. They all went to the house of John Mark, to pray for Peter.

That night Peter went to sleep in prison. The soldiers went to sleep, too.

But in the middle of the night, when it was very dark in the prison, an angel came. The angel was a bright light shining in the dark prison.

The angel went to Peter and shook him. The angel said, "Wake up!"

Peter opened his eyes. He thought he was dreaming.

The angel took hold of his hand and said, "Get up!"

Then Peter stood up. And the chains fell off his hands.

"Dress yourself, and put your shoes on," said the angel.

Peter dressed himself. He put his shoes on. He still thought he was dreaming.

The angel said, "Now put your coat on, and follow me."

Peter put his coat on. The angel walked away, and Peter followed the angel. The two soldiers were still sleeping.

The angel came to the door of the prison. The soldiers by the door did not see Peter and the angel. The big door went open for them. The angel went out, and Peter followed him.

The angel walked down the street, and Peter followed him.

And then the angel was gone.

Peter stood still. He rubbed his eyes. He was awake. It was not a dream at all. He was really out of prison.

"Oh!" said Peter to himself, "God truly sent an angel to take me out of prison, so that Herod cannot kill me!"

IV

Peter Tells His Story
(Acts 12:12-17)

Peter's friends were in John Mark's house. They were praying for Peter. They asked God to take care of Peter, so that King Herod would not kill him.

The door of John Mark's house was locked. All the Christians were afraid of wicked King Herod.

But in the middle of the night they heard a noise. Knock, knock, knock. Somebody was at the door.

A girl named Rhoda went to see who could be there. She did not dare open the door. She called, "Who is there?"

A voice came out of the dark night, "It is I, Peter."

Rhoda knew Peter's voice. She turned around and ran back to the others.

"Peter is there!" she told them. "Peter is at the door!"

They said, "Why, that cannot be. Peter is in prison."

Rhoda said, "I'm sure it is Peter."

And they heard the noise again, knock, knock, knock, at the door.

Then they went to open the door. And it was Peter.

How surprised they were. They all asked Peter, "How did you get out of prison?"

Then Peter told them about the angel — how the angel had come into the prison, how he woke Peter up, how the chains fell off his hands, and how the prison door went open for them.

Peter said, "Tell this story about the angel to all the Christians."

Then Peter said goodbye, and he went away to another city.

V

King Herod Dies
(Acts 12:18-24)

It was early morning.

King Herod woke up. He said, "Today I will get Peter out of prison. Today I will kill Peter."

In prison, the soldiers woke up. They looked around — and Peter was not there! They jumped up. They saw the chains on the floor. They saw the door open. Peter was gone!

Then they began to hunt for Peter. They hunted and hunted. They looked everywhere. But they could not find Peter.

They said, "How did he get out of prison? How did the chains get loose? How did the door come open?"

Nobody knew.

At last they had to go tell King Herod, "Peter is gone. He got out in the night. We do not know how he got away. We cannot find him."

Then Herod was angry. He sent more soldiers to hunt for Peter. But they could not find him.

Herod said, "You soldiers must die, because you did not watch the prison." And he killed those soldiers.

After that, King Herod went away, to another city.

There, one day, King Herod called a big meeting. He dressed in his most beautiful robes. He sat on his throne. And he made a speech to the people.

The people said, "The voice of King Herod is like the voice of God!"

That made King Herod very proud. He wanted the people to say that he was like God.

But God in heaven was angry with wicked King Herod. God sent a sickness to Herod. He was very sick, and soon he died.

But the Christians told the story of Jesus everywhere. And very many people believed on Him.

21

PAUL THE MISSIONARY

I

Away in a Sailboat

(Acts 13:1-4)

By this time there were many Christian churches. Many people knew about Jesus, and many people loved Him.

But there were still very, very many people who had never heard about Jesus. Nobody had ever sailed across the big blue sea to tell the far-away people about Jesus.

One day, when the Christians were praying in church, the Holy Spirit came to them. The Holy Spirit said, "I need Paul and Barnabas. I have special work for them to do."

Then the Christians all prayed again. They wanted to do just what the Holy Spirit told them to do. They asked God to show them what they must do.

Then they sent Paul and Barnabas away. They sent them across the big blue sea, to the people who did not know about Jesus.

So Paul and Barnabas sailed away in a big sailboat. They were the first missionaries. They sailed across the sea to tell the story of Jesus to the whole world.

II

A Lame Man at Lystra

(Acts 14:8-18)

Far across the sea was the city of Lystra. In Lystra there was once a boy who could not walk. He could not even stand up. His feet were crooked. So he was lame.

The doctors could not help him. The boy grew up. He became a man. And still he could not walk.

Then, one day, two men came to Lystra. They came to tell a wonderful story. All the people of Lystra crowded around to hear the story. They carried the lame man, so that he could hear it, too.

Who were these men, who came to tell a wonderful story? They were Paul and Barnabas, the missionaries.

Paul and Barnabas told the story of Jesus. They told how Jesus used to make the lame walk, and how he opened the eyes of the blind. They told how Jesus came to die for us.

The lame man listened and listened. He wished that Jesus would make him well, so that he could walk.

Paul looked at the lame man. He saw that the lame man believed on Jesus.

Then Paul said, in a very loud voice, "Stand up on your feet!"

The lame man jumped up. And his feet were straight. He could walk!

The people all saw the lame man jump up and walk. And they said, "Paul and Barnabas are gods! Only a god can make a lame man walk! Paul and Barnabas are gods!"

Paul and Barnabas said, "No, no! We are not gods! We came to tell you about the true God."

Paul talked to them a long time. And some of these people believed on Jesus.

III

Preaching by the River
(Acts 16:12-15)

One day Paul and Silas went to Philippi. Silas was a missionary, too. They went to tell the people of Philippi about Jesus.

Philippi was a big city. But there was not even one church in that big city. The people did not know about Jesus at all.

Paul did not know anyone in the city. He did not know where to go. When the Sabbath day came, there was no church to go to.

Somebody said to Paul, "People go to the river, to pray there."

So Paul and Silas went to the river.

Paul and Silas found some women by the river. These women knew about God. They came to pray together. Paul and Silas sat down and talked with the women. They told the women about Jesus.

The women were glad to hear the wonderful story of Jesus. They had never heard it before.

One of the women was Lydia. Lydia loved God. When she heard the story of Jesus, she loved Jesus, too. And she believed that Jesus is the Son of God.

Then Paul baptized Lydia and her family.

Lydia said to Paul, "I love the Lord Jesus. And I want you to stay in my house."

So Paul and Silas went to live with Lydia. At last they found a home in the big city.

Every day Paul and Silas told the story of Jesus to the people of Philippi. After a while there was a big church in Philippi. Many people believed on Jesus.

IV

Paul Helps a Little Girl

(Acts 16:16-25)

In Philippi there was a poor little slave girl. She had to make money for her masters. This little slave girl had an evil spirit. The evil spirit talked through the little girl. That is how she made money for her masters.

One day the little girl saw Paul and Silas. She followed them. She walked behind them and called out, "These men are men of God. They show us the way to be saved."

The next day she followed Paul and Silas again. Again she walked behind them and called out, "These men are men of God. They show us the way to be saved."

The next day she did it again.

It was the evil spirit that made the little girl follow Paul and Silas.

One day Paul turned and looked at her. And Paul said to the evil spirit, "In the name of Jesus, I tell you to come out of the little girl."

Evil spirits must obey Jesus. The evil spirit went right out of the little girl.

Then the little girl was free and happy.

But her masters were angry. They said, "Now she cannot make money for us anymore."

They were so angry that they ran and caught Paul and Silas. They beat Paul and Silas with whips. Then they put them in jail.

They said to the jailor, "Take good care of these men. Do not let them get out of jail."

So the jailor put Paul and Silas deep inside the jail. He put their feet between boards, so that they could not stand up. He put chains on their hands.

There they sat, in the dark jail. But Paul and Silas were not afraid. In the middle of the night they prayed to God. And then they began to sing. The other men in the jail heard Paul and Silas sing songs about God in the middle of the night.

V

How Paul and Silas Get Out of Jail
(Acts 16:25-40)

It was dark in the jail. Some of the men went to sleep. But Paul and Silas did not sleep. Softly they sang their songs to God.

Then, suddenly, the earth began to shake. The whole prison began to shake. The chains fell off the hands of the men in jail. The boards fell off their feet. And the doors of the prison broke open.

The jailor came running. He saw the doors open. He thought surely all the prisoners were gone.

Then the jailor was afraid. He thought, "Oh, if all the prisoners are gone, then I will be killed!" And he took out his sword, to kill himself. But he was afraid to die.

Paul saw him. And Paul called to him, "Do not hurt yourself. We are all here."

The jailor could hardly believe that. He called for a servant to bring a light. Then he saw that all the prisoners were still there. He ran to Paul and Silas and fell on his knees.

"Oh, sirs, what must I do to be saved?" he asked.

Paul said, "Believe on the Lord Jesus Christ, and thou shalt be saved."

Then he told the jailor about Jesus, the Saviour.

And that very night the jailor believed on Jesus.

He took Paul and Silas out of prison. He took them to his own house. He washed their sore backs. He made supper for them. And Paul baptized the jailor and his family.

In the morning, Paul and Silas went to Lydia's house. All the Christians came to see them. Paul and Silas said goodbye to them all, and then went away. They went to another city, to tell people about Jesus.

VI

A Boy Falls from a Window
(Acts 20:7-13)

Paul went from city to city, to tell the story of Jesus.

One day he came to Troas. The people of Troas wanted to hear the story. They came together in a big upstairs room. Very many people came, and the room was hardly big enough. One boy, Eutychus, sat on the window sill.

Paul talked a long time. After a while it was dark, and they brought lights into the room. Paul talked on and on. There was so much to tell about Jesus. There was so much the people wanted to know. Paul talked till midnight.

But Eutychus, sitting in the window, was sleepy. He could not keep his eyes open. His head nodded, nodded, nodded. Soon he was fast asleep. And then he rolled right out of the window. He fell way down to the ground.

Paul and some other men ran down as fast as they could. They found Eutychus lying on the ground. He was dead.

Paul said, "Do not feel bad about it. He will be all right."

Then Paul laid down on top of Eutychus, and put his arms around Eutychus. After a moment Eutychus opened his eyes. He was alive again.

The people were glad when Eutychus was alive again.

They all went back upstairs. They talked till morning. In the morning they had breakfast together. Then Paul said goodbye. He was going away, back to Jerusalem.

VII

By the Seashore

(Acts 20:17-38)

Paul and Silas were on the way back to Jerusalem. Luke, the doctor, went with them. They sailed away on the blue sea.

A while later the boat stopped near Ephesus. There was a church in that city, too. Paul sent for the elders of the church. Paul sat on the shore with them, and talked with them.

Paul told them that he was going back to Jerusalem. And he said, "You will never see me again."

That made them all very sad.

Paul told them how they must always do right. They must always serve God and trust Him. He told them that God would always take care of them.

Then they all kneeled down in the sand. They prayed together.

The sailboat was ready to go. It was time to say goodbye. The elders kissed Paul, and brought him to the boat.

Soon the wind carried the sailboat away. The elders waved good-bye to Paul. They watched until they could not see the boat any more. They were sad, because they would never see Paul again.

22

PAUL THE PRISONER

I

Paul In Jerusalem
(Acts 21:17-40; 22:1-24)

The Christians in Jerusalem were glad to see Paul. Paul had many things to tell them — about all the new churches everywhere, and how God took care of him all the way.

But many of the Jews in Jerusalem still hated Jesus. And they hated Paul because he talked about Jesus.

One day Paul went to the Temple. He wanted to worship God in the Temple.

The angry Jews saw him there. They called a crowd of people. They said, "This is the man that makes trouble everywhere!"

They told lies about Paul. They pulled Paul out of the temple. They dragged him down the street. They wanted to kill him.

Somebody ran to tell the captain. The captain and his soldiers ran into the crowd. They took Paul away from the angry Jews. They carried Paul away, up the steps to the castle prison.

Paul said to the captain, "Please let me speak to the people."

So the captain let Paul stand on the steps. Paul looked down on the noisy crowd. They shook their fists at him. They wanted to get hold of him again.

But Paul held up his hand until they were all quiet. Then Paul told his story.

Paul said, "I used to hate the Christians, too. I put many of them in prison. One day I went to Damascus. I wanted to take the Christians of Damascus to Jerusalem and put them in prison. But on the way I saw a bright light — brighter than the sun. And Jesus called to me from heaven. Then I believed on Him. And He sent me to tell people everywhere about the Saviour."

For a little while the crowd listened. But then they would not listen any more. They began to throw dust at Paul. They screamed at the captain and at the soldiers.

So the captain took Paul and put him in prison, where the Jews could not get him.

II

God's Plan and the Jews' Plan
(Acts 23:10-35)

It was night. Paul lay in his dark prison. He wondered what would happen to him tomorrow.

In the dark night, Jesus came to Paul. Jesus stood by Paul and talked to him.

He said, "Be happy, Paul. You have told the people of Jerusalem about Me. Now I shall send you to Rome, and you will tell the people of Rome about Me."

That was God's plan. He would send Paul to Rome.

Rome was a big, big city. It was the biggest city in the world. It was far, far away. Paul was happy to think God would send him to Rome, to tell about Jesus there.

But the Jews hated Paul. They said they would not let Paul tell the story of Jesus any more. They said they would kill Paul.

In the morning they made a plan. They said, "We will tell the high priest to call a meeting. Then the high priest must ask the captain to send Paul to the meeting. We will hide by the roadside. And when Paul comes by, we will catch him and kill him."

There was a boy who heard the men talk about Paul. He listened carefully, because Paul was his uncle. And he did not want Paul to be killed.

When the boy heard what the men wanted to do, he went to tell Paul.

Paul called a soldier. He said to the soldier, "Bring this boy to the captain. He has something to tell the captain."

The soldier took the boy to the captain. The captain listened to the story about the men who wanted to kill Paul.

The captain said, "It is good that you told me. Do not tell anybody else." And he sent the boy home.

Then the captain quickly called his soldiers. He told them to get ready to go away.

By night they were all ready. They gave Paul a horse to ride on. When it was dark, they all rode away — Paul in the middle of all the soldiers.

The soldiers took Paul to another city, to Felix, the governor. So the Jews did not get Paul. Their plan did not work.

Felix put Paul in prison. But Paul knew that some day he would go to Rome. He knew that God works out all His plans.

III

Paul and the Governor

(Acts 24:22-27; 25:1-12)

Felix, the governor, was good to Paul. He let Paul's friends visit him in prison. Paul had many friends.

Felix wanted to know about Jesus, too. So one day he sent a soldier to get Paul. He asked Paul to tell him about Jesus.

Paul told Felix how Jesus came from heaven, how Jesus died on the cross, and how Jesus is alive now, in heaven.

Then Paul told Felix that some day we will all see Jesus. And on that day God will ask us if we have done right. And God will punish us for all the wrong things we did – unless Jesus is our Saviour.

Then Felix was afraid. Felix had done many things that are not right.

But Felix did not want to believe in Jesus.

He said to Paul, "That is enough. I do not want to hear more now." And he sent Paul back to prison.

Paul was in prison for two years. The governor said, "Paul has done nothing wrong." But he kept Paul in prison just the same.

At last Paul said, "I want to go to Caesar. I have done nothing wrong. Let Caesar say if I must be killed or stay in prison."

The governor said, "All right. You shall go to Caesar."

Caesar was the great king of all the peoples. Caesar lived in Rome. So at last Paul was going to Rome.

But he had to go back to prison to wait for a boat.

IV

Paul Talks to a King and Queen
(Acts 25:13-27; 26:1-32)

One day King Agrippa came to visit the governor. Paul was still in prison. The governor told King Agrippa about Paul.

King Agrippa said, "I should like to see this Paul."

The governor said, "That is fine. Tomorrow we will call him."

So the next day king Agrippa came to the governor's big house. The queen came, too. The king and queen wore beautiful robes and sparkling jewels.

The governor sent for Paul. Paul stood before the king and queen. He was not afraid. He was glad to tell King Agrippa about Jesus.

So Paul told his story. He told about the bright light on the road to Damascus. He told how Jesus talked to him from heaven. He told how Jesus sent him to tell people everywhere the story of Jesus.

Then King Agrippa said, "Paul, you almost make me want to be a Christian."

Paul said, "Oh, I wish that you, and all the others here, were Christians!"

But King Agrippa shook his head. No. He would not be a Christian.

After that, they sent Paul back to prison.

King Agrippa said, "Paul has done no wrong. But he wants to go to Caesar. And you must send him to Caesar."

V

Paul Sails Away to Rome

(Acts 27)

At last there was a ship ready for Paul.

Rome was far, far away, across the big sea. The soldiers took Paul to the ship. When all was ready, the sailors put up the sails, and the wind carried the ship out to sea.

They sailed for many, many days. After a while they were far out on the sea. They could not see land anywhere. There was just water, water, all around.

And then, one day, a big storm came. The wind began to blow. It blew harder and harder. Big dark clouds covered the sky. All day long the sun did not shine. And at night the moon and stars did not shine. Rain came pouring down. The waves grew bigger and bigger. The waves almost tipped the little ship over. The sailors were sure they would all drown. Everybody was afraid.

Day after day the wind blew, the big waves rolled the ship, and the rain came pouring down. Everybody said, "Surely the ship will break. We will all drown."

But at night an angel came to Paul. The angel said, "Do not be afraid. You must go to Rome. And God will save all the people on the ship. They will not drown."

In the morning Paul talked to the soldiers and the sailors, and to all the other people, too. He said, "Do not be afraid. Not one of us shall drown. Last night an angel came to me and told me so. The ship will break. But we shall all be saved."

Then he told them they must eat, so that they would be strong.

They were too afraid to eat. But Paul took bread. He looked up to heaven and asked God to bless the bread. And he began to eat. Then the soldiers and the sailors ate. And all the other people ate, too.

The sailors said, "We are near to land."

After a while they saw the land. It was an island in the middle of the ocean. But the sailors could not steer the ship to shore. The big waves pushed the ship and made it crash into a big rock. The ship stuck tight on the rock. And the big waves began to break the ship.

Then all the people jumped into the water. Some could swim. Others took hold of boards from the ship. And they all got to land safely.

VI

On an Island

(Acts 28:1-10)

The soldiers, and the sailors, and Paul, and all the other people were glad to be safe on shore. The men of the island came running to help. They helped pull people out of the water. Then they built a big fire. The soldiers, and the sailors, and Paul, and all the other people stood by the fire to get dry.

After a while Paul went to get more wood for the fire. He came back with pieces of wood piled on his arm. He threw the wood in the fire.

But when Paul threw the wood in the fire, a snake came out of the wood. The snake curled around Paul's arm.

The people said, "Oh! look at the snake! Paul must be a bad man. The water did not drown him. So God sent a snake to bite him."

The people thought, "Paul will surely fall dead." And they watched to see Paul fall dead.

But Paul shook the snake off his arm. It fell into the fire. And Paul did not fall dead.

Then the people said, "The snake did not hurt Paul. He must be a god!"

The people of the island were very kind. They took the soldiers and the other shipwrecked people into their homes.

Paul went home with a man named Publius.

Publius' father was sick. When Paul saw the sick man, Paul put his hands on him and prayed. Then the man became well.

Publius was very glad. He told the story to his friends — how Paul could make a sick man well. Then they brought other sick people to Paul. He touched them and made them all well.

Paul had to stay on the island all winter, waiting for another ship. So Paul had time to tell the people about Jesus. He did many wonderful things to show them that Jesus is the Son of God.

VII

Paul in Rome

(Acts 28:11 ff)

In spring, another ship came to the island. The soldiers took Paul on this ship. Publius gave Paul many presents to take along. And then they sailed away, to Rome.

They sailed for many, many days. At last they came to land. They had to walk the rest of the way to Rome.

The people in Rome knew that Paul was coming. The Christians came to meet him. They were glad to see him. And they all walked to Rome together, with the soldiers.

The soldiers did not put Paul in prison in Rome. They found a house for him to live in. And a soldier lived with Paul, to watch him.

Many people came to Paul's house. He told them all about Jesus, and about the wonderful love of God.

Paul was happy there. He was happy because he could preach about Jesus.

Paul wrote many letters, too. He wrote letters to all the churches, all over the world. He told the Christians that they must be happy in Jesus. He told them to live for Jesus every day.

Some of Paul's letters are in the Bible, where we can all read them.

VIII

A Runaway Slave

(Philemon)

In the city of Colosse there was a slave boy named Onesimus. His master's name was Philemon.

Onesimus did not like to be a slave. And one day he ran away.

After a while, Onesimus came to Rome. He thought his master, Philemon, would not find him in Rome.

But one day Onesimus met Paul. Paul told him about Jesus. Onesimus learned to love Jesus. He became a Christian.

Then Paul said to Onesimus, "You belong to your master Philemon. You must go back to him."

Onesimus was afraid to go back to Philemon. But a Christian must do what is right. So he had to go back.

Then Paul wrote a letter to Philemon. He told Philemon that Onesimus was a Christian now. He said Onesimus was coming back, to be a slave again. And he asked Philemon to be kind to Onesimus.

Onesimus took the letter and went away, back to his master in Colosse.

Philemon was a Christian, too. So he was glad that his slave boy loved Jesus. And Onesimus was a good slave for Philemon.

Many other people learned to love Jesus when they heard Paul preach.

23

JESUS TALKS TO JOHN IN A VISION

(Revelation)

Do you remember how many disciples Jesus had when He walked on earth? Yes, twelve.

After Jesus went to heaven, His twelve disciples told the story of Jesus to people everywhere. They told the people they must believe in Jesus, the Saviour.

Many of the disciples were put in prison because they loved Jesus. After a while John was sent to a little island, because he loved Jesus. The blue sea was all around the little island. The blue sky was above it. And John lived there alone.

When Sunday came, John could not go to church. There was no church on the little island. So John sat down by the sea, to think of Jesus and to pray.

And then John heard a voice behind him. It was a very loud voice, like a horn.

The voice said, "Write in a book the things that you see. And send the book to the churches."

John turned around to see who was talking. And there he saw Jesus!

Jesus was all bright with shining glory. His face was bright as the sun.

John was afraid when he saw Jesus all bright with shining glory. John fell down. He covered his face. He did not dare look at Jesus.

But Jesus put his hand on John. Jesus said, "Do not be afraid. I will show you the things that are going to happen."

Then Jesus showed John many wonderful things.

Jesus showed John the troubles that will come to men on earth.

Jesus showed John how all the dead will live again.

Jesus showed John the Book of Life, with the names of all who love Jesus.

Jesus showed John the new heaven and the new earth. In the new heaven and on the new earth there will be no sorrow. There will be no sickness. There will be no night. All who love Jesus will live with Him there, and be happy forever.

Jesus said to John, "I am coming again, soon."

And today we are waiting. Soon Jesus will come again, and we shall all see Him.

Guide to Old Testament Characters

Guide to New Testament Characters

Guide to Parables of Jesus